Advance Reviews for

The Dance Gods: A N̶e̶w̶ ̶Y̶o̶r̶k̶ ̶M̶e̶m̶o̶i̶r̶

"Kenny Pearl has crafted a vivid and absorbing evocation of one dancer's life over the span of two important decades in New York, offering not only the honest story of his own awakening as an artist but also a series of insightful, sharp-focused portraits of the great artists he worked with— Martha Graham, Alvin Ailey, Pearl Lang—as well as memorable vignettes of bit players in his story such as Leonard Bernstein and Doris Duke and (always tastefully) the many ladies he pursued. His powers of recall are prodigious; we relive with him many of the struggles of an illegal Canadian making a life as a performer in New York. We also experience the thrill and challenge of working with great choreographers on some of their most important works, though his self-deprecating humour and clear-eyed self-awareness keep everything in modest proportion. This feel-good story is not only an inspiration to any young dancer; it is a delicious read for anyone interested in getting an insider's track on the unfolding story of modern dance in America."

Max Wyman
Dance Historian, Arts Critic, 1968–2001
The Vancouver Sun

"When a dancer has performed in the companies of both Martha Graham and Alvin Ailey, particularly since he came to dance late, attention must be paid. Kenny Pearl's vastly enjoyable autobiography, *The Dance Gods: A New York Memoir*, is a candid account of his 13-year stint in the Big Apple. His descriptions of his intimate encounters with both Graham and Ailey, two of the world's great dance icons, are just one of the many pleasures of the book. Pearl writes in an easy manner touching on both his personal and professional life, and he doesn't shy away from discussing the losses as well as the triumphs. In particular, his almost willful disregard of his injuries, which clearly shortened his dance career, is a cautionary tale. On the plus side, finding out that Pearl gave private Graham technique classes to tobacco heiress Doris Duke is just one of the many delicious surprises of his New York sojourn. In terms of the big picture, Pearl provides some deep insights into his philosophy behind being a dancer, which makes this book compulsory reading for young people contemplating a career in dance. His chronicle about how he found the pathway to being an inspired dance teacher is truly instructive. I read the book in one go. Pearl had me hooked from the first page."

Paula Citron
Senior Dance Writer
The Globe and Mail

"Kenny Pearl's *The Dance Gods is* the sweaty, gritty, insightful story of his amazing dance career. His memories of touring internationally with Alvin Ailey's company, close encounters with modern dance icons including Martha Graham, his forthright, funny, sometimes wrenching recollections of coming of age, and his passion for dancing during an intense decade in New York City are woven into a compelling memoir—a must-read for dance lovers."

Carol Anderson
Choreographer, Author
Chasing the Tale of Contemporary Dance

"Writing with eloquence, wit, and tremendous honesty, Kenny Pearl details his harrowing and exalted path to becoming a dancer. His memories are crystal clear, and each eventful episode is brought vividly to life in relation to the social, political, cultural, creative, and personal influences of the moment. This is a journey of epic proportions in which iconic choreographers and dancers play pivotal roles in the realization of a dream achieved through ferocious exertion and passionate commitment. I couldn't put this book down, and I will never forget it."

Peggy Baker
Dancer, Choreographer

"*The Dance Gods* is an engrossing look into the life of a dancer in New York City, during the heady decades of the '60s and '70s. Through the incredible experiences of Kenny Pearl, we are immersed in the feeling of this significant and singular time in history. With remarkable clarity and detail, Pearl recounts his rise from aspiring novice to sought-after performer and teacher, bringing us deep into the inner sanctums of dance icons Alvin Ailey and Martha Graham along the way. Divulging vivid anecdotes of both a personal and professional nature, Pearl astutely reveals the multifaceted existence of the dancer, giving equal attention to his struggle (and ultimate success) as an artist as to the personal and emotional roadblocks that challenge us all. *The Dance Gods* resonates for this reason in particular—it charts an extraordinary period of time for an exceptionally gifted man, all the while maintaining Pearl as a beautifully ordinary and extremely relatable personality. An absolute page-turner and a brilliant tribute to a pivotal time in modern dance."

Molly Johnson
Writer
The Dance Current Magazine

THE DANCE GODS
A New York Memoir

Kenny Pearl

 **FriesenPress**

Suite 300 - 990 Fort St
Victoria, BC, Canada, V8V 3K2
www.friesenpress.com

Copyright © 2015 by Kenny Pearl
First Edition — 2015

Edited by Karen Shenfeld, Susan Turner and Barbara Laskin

Front Cover Photograph: Kenny Pearl
Kenn Duncan/©The New York Public Library

ISBN
978-1-4602-6269-6 (Hardcover)
978-1-4602-6270-2 (Paperback)
978-1-4602-6271-9 (eBook)

1. Performing Arts, Dance

Distributed to the trade by The Ingram Book Company

for Lil and Al

I have used the real names of all the people in this book who were a part of my professional life. I have changed the names of some who figure in my personal stories.

It's permitting life to use you in a very intense way. Sometimes it is not pleasant. Sometimes it is fearful. But nevertheless, it is inevitable.
—Martha Graham, on being a dancer, in *The Dancer Revealed*

Showing up is not all of life–but it counts for a lot.
—Hillary Clinton

The trick is not minding that it hurts.
—Peter O'Toole, from the film *Lawrence of Arabia*, as he snuffs out a burning match between his fingertips

CONTENTS

1
Leaving and Arriving

2
Climbing

3
Reaching

4
Digging In

5
Contracting and Expanding

6
Releasing

1

LEAVING AND ARRIVING

October 11 and 12, 1967

Being Invisible

I looked the U.S. Immigration Officer in the eye and lied. The lie was planned and consisted of one sentence; my hopes of having a New York City career, dancing with the legendary Martha Graham Dance Company, depended on me saying it convincingly.

I had spent the past two hours on a packed train, travelling from Toronto to the Canada–U.S. border near Buffalo, practising "the lie." Now the moment had come to sell it. The officer standing beside my seat was tall, thick and anonymous behind blue-tinted sunglasses. He asked the expected question: "What is the purpose of your visit?"

The truth would have been: "I'm planning on living and working in your country illegally for many years without the required visa or Green Card." I gave my rehearsed answer instead, somehow managing to direct it intact through the butterfly wings beating frantically in my gut: "I'm going to spend a week in New York as a tourist to see the sights."

The officer frowned as he examined my passport. Then he took a pen from his pocket and began writing slowly on a pad. If he believed my story and let me through, I would be an illegal alien. If discovered, I would be deported, never to return again.

As a twenty-one-year-old, intermediate-level dance student, I could have entered legally with a student visa. The Martha Graham School of Dance, my immediate destination, had offered me one. I had turned it down because the visa would have made me visible at a time when I needed to be invisible. I needed to be invisible because of Vietnam.

In spite of massive demonstrations against the Vietnam War, President Lyndon B. Johnson had recently confirmed his commitment to it and, in the month of my departure, October 1967, had sent 45,000 new soldiers to join the 475,000 already there. Contributing large numbers to this total was the much-feared military draft.

Earlier in the year, heavyweight-boxing champion Muhammad Ali had been denied the right to escape the draft as a conscientious objector and, for refusing to serve when drafted, had been stripped of his title and sentenced to five years in prison. If all this could happen to an American hero, then who was safe? The rumours were that a Canadian with a visa could be inducted. I had recently read a newspaper story about a German man who had a U.S. work visa. He could have entered and worked legally, but he decided to stay in Canada after receiving a letter requesting him, upon arrival, to show up for a military hearing.

A Canadian dancer living in the U.S., who had headed back home after the war started, offered me advice on how to be invisible. He told me to buy a round-trip ticket, with the return to Toronto a week later. At the border, I could then tell the immigration officer that I was going to New York for a brief visit. In that way, the ticket I showed him would prove that my trip was really a short vacation to see the sights. When I arrived in New York, I was to change the return date to whenever I was really planning to go back home.

I felt guilty about my lie. But I rationalized: It's all fair. Thousands of U.S. citizens are making themselves invisible by dodging the draft and heading north. The few Canadians like me heading undercover to the U.S. won't come close to filling the gap that their absence is creating.

And in true '60s spirit, I wholeheartedly believed that artists, who wanted to bring peace, love and happiness to the world, should be allowed to live by John Lennon's words, "Imagine there's no countries," and should not have to deal with border regulations.

In the end, I had two choices: enter with a student visa, be visible and take my chances with a possible military hearing, or go in illegally and be invisible.

The officer finished his notes and looked down at me: "Ticket please." My hand shook as I handed it to him. He took off his sunglasses to have a better look, squinted at it and then squinted at me. The squints made me feel he was close to catching me in my game. Then he handed it back and moved on.

Fifteen Hours to Think about Myself

Sitting on the train, watching the blaze of autumn colours along the Hudson River pass by, I felt for the keys in my pocket. They had been given to me by Susan Macpherson, a Toronto dancer who had recently returned home after living in New York for several years. When she had heard I was moving to New York, she generously transferred her apartment to me. The fact that I had four keys to open the door of one apartment confused me, since I was coming from a part of Toronto where we felt safe not locking up at all.

The train ride from Toronto's Union Station to New York's Penn Station took fifteen hours; fifteen hours between the departure from my family's elegant Toronto home, with its polished oak floors and lilac gardens, and my arrival at a broken-down tenement building on the Lower East Side of Manhattan. I had a lot of time to think about the events that had led me to be on that train.

Camp Moments

My first experience as a performer was at Camp Northland, a summer camp located on a pristine lake a few hours north of Toronto. I was seven. I had been inspired by my dad, who always sang Al Jolson songs around the house. I didn't know back then that Al Jolson had been a singer and actor, renowned in the early 1900s as "The World's Greatest Entertainer." I had just sung his songs to copy my dad, and I did so at camp in my cabin. My counsellor, Harold, who happened to be planning the inevitable closing-night talent show, thought it would be terrific if I added my vocal skills to the proceedings. He rehearsed with me every night for a week, teaching me some of Al Jolson's moves, such as dropping down to one knee and stretching my arms out wide as I belted out the song.

The camp theatre was an old barn covered with peeling green paint. On the night of the show, I waited behind a curtain on one side of the tiny stage. I felt good. My cabin-mates had told me I was great singing *Swanee*, one of my favourites. But my mood shifted when, in the few minutes before my entrance, Harold suddenly pulled out a cloth and a tin of black shoe polish, and started to cover my face. I struggled to get away from him, but he grabbed me, holding me back.

At camp
before the show.
Author's personal
collection

"No!" I shouted. I didn't know that Mr. Jolson often employed a theatrical tradition called black-face to project the stereotype of the happy-go-lucky African-American entertainer.

"No, I won't do it!" I shouted again.

"You have to do it Kenny," he responded, holding tightly to my shoulders, his nails digging into me. "What will I tell your parents?"

I stopped struggling. The applause ended for a baton-twirling act and Harold gave me a not-so-gentle push, aiming me towards the red piece of tape that marked centre stage.

I slowly made my way, my head turned to the back, praying for lightning to strike and set the barn on fire. As I got down on one knee and faced front, there was a scary silence, only interrupted by the flapping of bat wings in the rafters, which was where I wanted to be. I sang, "Swanee, how I love ya, how I love ya, my dear old Swanee." I heard a few chuckles; when I got to, "even tho my mammy's waitin' for me, prayin' for me," there was a barrage of laughter; by the time I belted out the last line, "the folks up north will see me no more, when I get to that Swanee shore," drawing out the "ee" of "Swanee" as directed, the howling was deafening.

On the way home in the bus the next day, streaks of hard-to-remove shoe polish still decorated my face. Every so often one of my fellow campers shouted, "Swanee, Swanee!" and everyone just about fell on the floor, they were laughing so hard. During the two-hour trip, I repeated over and over, "I will never go on stage again." For the next nine years I talked my way out of being in every camp show and school play that came my way.

Bar Mitzvah Jitterbug

My only experience of dance before I turned sixteen was the series of Saturday classes I was forced to take at Sam and Sandy's School of Ballroom. Sam and Sandy were husband and wife—slim, olive-skinned, high-spirited Israelis, who sincerely wanted to bring the joys of the polka and foxtrot to twelve-year-olds.

I was about to take part in a rite of passage called the Bar Mitzvah, which would mark my unlikely transition at the age of thirteen from boy to man. On a Saturday morning, invited guests would fill a synagogue called Shaarei Shomayim, the Gates of Heaven. I would stand on a stage in front of the Holy Ark, the Ten Commandment tablets sculpted into its doors, and sing carefully rehearsed Hebrew verses from Judaism's holy scroll, the Torah.

For me, however, the real challenge would take place at the celebration in the evening. Two hundred guests would form a circle around my mother and me, and watch us dance the waltz. This was the reason for the ballroom classes with Sam and Sandy.

Their studio, with its matted orange carpet and cracked mirrors, was located in a strip mall just north of downtown, right above a fish market. It must have been the smell rising through the floor vents that drove Sam and Sandy to douse themselves with vanilla cologne. My favourite style was the jitterbug, because I could dance holding onto only one of Sandy's hands most of the time. Whereas the waltz brought us chest to chest, so that I could not avoid being enveloped by her perfume, the jitterbug allowed me to stay a secure, two-arm distance apart.

On the night of the party, I had not yet mastered the waltz. I secretly asked Murray, the leader of the five-piece band, *The Murray Brown Band of Renown*, to play a jitterbug instead. My mom, in her puffy, pale yellow gown, stood at the centre of the floor smiling, her arms reaching towards me. Photographers stood ready, cameras pressed against their faces. The music started. It was Carl Perkins' *Blue Suede Shoes*: "Well, it's one for the money, two for the show, three to get ready, now go cat go." I grabbed Mom, whose expression was incredulous, and started swinging and twirling her, doing the jitterbug. Unexpectedly, she shrieked with delight. After a few spins and turns, my Dad cut in and picked up the energy. Then my sister Toba, two years younger than me, pulled in our three-year-old sister, Wendi, as 200 guests clapped and laughed. Murray Brown wrapped it up, belting out, "Well you can do anything but lay off of my blue suede shoes."

We all hugged; everyone applauded.

Bar-Mitzvah family photo.
Author's personal collection

Rags to Riches

The Pearl family in Poland, around 1912. My dad is the little guy with
the bangs. My grandfather was already in Toronto.
Author's personal collection

My high-spirited mom and dad had both grown up in poverty. Born in Poland,
my dad, Albert Pearl, came to Toronto as a child before the First World War,
narrowly escaping the destruction of his family's shtetl, a village of unknown
name, somewhere north of Lodz, by anti-Semitic Cossacks. When he was a
kid, his dad died from tuberculosis, leaving his devoted wife, who had to
support five children, running a tiny grocery stand in Kensington Market, an
area of Toronto then populated largely by Jewish immigrants. They were so
poor that they had to use the paper wrappings that covered oranges in those
days as toilet paper.

Mom, Lilyan Greenbaum, was born in Toronto into a family of eight: seven
girls and one boy. Her parents were Orthodox Jews. Like a fair number of his
contemporaries, her father was a ragman who bought and sold used clothing.

He was also known as "The Judge," because he unofficially assisted the Jewish immigrant community in resolving their local conflicts. Her mother, as required by religion (and eight kids), was a full-time homemaker. My grandparents had been brought together at the age of sixteen in Poland by a matchmaker. They raised their family lovingly, but with strict guidelines set out by the rules of their religion. They even refrained, as stipulated, from turning on and off the lights on the Sabbath.

The families lived only a few blocks apart, but my mom and dad, Lil and Al, didn't see each other until they were young adults. Dad walked past Mom's house one day and saw her on the porch. He told me he fell in love instantly, but couldn't get up the nerve to approach her for years.

As adults, they moved away from the religious tenets and restrictions of their childhood. They became members of a new breed of urban professionals and enjoyed the cultural life that the evolving city of Toronto had to offer. Their frequenting of theatres, museums and concert halls represented their newfound sophistication and assimilation into Canadian life.

Dad was a chartered accountant with the heart sometimes of a poet, sometimes of a comedian. Away on trips with my mom, he wrote lively letters to us about the *Carnaval* in Rio de Janeiro, the changing of the guard in London and the hula dancers in Hawaii. He liked to make up humorous lyrics for well-known songs. Instead of singing "All of me, why not take all of me?" from the song made famous by Billie Holiday, Dad liked to sing "Olive trees, plant me some olive trees." Mom, too, had her own artistic gifts. She had a feel for texture and design, and created beautiful homes and gardens wherever we lived. Neighbours loved to drop by to take in the colours of her spring garden of tulips, lilacs and peonies, and the late summer blast of her roses. When I was six, my mom helped me plant a vegetable garden. I watered it and pulled weeds, and by August was thrilled to see perfect, parallel rows of carrots, green beans and stalks of corn that were twice my height.

The Greenbaum family, with early twentieth century Hebrew tagging.
My mom is fourth from the left, bottom row.
Author's personal collection

I never saw my parents happier than when they were dancing the waltz or a foxtrot at family celebrations. Dad, slim and athletic, with his Clark Gable moustache and sleek black hair combed straight back, and Mom, with her soft auburn curls and warm smile, lit up the room as they moved confidently around the floor.

In spite of their natural abilities, neither of my parents would ever have seriously considered a career in the arts. The idea of sitting down to write a novel, or going to school to study landscape design, would never have occurred to them. Work was about earning money to live on, and saving for well-deserved vacations and the future education of their children.

While they believed it was fine to dabble in the arts, pursuing a life as a writer, dancer or actor was a sure way to slide back into the poverty they had spent their adult lives struggling to leave behind.

Right is Wrong

Perhaps inheriting my parents' natural talents, I had been artistically expressive as a little kid. I loved to paint and draw. Mom and Dad, always loving and generous, supported these activities. They showed their pride as I worked at the kitchen table, telling me how lifelike my horses and cats were, and inviting the neighbours in to admire them. Encouraged, I added writing stories and creating puppet shows to my activity list. But when I hit the age of eight, the attitude of my parents suddenly changed. Whenever my creative impulses rose to the surface, they expressed disapproval: "Kenny, leave that drawing. Why do you want to waste your time with that nonsense?"

For a while, I continued to draw and write, but only at school or behind my closed bedroom door. I gave away all my pictures to friends—no refrigerator art in our home—and hid my stories in a box in the basement. One day I went to retrieve them and found that the box was gone. "Mom," I asked, "what happened to all my stories?"

She replied casually, "I threw them out. The basement was too messy."

Soon after, my paintings met the same fate. Then my stamp collection and puppets disappeared. With each incident, I felt like a precious part of me was being tossed away. Right became wrong as I quickly learned that people who loved me could be unkind. I managed to suppress my anger, afraid to lose my parents' love, anxious about making things worse if I expressed myself.

Seeking my parents' approval, I set aside drawing and puppet shows and got on with "more important things." I pretended to read the business section of the newspaper for a while because it made Dad happy. In my early teens, I began getting violent stomach cramps whenever I held back my feelings. They left me doubled over, unable to walk. Trips to the emergency room of the hospital usually followed. Mom and Dad were deeply concerned, telling the doctors that homework must have been the cause of my distress. The doctors always gave me a bottle of tranquilizers. A couple of times they were sure I had acute appendicitis and were ready to operate, but in the end, I got the little white pills and was sent home.

At school we were required to learn how to play an instrument. My dad, proud that so many of the world's greatest violinists were Jewish, encouraged me to choose the violin. He liked to ask the riddle: "Why are there so many great Jewish violinists?" Answer: "Because you can't quickly pack up a piano and run from the enemy." I later switched to string bass—an instrument too large for a quick getaway—so I could play in dance and jazz bands. Without the music, I would have exploded.

The "A" Word and Talking to My Pizza

At thirteen, I was an outgoing kid at school, class president and member of my school's junior basketball and football teams. By fifteen, I felt I was already past my prime and would be living the rest of my angst-ridden life on a never-ending downward slope. I had been hit by the teen destroyer, the relationship spoiler, the "A" word: acne. No medication or change of diet could cure it and no amount of Clearasil could cover it. There was more to my insecurity than bad skin, but its arrival was a moment I recognized as life altering.

I quickly dissolved into myself. Watching clear-skinned boys going out with cute girls, my skin got worse. Though I did have some dates, every relationship ended quickly as I couldn't handle anyone looking at my face. Making eye contact with girls was impossible. One night at Mario's Pizzeria, when I was sitting across the table from fair-haired Rachel Goldstein and chatting away about our teachers, she abruptly changed the subject: "Kenny, what colour are my eyes?" I had no idea, as my own were focused downward.

"You're not looking at me! You haven't looked at me all night," she shouted as she got up and stormed out, while classmates at nearby tables stared.

When You're a Jet

One day in 1962, when I was recovering from one of my stomach-cramp episodes, a couple of friends took me to see the movie *West Side Story*, to cheer me up. Our teacher at school had prepared us to see it by having us read scenes from William Shakespeare's *Romeo and Juliet*, the play that had inspired the movie. I went to the film knowing that the feuding Italian families from long ago would be replaced by New York street gangs, the mainland American Jets and the Puerto Rican Sharks. While listening to the overture, hearing for the first time the drama in the music of "Maria," "Tonight" and "Something's Coming," I had the feeling that something special was about to leap out at us from that screen. The camera zoomed in on a playground and then onto the snapping fingers of Riff, the leader of the Jets. With his focused gaze and clear skin, he looked utterly self-confident and perfectly in control. The camera then pulled back to reveal a group of young, tough guys in jeans and tight T-shirts. They got up, intimidated a few kids and then did the unexpected, the unimaginable, the incomprehensible: they started to dance! Gang members were twirling, jumping, gliding, leaping into the air and kicking their legs up over their heads!

Riff, Bernardo, Ice and Action were outgoing and fearless. At a dance in their school gym, each one of them showed up with a beautiful girlfriend. Their relentless energy as they danced, whether in a gym, a playground or on New York City streets, shook me to the very core of my sixteen-year-old soul. The desire I had once shown for expressing myself was re-ignited that afternoon. Sitting in the cool darkness of the Carlton Cinema, I knew I would never be the same.

For this acne-scarred guy who was sexually shut down, dancing, at least as done by two choreographed street gangs, came to represent the most masculine activity imaginable, and I latched onto the idea of dance as the path to uniqueness, clear skin and popularity. Dance seemed like the magic elixir: as a dancer I would be able to express myself without having to speak. It would surely transform me from the shy teenager I had become to the real me who was expressive and outgoing. The men's dancing in *West Side Story* became a guiding force that, slowly and unsteadily, propelled me forward.

I had already grown into a teenager who loved to move, but did not like to speak; who was emotional, but rarely expressed any feelings. I was a good athlete in just about every sport I tried; my strengths were in my ability to duck, twist and turn, whether that meant getting to the ball as a tennis player or eluding opposing players as they lunged at me on a football field. So even though dance was foreign to me, dynamic movement was natural.

I had no one to talk with about what I was experiencing, nor was I able to imagine how, in Toronto in 1962, a teenager might set out on a path that involved even *thinking* about dancing. I had no guide. At that time there was not even one performing arts high school, nor one university dance program in the city. And I knew that, if I ever figured out how one could learn to dance, I would have to hide all such activity from my parents.

Dance Steps

That summer, I attended a fine arts camp called Manitou-Wabing, another idyllic lakeside retreat north of Toronto. I had gone there for sports and to play the string bass in the camp orchestra. At a staff concert, two dancers from Toronto, Yoné Kvietys and George Donnell, performed something I was told was modern dance. Mr. Donnell did not wear blue jeans and did not snap his fingers and rumble under the highway. He partnered Ms. Kvietys lovingly and playfully with athletic and muscular moves. I watched him somehow leap into the air sideways with his legs split, and then do a roll on the floor as he came down. Then he bounced up into the air and jumped towards Ms. Kvietys who was doing a series of crazy spins. He took her by the waist and lifted her straight up over his head, making that impossible feat look easy. How did they do that? I watched them perform all through the summer and was aching to learn how to move the way they did, but never thought of taking one of their classes.

The next summer, I dared to dance in a Manitou-Wabing production of the musical *The Pajama Game*. The plot concerns the members of a workers' union in a pyjama factory who go on strike for higher wages. I was surprised to see how song and dance could transform this seemingly serious and dry story into something that was upbeat and fun. Three hours north of my parents' critical eyes, my need to try this activity called "dancing" (an activity which I had only previously experienced in the arms of the perfume-drenched ballroom instructor, Sandy) won out over my fear of being caught and censored. The camp had a dance program in which lots of girls had enrolled, but no boys. So all of the guys interested in performing were accepted into the musical cast by default. We performed very simple movements. One of the girls told me I was graceful and stayed on the beat.

At the end of that summer, Yoné Kvietys gave me the location of her Toronto dance studio, but I didn't find my way there. I did, however, take some gymnastic classes and learned to do a flip.

A Golf Trophy

The next summer at camp, I auditioned for the role of finger-snapping Riff, the leader of the Jets in *West Side Story*, and I got the part. Garbut Roberts, our camp choreographer, created movement for the guys that, in spite of our total lack of training, was manageable and felt good. He was the first adult working in the arts with whom I spent time talking—easy to do as he was sincere and treated his young students with respect. With his broad shoulders, long lyrical arms and beak-like nose, he reminded me of a gentle vulture.

Playing a leading character for the first time was a challenge. I was slow memorizing my lines and nervous saying them in front of everyone. Garbut, however, was both a sympathetic director and a patient choreographer. He brought out the best in everyone. I experienced the wonder of seeing all the elements of the musical come together, participating in a journey that, at times, resembled an obstacle course.

During the three performances, with lights, costumes and makeup to smooth out my skin, with dialogue, songs and dance steps, I became one of those cool guys in jeans whom I'd seen on screen, who was outgoing and mas-culine. After the shows, girls who hadn't looked at me all summer were lined up at the stage door. They talked to me as if I really was Riff, the gang leader of the Jets.

At the camp's closing ceremony, I was voted "Best Actor" of the summer. The Theatre Department was short on trophies so I didn't get mine that night.

A few weeks later in mid-September, back in Toronto, I was doing some gardening in our front yard with my parents when a car drove up unexpect-edly. The Camp Director got out and presented me with my award. I guess he had forgotten what I had actually won it for, because the trophy I received was of a woman swinging a golf club. In any case, my secret was now out in the open. Both Mom and Dad gave me a quiet "congratulations," and walked away.

Cabaret Drumming and Hawaiian Dance

Back in Toronto, Garbut made a living performing South Asian-style dances with dance partner Suzanne Charlton. He taught me a few rhythms on conga drums and, at seventeen, in Grade 12, I became their accompanist—underage, but playing in clubs for their shows around the city.

I made my professional dance debut performing his choreography. Still untrained, I was part of a trio of dancers that included Garbut and summer camp friend Lorne Weil, faking my way through some Garbut-inspired "Hawaiian" steps. Garbut had been hired to stage a Hawaiian cultural festival at Eaton's Auditorium, now an upscale Toronto arts venue known as The Carlu. I had to dye my light-brown hair black, wear a grass skirt and, for the second time in my limited performing career, had to colour my skin with dark make-up. "Please God," I prayed, "don't let my parents or friends come to this show!" Looking at myself in the mirror, I realized it didn't matter if they came or not. I didn't even recognize myself. I thought the dance would be a nightmare, with me wearing a skirt in front of a big crowd, but I really got into it, vibrating my knees and swinging my hips. The body makeup must have been cheap, because once the sweat soaked in, it dripped off my chest. After the show, when I saw myself in the mirror, I looked like a zebra.

A Good Mark

During my final year of high school, I quietly searched through the shelves of the library and found a tiny section devoted to theatre. There on the spine of a thin volume was the word "Dances," preceded by a name as yet unknown to me: *Martha Graham Dances.* My heart started pounding. I felt like I was breaking all the rules as I pulled that book off the shelf, held it with the cover pressed towards my chest and snuck off to a corner of the room furthest from the librarian. The book creaked when I opened it to the middle, making me believe that I was the first one ever to look at it. I studied a full-page picture whose content was totally unfamiliar. An angular woman with flaring cheekbones sat on a bench that looked like an amoeba. She wore a hair ornament that resembled a big key. Hovering over her was a bare-legged man, wearing a cape; he held a small tree branch over his right leg that was extended at right angles from his body. I could see that they were both characters in a story. But which? Underneath the photo, the caption read: "Martha Graham, Bertram Ross in *Night Journey,* the story of Oedipus and Jocasta." I flipped through the pages, mesmerized by the athletic shots of the dancers and the designs of the theatre sets. Finding that book was a whisper, a small act that pulled me in a direction I had never anticipated.

Later that year, I terrified our teacher with my essay on the subject: "What do you want to do with the rest of your life?" I wrote about why I wanted to be a dancer: "Since dance is a highly creative art, the high school curriculum will have little effect upon my personality or abilities as a dancer." I received a grade of "Good."

Shortly after, I was awarded an Ontario Scholarship. I put the money towards tuition for my first year at the University of Toronto. A lover of Charles

Dickens' Pip, David and Oliver, kids who had lived remarkable lives, I chose to major in English literature, focusing on the Victorian classics.

Light Bulb Moments

At the age of nineteen, with only a little beginner, informal dance training from Garbut Roberts, I performed in university shows, written and directed by the one and only Lorne Michaels, later of *Saturday Night Live* fame. Lorne was a year ahead of me in school and a great guy. His shows included jazzy dances, set to show-tune melodies. Lorne made up funny lyrics that satirized the school and our teachers. Around the same time, I auditioned for a CBC TV new year's variety show and was accepted. The musical numbers were Broadway-style dances. There were lots of fancy turns and high leg kicks, which I couldn't do. Strangely, although I was the least experienced in the cast, the camera focused on me for what I thought was far too much of the time.

On New Year's Eve, with my parents out celebrating at a dinner-dance, I stayed home to watch the show. I got excited when I first saw myself on our little Philips black-and-white TV screen. My excitement quickly faded though, as I watched myself moving beside the other dancers, their legs high, mine low, with my feet hanging off them like soggy pancakes. I began to suspect that something was missing.

My moment of real awareness came on the day of another audition, several months later. The musical *Guys and Dolls* was going to play at the Royal Alexandra Theatre, a 2,000-seat, ornate Victorian-style building in downtown Toronto. The producer was looking for local dancers. The choreographer was Noel Swartz, who had been a Shark in the Broadway production of *West Side Story*.

Before the start of the audition, as I stood on the stage in a row with twenty other men being scrutinized by Mr. Swartz, I looked out towards the audience. All I could relate the scene to was what I thought a professional baseball batter must see looking out from home plate to the layers of seats rising up in front of him. Having won the role of Riff at Camp Manitou-Wabing and having been a dancer on a TV show, I felt optimistic. But even though I gave the audition my best shot, watching my competitors sail through the air and spin many times on one leg while I flapped about once more, I knew there was something wrong. My suspicions were confirmed when Mr. Swartz pulled me aside and said, "You have wonderful energy, but if you ever want to dance, you're going to have to get to a studio and take classes every day." He was nice—and he was right. And the next moment, I was gone. The first person to be dismissed, I felt humiliated as I walked the lonely walk up the theatre aisle. In my imagination, I heard whoops of laughter after I had gone.

I swore that I would never make that kind of exit again, so I listened to Mr. Swartz and began finding my way, but only once in a while, to two studios. I took classes taught by Yoné Kvietys at the YM & YWHA (Young Men's and Young Women's Hebrew Association) at Bloor Street and Spadina Avenue and by her dance partner George Donnell at the United Church on St. Clair Avenue. I always made up a good story for my parents, such as saying that I was going to study at a friend's house, to keep the peace. I only trained sporadically because the more time I spent in a dance studio, the worse my university grades got. I hoped that one day I would come out of the dance closet, stand firm and confidently tell the world what I wanted to do with my life.

Reality

I became truly serious about dancing, accidentally, after my first year at university. Looking for a summer job, I wandered into a building on King Street, a major thoroughfare in the heart of downtown Toronto, thinking it was a warehouse. I heard a piano being played and followed the sound to a large room with a high ceiling, grey floor and mirror-covered walls. Muscular men were practising spinning on one leg, some of them an impossible six times. Long-legged, elegant women were turning diagonally across the floor, whipping their heads around, moving with such speed I couldn't figure out how they were keeping their balance. Everyone wore tights, the men in black, the women in pink. Seeing everyone dressed this way, with their bodies so clearly revealed, both surprised and intrigued me. No one kicked me out, so I stayed. This was my first look at ballet.[2]

At the end of the class, the teacher told me that the dancers were from the renowned National Ballet of Canada and that the National Ballet School was having a summer course. Not having a clue what I was getting myself into, I signed up, telling my parents that I had a job as a lifeguard at the local pool.

Every morning, I stuffed a bathing suit into a backpack along with my newly purchased black tights and ballet slippers. My deception made me feel uncomfortable, but the desire to learn to dance had me pulling on those tights for an unimaginable day of physical exertion. Every night, I returned home, exhausted and aching from the efforts of learning to use all my muscles in unexpected new ways. I headed for a washroom, soaked my unused bathing suit in the sink and then hung it up on a clothesline in the backyard, just to make sure my parents thought I had been teaching swimming classes all day. Then I would rinse out my tights and hang them in the most secret place I had access to, my bedroom closet.

One Friday, at midnight, when I returned home from watching a movie with friends, Mom and Dad confronted me. They seemed twelve-feet tall as they sat me down on a kitchen chair and glowered at me. Holding up my damp tights, Dad asked slowly, with lots of space between each of his words: "What are these? Are you wearing these?"

I thought of saying that tights were the required outfit for lifeguards at the Y because of ultra-religious Jewish swimmers, but thought better of it and told their unbelieving ears: "I'm taking ballet classes. All day every day."

Chaos followed. Dad tried to talk me out of going to my classes, Mom at his side: "Why choose to dance when you have the grades to be a doctor or a lawyer? Why choose poverty?"

But never having experienced poverty, I wasn't troubled. I continued going to the ballet school and put up with "the silent treatment" during our family meals. My abominable abdominal cramps got worse. I popped the familiar little white pills so I would not miss a class.

In the fall, Betty Oliphant, the National Ballet School's director, generously accepted me into the full-time program with a partial scholarship, while I was already struggling full time during my second year at the University of Toronto. Because of my lack of training, I took class with nine-year-old boys who had already been training for two years. I felt like a fool, struggling to keep up as they all jumped and turned much better than I could. The boys snickered at me a lot, while my teachers seemed surprised at my presence there and largely ignored me. Maybe they felt I would never dance professionally because, as a nineteen-year-old beginner, I didn't fit into the ballet school mould: many male dancers were professionals at my age. Anxious to prove them wrong, I worked ferociously, missing most of my university classes in order to dance.

Four teachers, however, who taught later in the year, gave me hope and were very supportive *because* I was "an old man." They were Joyce Shietze, Shirley Cash, Sandra Caverley and Nancy Shwenker. They valiantly persisted in teaching me the subtleties of the technique. Over and over again, day after day, they urged me: "Align your hips over your heels; rotate your legs from the hips." They went on to push me to make difficult movements look effortless, and to defy gravity with a variety of jumps and leaps.

To complicate my life even further, I saw an article published later that year in the *Toronto Daily Star* and, accompanying the article, a photo of one Patricia Beatty making an angular dance shape with her long, lean body on the city's main artery, Yonge Street. A Toronto native and former modern dance major at Bennington College, Vermont, she had been studying and working in New York as a dancer for several years; she had now returned home to teach the modern dance technique created by Martha Graham, the very woman whose theatrical vision was represented in the book that I had discovered in my high school library years before.

I went to watch one of Ms. Beatty's classes (she liked to be called Trish). A drummer, a defector from Cuba named Ricardo Abreut, improvised fiercely on two congas, sending a group of rugged-looking dancers through an evolving pattern of dramatic floor movements. Their raw energy seemed to me far removed from the nineteenth-century romanticism that I was struggling to embrace in my ballet classes, transporting me into more visceral territory. The darker palette of the dancers' movement was appealing to someone who found the nobility and grace intrinsic to classical ballet quite unnatural. And, I noted thankfully, everyone was closer to my age.[3]

Soon after, David Earle, a dancer in his mid-twenties, began teaching his own modern dance classes at the Artists' Workshop, in an area called the Annex, not far from the University of Toronto. David, with his fair hair, sparkling eyes and pale skin, looked to me like a prince. A former National Ballet of Canada advanced student, he, like Trish, had recently returned from New York. Because of his generous encouragement, he became the role model I desperately needed, the pathfinder who believed in me, who helped me envision possibilities.

All the dancers in my modern classes were adults, aged sixteen to thirty. Many had already trained for years in ballet, but some, like me, were novices. We were all in good condition, but unlike traditional ballet dancers, whose bodies had specific proportions and who could "turn out" or rotate their legs fully within their hip sockets in order to realize the classical lines of such works as *Swan Lake* and *Sleeping Beauty*, we came in a variety of shapes and sizes.

Trish and David showed us how to move as if we were willing servants of gravity. We jumped less and practised dramatic falls to the floor. We danced barefoot instead of wearing ballet slippers. Bare feet, often sticky from sweat, didn't allow for the multiple turns ballet dancers do wearing their slippers, but did allow for a stronger connection to the floor and better balance. Trish told me that Isadora Duncan, a pioneer of modern dance in America, had shocked early twentieth-century audiences by refusing to wear shoes when she performed. Her act, considered rebellious, represented her desire to push dance in a new direction, away from ballet.

Ballet and modern dance, as I understood them, had certain similarities that were mainly to do with the use and positioning of the legs and feet. A big difference between the two dance forms seemed to be in the training of the torso. In my ballet class, we danced with our torsos upright most of the time. But in modern, the torsos curved and spiralled, making me aware of an unlimited range of physical possibilities.

I saw that another big difference between the forms was in how dancers presented themselves. In ballet class, I usually saw dancers trying to be pretty or princely. In Graham classes, they didn't seem to be trying to be anything. They were just people. Both ballet and modern dance captured my imagination. I saw that studying each would be essential if I were to one day both defy gravity and give in to it.

I continued with dance classes, as many as I could fit in, as I struggled to get through a nineteenth-century novel every week. Somehow over the next two years, I took at least one class a day with David or Trish, as well as classes at the National Ballet School, along with all my courses at the University of Toronto. In addition, I worked as a theatre usher and co-presented a weekend film festival with my friend Joel Siegel. I performed in two children's theatre shows with David Earle and did the Charleston in a professional theatre production of the '20s musical *Good News*. I was pretty much stoned on fatigue all the time, photocopying my friends' notes from all the university classes I missed and inhaling coffee so I could keep my eyes open late into the nights to try to keep up.

Inspiration in Rochester

In the winter of 1966, Trish crammed David and six of us modern dance students into her station wagon and drove around Lake Ontario to Rochester, New York, to see the Martha Graham Dance Company.

The first dance was the 1948 piece *Diversion of Angels*. Ms. Graham, in her biography, *Blood Memory*, describes it as a dance about "the love of life and the love of love." It's a lyrical piece, with a driving score by Norman Dello Joio, showcasing men and women moving with a joyful and rich physicality. In addition to the ensemble work, three women, each joined by a male partner for a striking duet, define different aspects of love: adolescent, mature and erotic. The company members, gliding and leaping through space, their energy reaching past the footlights to where we sat twenty rows back, seemed to represent the fulfilment of everything I wanted to be as a dancer, at least until I experienced the closing act.

The final piece was *Seraphic Dialogue*, Ms. Graham's exploration of the story of Joan of Arc. When the curtain opened, there was a collective gasp from the audience. Graham and set designer Isamu Noguchi had created a Gothic cathedral of symmetrical golden rods. St. Michael, played by Bertram Ross, the man in my high-school picture-book, stood at its centre. Kneeling beneath him was Joan, danced by Mary Hinkson and, beside them, Saints Catherine and Margaret. Wearing costumes of brilliant blue, red and purple, their stillness at the centre of the shimmering golden set convinced me that they were medieval glass figures set into a soaring stained-glass window, flooded with sunlight. So perfect was this illusion that it was shocking when they suddenly moved.

Seraphic Dialogue uses retrospective storytelling to propel the drama. A "central" Joan recalls the stages of her life as maid, warrior and martyr. A different dancer performs each incarnation, conveying character through passionate choreography.

All elements of the piece, including the dancing, set, costumes, lighting and music, once again by Norman Dello Joio, came together to create a transforming and convincing journey. The performance of Mr. Ross stood out. He did not act the part of St. Michael; he *was* St. Michael. With that performance he set a standard for dancer-actors that was inspirational. I felt that if I were ever to bring such passion to my dancing, I would have to go to New York and study with this great artist.

The two dances reached out to me, took me by the shoulders and pointed me toward New York.

Free Love Anticlimax

The visceral dancing that I had witnessed in Rochester was reflective of the ethos that was all around me in 1966. Free love—love without complications, without commitment, without dating, without marriage—had been made possible by the invention and wide distribution of the birth control pill.

Fellow dancers talked over coffee after class about how a person had to experience all that life had to offer in order to become an artist. A big part of that, they all said, was lovemaking: uninhibited, free, become-one-with-the-cosmos lovemaking. I nodded knowingly in agreement whenever the topic came up, even though, at nineteen, I had still not become one with the cosmos.

My goal was to lose my virginity before I was twenty, but with only three months to go, and too shy to make the necessary advances, I was losing hope. During high school, I had managed to look up from my pizza once in a while on dinner dates to see a beautiful face looking back at me with interest, somehow not minding my blemish-covered face. Hooking up usually resulted in extended periods of high-velocity making-out in my parents' car, or on the grass in deserted parks and schoolyards. But for me, entry into the exalted territory beyond "third base" appeared to be impossible. It seemed that free love was restricted to the fortunate few, namely the boys who had longstanding girlfriends, or the ones who got together with one of the school's few "bad girls."

My friend Bobby Weinberg approached me after university classes one afternoon, with a big smirk on his face: "I had sex yesterday with this older woman, maybe twenty-five, really cute, our family's housekeeper. She grabbed me in our kitchen and we did it under the table. She taught me some cool tricks. You gotta learn these 'tricks' from someone, Kenny, or you're not gonna do it right."

I had no clue what these "tricks" might be and was instantly worried that, without them, I would never be a successful lover or, by extension, a successful artist. A helpful housekeeper who would throw me down on the kitchen floor would have been an ideal teacher; but our family's housekeeper, who visited every other Thursday while my mother was home, was a married grandmother named Mrs. Kaplotnik.

Then, at a party of dancers in a classmate's apartment one cold January night, a long-limbed dancer with a perky pony-tail started a conversation with me. She was someone I had seen in class a few times, but knew little about. I didn't even know her name. I did know that she had a well-muscled boyfriend who eyed us suspiciously as we talked about her aching back and my sore knees.

"I want to show you some therapeutic moves that will definitely help you feel better," she said, her boyfriend now engaged in conversation with his back towards us. She led me from the kitchen, down the hallway to the bedroom. "Get ready for the healing," she announced, and she shoved me through the door onto a bed covered with dozens of the partygoers' winter coats. Executing a dancerly leap, she pounced on me and pulled a bunch of coats and scarves over us. With no knowledge of Bobby Weinberg's tricks and distracted by visions of her boyfriend bursting through the door with a kitchen knife, I became a man.

The Right Choice

I wrote my final exams at the University of Toronto in mid-1967. Around that time, my teachers, David and Trish, and their friend, New York born dancer Peter Randazzo, generously invited me to dance in their upcoming performances. Their invitation was a great opportunity, but my deep admiration for their work prevented me from taking them up on it; ironically, it convinced me that I should leave Toronto. I knew that all three of them had spent years in New York. And I felt that, if I were to reach their level of excellence, I needed to head to New York, too.

But there was a more personal reason for my quick exit. If you were a young man living in 1967 in Toronto's Jewish community, and if you had good grades, you became a doctor or lawyer. If you didn't, you went into a family business.

Mom and Dad thought—they prayed—that I would soon come to my senses and learn to heal the sick, like the sons of their friends. But I knew I had already come to my senses. Dance was a lifeline I couldn't abandon and I knew it would be easier to pursue my dream in a city far from my parents' disapproval.

It was a rough day for all of us when I finally told them I was not only choosing dance, but also leaving for the U.S. They were disappointed and afraid, but the night before my departure they gave me a sort of blessing: "We don't want you to go, but if you must, we'd like to give you some money so you can afford to stay in a safe neighbourhood." Even though I was close to broke, I was too proud to take anything from them.

Into the Light

My *West Side Story* look
Author's personal
collection

The train stopped at Penn Station, 33rd Street and 7th Avenue. As I stepped in front of the glass doors, ready to leave, I paused to look at my reflection: a slender, six-foot-tall guy with an oval-shaped, serious face showing only a little of the teen spoiler. Fifteen hours after setting out, my curly brown hair, tamed every morning with a handful of gel, had remained slicked down in a James Dean–style pompadour, parted on the left. Wearing a T-shirt and tight Levi's, I felt my *West Side Story* look was perfect for my imminent entry into the island of Manhattan.

I had no money, no work, no friends and no legal status. Who cared? My dreams were just going to come true, no matter what.

I gave myself a quick smile and grabbed my bag, filled with only a few articles of clothing, dance clothes, a bar of soap, a toothbrush and a razor, and headed for the subway. My mind was racing, full of questions. Would I be good enough one day to join a company? How could I receive a salary when I didn't have a Social Security Number? Would I be drafted? Would I be deported?

I took the No. 2 train north to Times Square, then walked carefully along endless underground passageways, working my way through charging crowds of people, all of whom seemed to be aiming straight at me. I searched for the SS crosstown shuttle that would take me eastward to Grand Central Station, locating its symbol in a jumble of letters: A, AA, B, C, D, E, SS. A short ride later, I took another hike underground to the Lexington Avenue line, and headed south to my final destination, the East Village, Lower East Side.[4]

Climbing the stairs to the street, all the clatter in my head about the draft and visas became background noise. I felt all-powerful, fortified by the excitement, dreams and strength-giving naiveté I had needed to make my big move to the dance capital of the world.

I exited into sunlight at Astor Place, right across from the Cooper Union Hall, a place where Abraham Lincoln once spoke. In front of me there was, and still is, a ten-foot high black cube sculpture balancing on one of its corners. Three guys around my age, with hair long and loose, wearing wide bellbottoms, were slowly turning it. Painted in pink on one side was a peace symbol. On another, as the cube turned, I read, "Screw Vietnam, I'm going to Canada."

I looked at my map, turned left along St. Mark's Place, the main east-west street through the East Village, and started walking.

The Cube, 2010.
Photograph: Kenny Pearl

Life is Different on the Lower East Side

I found myself in a tie-dyed world saturated with the scent of marijuana, the lazy strumming of guitars all around. The lyric from the Beatles' new song, *Strawberry Fields*, "Nothing is real and nothing to get hung about,"[5] played over and over in my head. With my *West Side Story* look I felt like an outcast as I walked past white guys with ponytails and beards, and women with long, lanky hair entwined with colourful love beads. An African-American man with a massive Afro called out, "Welcome white brother," figuring that the non-tie-dyed, narrow-panted, short-haired guy lugging a suitcase and looking stunned was a newcomer.

I passed "head shops" with drug paraphernalia on display; vintage clothing stores showcasing navy pea-jackets; and a bookstore, where, through the front window, I saw volumes written by thinkers still unknown to me, including *Autobiography of a Yogi*, by Swami Yogananda, and *The Feminine Mystique*, by Betty Friedan. The only author I recognized was Martin Luther King Jr., the African-American civil rights leader. I passed the Electric Circus, a psychedelic dance club painted navy blue, and the St. Marks repertory cinema, advertising a $2 double bill of *Bonnie and Clyde* and *Cool Hand Luke*. Lamp posts were covered with fliers announcing an upcoming anti-war demonstration in Washington, D.C. On one wall someone had spray painted, "No nukes is good nukes;" on another, "Burn baby, burn." Coming from a culturally homogeneous neighbourhood of Toronto, I was surprised to see so many people with skin much darker than mine.

Heading south on 2nd Avenue, I stopped at the corner of 7th Street and listened to the sounds of Spanish being heatedly spoken by a group of men. At 6th Street, I passed the celebrated Fillmore East Theater. On the marquee I saw an announcement for the premiere of the Beatles' new film, *Magical Mystery Tour*. Posters in display boxes advertised upcoming shows by the most famous rock bands of the day, including The Doors, Jefferson Airplane, Jimi Hendrix, and Big Brother and the Holding Company, featuring Janis Joplin. Just south of the Fillmore, I walked past a Kosher vegetarian restaurant called Rappaport's. I saw elderly waiters through the window dressed formally in black and white, and a mix of blue-haired seniors and long-haired hippies seated at the tables. At the corner of East 4th Street, I picked up a free *Village Voice* newspaper and then turned right. Along the way was an experimental theatre called La MaMa.

I arrived at the front entrance of my new home, 69 East 4th Street, noticing the lock was broken and the intercom was smashed, and got ready to figure out how to use four keys to open one door.

2

CLIMBING

October 1967 – August 1970

Home

East 4th Street resisted sunlight. The block was a stretch of blackened, grimy brick divided into five-storey tenements, criss-crossed by rusted fire escapes. Along the street, a few scraggly trees somehow managed to grow a few leaves. They were barely noticeable alongside the rows of garbage cans that over-flowed with reeking trash, days before Friday pickup. Men from the Bowery ("skid row," a resting place for the homeless, at the end of the block) had established a permanent meeting place by the curb in front of the apartment door. Most mornings, a few of them lay contorted on the sidewalk, their liquor bottles clutched firmly to their chests, broken glass everywhere.

I learned from my new Puerto Rican neighbours that the local Hell's Angels had set up their headquarters a block further south, and that to the southeast there were actual street gangs, but without the dance steps.

By day, the most noticeable feature of my building was the disinterested, round face of the superintendent's wife. It perched over crossed hands that rested on a windowsill behind a cage of security bars. The face was always there, watching life on East 4th Street go by, giving away nothing. Her husband, a stick with a belly, could usually be found leaning against the front doorpost, Budweiser in hand, glazed eyes fixed on overflowing garbage. His wire-rimmed eyeglasses teetered on the end of his nose, held together at their centre by what looked like a decaying band-aid.

He told me with a slurred Puerto Rican accent that, for one day of the year, the building's intercom was usable and not ripped out of the wall. That was the day the city's maintenance man came and repaired the system that would get torn off the wall later that night. Then, for about a year, the speaker would just hang by a few wires, a reminder that city officials don't care that much about what goes on in a City of New York rent-controlled apartment that goes for $36.50 a month. The front door of 69 East 4th Street was therefore left unlocked and street people from the Bowery often hung out inside as well as outside. With visiting privileges guaranteed, no tenement was more popular than number 69, already known as the Bowery Hotel when I arrived.

69 East 4ᵗʰ Street, 2010. All cleaned up, but with security bars and garbage cans still intact.
Photograph: Kenny Pearl

Inside the front door was, to be kind, the foyer. The floor, large enough to accommodate one person only, was a square covered with black and white mosaic tiles. It seemed that these tiles had once been set down carefully and cleverly in the shape of an eagle with outstretched wings. Likely meant to greet the newly arrived immigrants who had always populated the building, this great American symbol of freedom, with its tiled beak broken off and the tail almost gone, now looked like a bat.

A few feet down the hall on the right was the super's apartment. Next, on the left (hard to imagine, coming from a middle-class home with three full bathrooms) was the door to my toilet. It was like an indoor outhouse and was about ten feet down the hall from my front door. This distance taught me terrific bladder control, especially on cold nights, when the Bowery Hotel was doing good business. Next to my apartment door, and to its right, was the third ground-floor apartment, whose tenants were constantly changing.

Getting to my apartment door was an adventure. I always moved slowly down the hallway, listening and sniffing for signs of life. The smell of urine and unwashed bodies indicated someone from the sidewalk had migrated indoors. If there was snoring coming from under the stairwell, I was safe. But if there was silence, it was good to be careful. Someone might be awake and lying in wait.

Of the four locks on my front door, the most impressive one, the enforcer, was the "police lock." This was a four-foot-long steel bar that lodged into a hole in the floor inside the apartment a foot from the door. It rose on a sharp angle to the lock where it fit into a slider that moved from side to side when you turned the key. I was pretty confident that it, at least, would serve its function if an interested burglar decided to check the place out.

After a bit of practice, going through the many moves necessary to unlock my door became a fluid piece of satisfying hand choreography—slide, turn, lift-slide, turn again.

I had grown up in a home with a kitchen so clean and shiny that I could see my reflection in our grey and lime-green linoleum floor. So I had to get used to sharing space with a thriving cockroach community. In most parts of town, cockroaches would dive for cover as soon as someone flipped on a light switch. But the ones that had evolved on the Lower East Side were fearless. Arriving home each night, I turned on the light, which was their signal to get into marching band formation and parade confidently around the sink.

The front room was kitchen as well as bathroom. The sink was to the right of the front door and to its right was a deep, clawfoot bathtub. Across from the bathtub were the stove and fridge. I found that having the bathtub in the kitchen, right by the front door, wasn't such a bad arrangement and was actually timesaving. I could have a bath and greet guests at they arrived.

There was no hallway. To the right of the kitchen was the living room, that doubled as a guest room. To the left was my bedroom, with space only for my queen-sized waterbed. As mentioned, the toilet was outside the apartment, down the often-populated hall.

I found most of my real furniture on the street. One piece I picked up on garbage night was a bureau with a sailboat carved into the top drawer. Aside from that, my apartment was entirely furnished with wooden orange crates. No one would have guessed that these humble crates would be for sale twenty years later in designer stores after plastic furnishings flooded the market. At the time, there were a few in the garbage every week in front of the little grocery store next to our building. At the peak of my crate frenzy, I had twenty-eight. I painted some white and stained others walnut. I used them for all my shelves and for my kitchen chairs and table.

The bedroom and the kitchen each had one window, which looked out onto airshafts, narrow spaces between the buildings. A twin window looked right back at each one, but there was so much dirt caked onto them that privacy was no problem. Occasionally, a falling beer bottle would catch my attention through the haze, the glass smashing, people somewhere laughing. Sometimes there were loud arguments; occasionally, screams.

Two security-barred living-room windows at the end of the apartment looked out onto a dull concrete courtyard, with the opposite building fifteen feet away. If I pulled back the security bars, pressed my face against the glass and strained my eyes upward, I could just see a tiny triangle of blue sky. So I called the apartment "the Cave": twenty-four hours without daylight.

I painted the floors dark green, tore the plaster off a few of the walls to expose the brick and painted all the other walls white. On them, I scotch-taped a print of Matisse's five dancing figures and a poster of Martha Graham with prominent cheekbones emphatically catching the photographer's lights. Between the two courtyard windows, I hung a found square of spiralling mattress springs and a dinner plate with a sun painted on it.

While painting the floor, I noticed a few floorboards that were cut into a small square. They lifted up easily and underneath was a small compartment containing partially filled bottles of whiskey and gin. I thought they might have dated from prohibition days, but the labels were recent. Maybe someone had been hiding booze from a partner to whom a promise of abstinence had been made.

A used sound system, consisting of a low-end record player, amp and speakers, represented my one "extravagant" bit of spending. I clipped a lamp onto the edge of an orange crate, aiming it a few inches from a peace lily plant, further pushing back the gloom in what I had turned into a colourful and light-bulb-bright place.

One night during my first week, after moving quietly past a man snoring under the stairwell, I was going through the find-the-right-key ritual, when someone grabbed my shoulder and spun me around. It was the stairwell man. "I want a picture. Take our picture together," he screamed in my face, his breath overwhelming. There was a broken wine bottle in his right hand aimed at my head. The fingers of his left hand dug into my throat.

"I can do that. Let me go inside," I responded quietly. "I'll get my camera."

He held onto me. "Now. I want it now. Before the wedding, before she sees me."

This guy thought he was getting married and wanted a picture without a camera. I pretended to take a picture. No luck. He shoved me and screamed his orders again.

The superintendent's door opened. There she was, the super's wife. It was the first time I had seen her away from her barred window and upright. She was short and round, calm and menacing, and she held a steaming frying pan in her hand. Her husband cowered behind her, a Bud in his.

Even with my assailant's bottle aimed at my head, the smell of garlic surprisingly made me think of what I hoped to make for dinner a little later.

"Not in my hallway," the super's wife said quietly but firmly, her Puerto Rican accent exotic and theatrical. For a big woman, she moved well. With two long strides she was beside my assailant. Raising the pan over her head, vegetables flying off behind her, she brought it down with just enough force. He fell and stayed down. Following her directions, I dragged him to her, thanking her, praising her cool attitude and deft moves.

With a foot on his chest, frying pan raised overhead triumphantly, she looked as heroic as the Statue of Liberty with her torch. And her message was the same: "Welcome to New York."

First Class Catastrophe

The clock above the mirror read 9:55. The date was an auspicious one—Friday, October 13, the day of my first class at the Martha Graham School of Dance (the Graham School). Thirty intermediate-level students, most of us late starters to dance already in our early twenties, sat nervously on the floor of Studio One. We had arrived that morning to find a note on the bulletin board beside the class schedule. It said that Mary Hinkson, our teacher, was sick, and that the legendary Martha Graham, who rarely taught the intermediate level, would be teaching in her place. The shockwaves generated by that note had us all vibrating.

In 1967, the school was the temple of modern dance and its high priestess was Martha Graham, choreographer, dancer, teacher and genius. The oak floor on which we were stretching and fidgeting was, for us acolytes, sacred ground. It had been oiled and smoothed for many years by the moving feet of both aspiring students and seasoned professional dancers, by the dancers in her company who had executed thousands of turns and leaps as they prepared to embody the great protagonists of the Graham repertoire: Jocasta and Oedipus, Medea and Joan of Arc; dancers whom Ms. Graham had called "Acrobats of God."

Renowned lighting, costume and set designers, as well as gifted composers, had all sat on the flowing wooden benches designed by the set designer and sculptor, Isamu Noguchi, that lined the front of the studio. A number of dinosaur-bone-like props leaned against the walls and a grand piano stood at the back, beside the entrance. Two windows, latticed with security wire, let in rays of dusty morning light. And there, waiting for Ms. Graham, front and centre, was a plain wooden chair upon which she sat each day holding court, teaching and creating.

When I later told this story to friends, I said that I had prepared for that class by letting the creative energies absorbed by and reflecting off the studio walls sink into my bones and inspire me to be my best. Actually, that day I had been sick with a temperature, a possible outcome of my stressful train trip and sleepless night after arriving. I couldn't stop blowing my nose into a huge wad of Kleenex, which, between blows, I stuffed under my belt. All I was hoping for was to get through class without my nose dripping, as I danced across the floor in front of Ms. Graham.

9:59. All eyes looked up at the clock. In one minute, the great star of modern dance, the very person who had been at the centre of the many photos I had studied in my high-school-library dance book, would be sitting in front of me. In the stillness of a picture, she had radiated enough energy to seemingly leap out at all observers. What would she be like in person, only ten feet away?

10:00. We all turned to the door at the back of the studio. It opened sharply and we sprang to our feet. The woman knew how to make an entrance, conscious of what she wanted our first impression of her to be. Lightning. Dressed in a black kimono embroidered with gold stitching, a black fan in her right hand, Martha Graham seemed to glide across the floor, streaking through the thirty of us mere mortals. Behind her walked her demonstrator for the day, the passionate and heroic Bertram Ross, the man who had inspired me in Rochester playing St. Michael in the dance, *Seraphic Dialogue*. She used a demonstrator because, at seventy-three, she might still indicate movement for her company members, but she would rarely agree to demonstrate a dance phrase before an intermediate class.

Ms. Graham stood at the front of the room facing us, shorter than I had expected, but filling space with her power, her will, her cheekbones. Her first words to those of us who didn't quite know what to do with our trembling arms were: "Don't ever stand in front of your teacher with your arms folded across your chests. You look resistant, defensive. A teacher wants to see that place where your heart beats."

With her unblinking gaze, she studied each of us, letting us know that, while she might be seventy-three, she could still, in a flash, transform herself into Clytemnestra, the murderous queen of ancient Greece, for many years one of her starring roles.

Then she gave us our cues. Her first was, "Please be seated." (The ritual of a Graham class begins with a sequence of movements on the floor.) I blew my nose one last time as she gave us her second cue, "and"—the word that in the

Graham lexicon implies continuity, that leads the dancers from their street life into their dance life.

What I remember most about that class was the final jump with which we all travelled diagonally across the floor, passing dangerously close to Ms. Graham. This movement was not radically different from a simple skip, much like you do when you're a kid. But in dance, not much comes easily. After being instructed to point our feet, drop our shoulders, pull up our leaping legs so their thigh muscles were long and stretched, and to position our arms so as to make a very specific shape, we set off, two at a time. I knew I could do this well. I ran and skipped, ran and skipped, covering space, feeling free, powerful, a new disciple and future company member. My nose did not run.

11:30. We finished our last jumps and Ms. Graham called us back to our starting positions. Sweating and panting, arms straight down at our sides, we were all careful to let her see that place from which our hearts were now rapidly beating.

As we waited for her parting words of wisdom, we all noticed that right in front of her, on that most sacred floor that our feet had just polished with our own leaps and turns, lay a big clump of used Kleenex. Judging by the look of horror on all the dancers' faces, a mangy dog may as well have come in and done its thing right there in front of Ms. Graham. We all knew she saw it, though she did not look at it. Apparently she was not going to let us leave until the offensive matter was taken away.

11:31. No one moved. Silence.

11:32. As I stepped forward, the whole class holding its breath, I felt that my life as a dancer was about to end. I picked up the Kleenex, mumbled, "I'm sorry, Ms. Graham," and went back to my place. She didn't look at me and said nothing. She was Clytemnestra on her throne.

She then made one last pronouncement. She stood. And with a voice that started quietly and then rose in volume to become an imperious growl meant for all in New York to hear, she exclaimed, "You all did well, but that is not good enough. From what I can see, there are only two of you in this room who will ever be dancers."

She emphasized ever.

Then, with the same lightning impulse that charged her entrance, she parted the waters once more, leaving us stunned.

With everyone shunning me, I headed for the changing room. An arm that felt as thick as a car tire wrapped around my shoulders. It belonged to one of my fellow dancers, a young woman who stood out in class not only because she seemed about as wide as she was tall, but also because she moved very gracefully. "That was a riot," she said through a big burst of laughter. "I'm Abie. I wish I'd thought of dropping a big wad of Kleenex in front of that prima donna."

I couldn't believe it. Here was someone speaking about "the legend" as if she were merely human.

"And don't worry pal," she continued, whispering confidentially, "I was watching you. If there are two people in this class who are going to dance in her company one day, they're going to be you and me."

A Few Notes About Martha Graham

Martha Graham was born on May 11, 1894, in Pittsburgh, Pennsylvania, into a prosperous, strict Presbyterian family. Her father, Dr. George Graham, was an "alienist," a physician who specialized in the study of human behaviour, with a specific interest in the way people used their bodies. Later in her career, Ms. Graham often used her father's saying: "Movement never lies." [6] The family moved to California in 1908, where she became interested in dance after seeing a performance given by Ruth St. Denis, one of the American founders of modern dance. Due to the principles of his faith, her father discouraged her from pursuing a life in the arts. In spite of his disapproval, at eighteen, Ms. Graham enrolled for classes at the Denishawn School of Dancing and Related Arts (named after Ms. St. Denis and her dancer-choreographer husband, Ted Shawn). After her father passed away in 1914, Ms. Graham felt free to follow her dream.

Aside from the exoticisms of Ruth St. Denis, whose work was characterized by its religious and Far Eastern content, and the Greek interpretations of Isadora Duncan, the young Martha Graham would likely have seen vaudeville acts, minstrel shows, ballroom exhibitions and Broadway shows. What was considered to be "serious" dance were the performances of visiting European ballet companies, which generally presented women as ethereal beings in fantasy romantic stories.

Martha Graham performed with the Denishawn Company until 1923, after which she took a job with the Greenwich Village Follies. Two years later, she left the Follies to teach at the Eastman School of Music and Theater in Rochester, New York, and the John Murray Anderson School in New York City.

Martha Graham and Bertram Ross, 1961, *Visionary Recital.*
Photograph: Carl Van Vechten,
Reproduction Number LC-USZ62-106859
Courtesy of the Library of Congress

Her influences were many. They included her father, her former teachers, the psychoanalytic theories of Dr. Sigmund Freud, European dance theatre, the South Asian practice of yoga, as well as the dance forms of Bali, Indonesia. Her technique initially departed from classical ballet with specific body movements, two of which she identified as contraction and release. These were based upon a principle initially propounded by a 19th-century French musician and teacher named François Delsarte. She told us in class that the contraction, a deep curve in the spine, became a part of her technique after she had studied the shape a body made when experiencing grief. Release, enacted by the straightening of the spine and expansion of the chest, evoked joy and extroversion.

In 1926, she established the Martha Graham Center of Contemporary Dance. Her initial programs were stylistically similar to those of her teachers, but she quickly found her artistic voice and began conducting sophisticated experiments in dance, based on her belief that the spiritual and emotional undercurrents in real people were largely ignored in Western dance forms.

Over seven decades, she conceived and shaped what was, arguably, the major dance form of the twentieth century. Martha Graham was to dance what Picasso was to painting, and Stravinsky to music. Ms. Graham broke barriers. Not only did she choreograph innovative works of art, she also created a dance technique that could teach an aspiring dancer to dance and to potentially develop the skill to perform her work. The Graham technique is possibly her greatest achievement.

Particularly in her early years, her choreographed movement was done percussively. This gave Graham's dancers a hard look, one that was unfamiliar to audiences used to the smooth, lyrical motions of Isadora Duncan and Ruth St. Denis, as well as to those of classical ballet. This hard look was often not "pretty," but it enabled Ms. Graham and her dancers to convey the emotional lives of real people. In early reviews, she was often accused of dancing in an "ugly" way. Ugliness did not scare her. She commented, "Ugliness may be actually beautiful if it cries out with the voice of power." [7]

She drew inspiration for her characters from many sources, including Greek mythology (Jocasta, for example, in her celebrated work *Night Journey*) and the history of women of stature (such as Joan of Arc, in *Seraphic Dialogue*). She explored the universality of her characters, using them to express life's journeys and passages. Unwilling to compromise, she courageously expressed ideas that were often dark, psychological and concerned with social injustices; strange subjects for audiences accustomed to Broadway showgirls and lovely maids in ballet fairy tales.

Martha Graham received an armload of honours for her achievements. In 1976, she became the first dance artist to receive the Presidential Medal of Freedom. In 1998, *Time* magazine named her "Dancer of the Century" and *People* magazine called her one of the female "icons of the century."

The First Months

Classes

As an "independent" dancer, I was not formally enrolled in any official professional training program. I was totally on my own, with only myself to trust to carve out a daily training routine. Young, with little experience, I somehow had to make the right choices.

During my first weeks in New York, I investigated different classes. I felt it was important for me to train in a way that would make me versatile. I saw that dancers who took classes in only one studio never really spread their wings. Choosing teachers, however, could be tricky, as it was easy to get pulled in by their personalities and neglect to assess what, and how well, they taught.

Most mornings, I'd wake up before 7:00, the pain in my thighs and butt a visceral alarm clock. I'd stuff a water bottle, dinner leftovers, three pairs of black tights, three white T-shirts, a pair of ballet slippers and three dance belts (uncomfortably tight, elasticized underwear, meant to stabilize and protect) into my backpack and head out to the Graham School.

The school, a three-storey, red-brick building that housed three dance studios, was located at 316 East 63rd Street, between 1st and 2nd Avenues, on a block lined mainly with high-end brick apartment buildings. With an ivy-covered garden to its left and a graceful ironwork fence out front, it was clearly the lone survivor of a more genteel age. Georgie Graham, Martha Graham's sister (whom Abie knowingly confided had been the better dancer of the two), worked in the office. Before my first class, she had given me an information sheet explaining how this unique former residence, in a ritzy part of town, had become a dance studio. Ms. Graham had been befriended by a remarkable philanthropist named Bethsabée de Rothschild, a member of the famous European banking dynasty; she in turn also happened to be married to Donald Bloomingdale, of Bloomingdale's department store fame. She had been a student at the Graham School, and for a short time she had provided the funding for the school. Later, she helped produce company tours. Ms. Rothschild settled in Israel in 1962, changed her name to the Hebrew, "Batsheva," and founded the Batsheva Dance Company, which Ms. Graham visited, teaching and setting her repertoire.

After being buzzed into the school, I'd head down a narrow hallway, past a small studio on the left, and turn right just before Studio One into the men's changing room. Its smell was a mix of Ivory soap and mould. After changing, I'd make my way into the main studio and stretch for an hour before the start of the 10:00 a.m. class.

The class was often taught by Robert Cohan. He was tall, dark and Hollywood-handsome, a Jewish man from Brooklyn: modern dance's Tony Curtis. He had served on a submarine in the Second World War, something I could barely comprehend, and began to dance before I was born. While Ms. Graham's voice had been all growl and snarl, Mr. Cohan's was warm and quiet.

One morning, unhappy with the way we were executing the basic movements of the Graham technique, the contraction and release, he gave us a talk: "As you exhale, a rounding movement travels from the pelvis to the top of the head."

He sat on the floor and showed us the right way to do it: his torso made the shape of a "C." "When done poorly, it looks like a hunching over." He then showed us the wrong way.

"Done well, the chest hollows, the lower back reaches and the shoulders stay over the hips. The release, the affirmation, is initiated by an inhalation." He then took in a quick breath and his spine unfurled with the speed and power of a whip being cracked. "It is the flow of energy upwards from the contraction."

His demonstration of these seemingly simple movements was spellbinding. I saw that a dancer didn't have to do big technical feats to be engaging. It was possible to curl and release your spine with a single breath and create magic.

One night, I was on the subway after an evening class. There, on a seat directly in front of me, sat Robert Cohan. I froze. Before I could move, he looked up, smiled and motioned for me to sit beside him. What was I going to say? I didn't have to worry. He was warm and nice, so I relaxed and talked about myself non-stop.

As Astor Place approached, I said, "Nice talking to you. This is my stop."

He replied, "Mine too." So the novice and the star climbed up into the light across from the black rotating cube with its pink peace sign and headed down St. Mark's Place. As we walked through the marijuana haze, I told him how sore I was. He said, "For dancers at your level, three classes every day will make for a solid routine, one that will leave you feeling pain in your thighs as you climb up every step of the subway stairs after the ride home."

I nodded.

"At twenty," he added, "I'm sure you can go full out all day and still get up the next morning more than ready to go."

I nodded again.

He went on to prepare me for my possible future: "Soon, after you start rehearsing, your thighs will feel like you're climbing those subway stairs when you're only just getting out of bed. That's when you'll realize how much discipline and love it takes to survive as a dancer."

Ballet at 2 p.m.

After my morning class at the Graham School, I took a crosstown bus to the West Side to an afternoon ballet class with Barbara Cole, a former American Ballet Theater soloist. I chose to study ballet with Ms. Cole because she was knowledgeable, had a great eye and, not incidentally, gave me a lot of attention. I preferred her class of only a dozen adult dancers over one of the crowded, super-popular ones at the big company studios, such as those of the Harkness and Joffrey ballet companies, because I didn't want to be lost in a crowd. Ms. Cole understood my passion for dance, and knew that I was training in ballet to make myself a better modern dancer, not because I was aspiring to be a professional ballet dancer.

My ongoing studies with Ms. Cole made me aware that ballet technique was not as flat as I had originally believed. A good dancer uses his whole body in a three dimensional way, no matter what the discipline may be. Principles learned in Barbara Cole's ballet class fed my work in modern, and vice versa. In her classes I worked on the quick footwork, turns, jumps and leaps that were now becoming more a part of the modern dance vocabulary.

The Choreographer Who Flipped Coins

Evenings, I often took the train to Merce Cunningham's studio, which was located back on the east side at 33rd Street and Lexington Avenue. Mr. Cunningham, a soloist with the Graham Company from 1939 to 1944, began creating his own work in the late 1940s. Along with his primary composer, John Cage, he became a leader of the avant-garde movement of dance in America. Many fellow dancers considered Mr. Cunningham's dances to be dry and abstract. True, there were no narrative "through lines," or stories told in his work, and the duets he choreographed did not convey an accessible meaning. But I found many of his dances to be compelling—not because the dancers who inhabited them portrayed characters enacting an emotional story, as in Martha Graham's dramatic work, but because of their movement and what was suggested through their physical relationships.

What was really new to me, when I first watched Mr. Cunningham's company perform, was the choreographer's apparent choice to direct dancers *not* to move on the beat. When I had previously watched dance, or danced myself, I had been conscious of listening for the accompanying music's rhythm. Seeing dancers move with no evident relationship to the music at all was initially confusing. But then I read in a review that Mr. Cunningham constructed his dances largely by chance: he would often use the flip of a coin to determine certain aspects of his choreography, such as which way a dancer would face, or how long she would spend dancing a phrase, regardless of the music.

Mr. Cunningham's dances, however, were not those that I hoped to perform, because I liked moving to music that triggered emotions and propelled one's physicality. But I acquired so much respect for this man, who was so inventive and defiant, that I rushed to his studio for classes. Surprisingly, but necessarily, we moved in class to precise beats. My elementary class, usually taught by company dancers Sandra Neels and Viola Farber, was a rigorous workout, without Graham contractions but with a variety of other torso curves, bends and twists. The most challenging parts of class for me were the movement phrases that involved quick changes in direction and sudden shifts in energy.

I didn't have the money to take all of the classes that I wished, so I asked Merce Cunningham's administrator, David Vaughan, if I could work in exchange for payment. The next day, he offered me a work scholarship. Three nights a week, I got to take class for free in exchange for washing the studio floor.

At the time, Merce Cunningham lived in his studio. His kitchen was located behind a sliding partition, which separated it from the dance area. Sometimes, after class ended, Mr. Cunningham would arrive, pull back the partition and get a beverage. Once, while I sloshed the mop up and down the floor, he offered me a beer and talked to me about dancing in New York. He asked about my finances, making sure I was getting by all right. Then he told me, "Good men usually get work more easily than women because there are so few of them. Many get overconfident and miss daily classes. So few reach their full potential as a result, so don't miss class!" I remember him looking me in the eye with his uniquely quizzical and penetrating gaze, bristling with energy as if a high-voltage current were passing through him.

Not long after, a few hours before an evening class at Mr. Cunningham's studio, I was waiting for a friend in the lobby of the Museum of Modern Art. I turned and saw a tall woman with long, straight black hair and a sorrowful look, who also seemed to be waiting for someone. Neither of our friends showed up, so we began talking and started brushing against each other in front of Van Gogh's *Starry Night*.

Her name was Alice. She told me that, a month earlier, she and her boyfriend, Rob, had been driving north from Mexico with a sack of marijuana in their trunk. United States customs agents had caught them at the border and had singled out Rob to do jail time. Caught up in thoughts about beginning a relationship with a beautiful drug smuggler, I asked her out for pizza. I did my best not to look down at my plate while talking. Her pizza-eating display drew my eyes: Alice's technique involved lifting a slice, tossing her head back and then lowering it seductively into her very wide open mouth. I thought she might be sending me a signal. I fantasized about our after-dinner romp, rolling in the waves of my queen-sized waterbed. But Alice couldn't stop talking about Rob: "I miss him so much. He has the cutest tattoo on his right arm."

"There's a tattoo place on St. Mark's, near where I live," I said. "Do you want to walk over after dinner?"

She responded, "His tattoo is a poppy with my name in the centre." Then she just stared off into space.

My waterbed stopped rolling as I quickly realized that the Stephen Stills lyric, "If you can't be with the one you love, love the one you're with," [8] was not going to apply here. My free love nights in New York would have to wait.

Arriving at the Cunningham studio the next night for class, I was met by the school administrator, who greeted me with the news that I had missed my floor-cleaning duties. Distracted by Alice, I had forgotten to show up.

Goodbye scholarship. Goodbye chats with Merce Cunningham.

Technique

Becoming a good dancer in any discipline requires ongoing, fanatical dedication. Becoming a great one requires gifts from heaven. When audiences see well-trained dancers performing seemingly impossible feats, they see the tip of the iceberg, the end result. Ms. Graham often said, "How many leaps did Nijinsky take before he made the one that startled the world?"

I had already learned that, before I could execute with skill the daredevil leaps and turns, I had to practise the basic learning blocks of each discipline, many of which were shared, every day of my dance life. In every sweaty class, there were never-ending knee bends, or *pliés*, in five different leg positions; endless rises to the balls of the feet, or *relevés*; detailed articulations of the feet, pawing and brushing the floor, called *tendus* and *degagés*; leg lifts high to the front, back and side, or *développés*.[9]

In every class, my teachers' words of encouragement had me multitasking with body-mind co-ordinations I had never imagined: "Pull up your thighs, drop your shoulders, use your abs; breathe, relax, rotate, expand, suspend, extend, project, reach, relate, stretch, lengthen."

All of this work was required so that, one day, the aspiring dancer could, for example, rise onto the ball of his foot on one straight leg, the other leg held straight and waist high directly to the side of his body with the knee facing the ceiling, with a perfect physical alignment of shoulders over hips over heels, and do two or three turns with the form, precision and power that could astonish an audience. After two years, I was still working on getting my lifted leg, fully stretched, up to waist height and keeping it there—without initiating a single turn.

Nevertheless, as I watched performances, I saw something that surprised me: there were dancers who could perform incredible feats, but who didn't dance well. They didn't make the smooth movement transitions between their technical feats that would give their dancing flow and continuity. As a result, they came off looking clunky and robotic despite their technical prowess. I realized that being able to do flashy steps well only gave one the possibility of dancing well. Virtuosic moves—big jumps, high legs, multiple turns—in themselves are not good dancing. Dancing well involves an almost indefinable layer of artistry that infuses the work and gives it quality, so that the movement goes beyond a mere physical display. Dancers must learn to express the emotional content of their movement; they must be musical in a way that is not rigid but enables them to dance with, through, or against the music, or with no music at all. They must learn to dance in ways that can transform movement through shifting dynamics—percussive, soft, playful, romantic—revealing subtle qualities of the choreography.

I tried to remember and write down impactful words Ms. Graham communicated to us in class. She often spoke about the many years it usually took to become a dancer: "It takes ten years of handling the instrument, handling the material with which you are dealing, for you to know it completely." She also said that, in dance ". . . there is fatigue so great that the body cries, even in its sleep. There are times of deep frustration, there are daily small deaths."

Bad News and Good News

After a month of study, I had no idea what anyone at the Graham School thought of me. Unlike those dancers who could participate in a full-time professional training program, I had no opportunity to take part in evaluation meetings with my teachers. One morning, however, a class pianist named Ed spoke to me. He would often hang out in the Green Room, a comfortable meeting place for staff beside the studio. He gave me some distressing news: "Some of the teachers don't think you have a chance of dancing professionally."

His words made me dizzy. They seemed to validate my parents' unwavering negativity regarding my passion for dance. I spent the night lying awake, angry at myself: "Why aren't you doing better? What's the matter with you?" A harsh self-critic, I never took the praise I got very seriously. But this bad review put me under a dark cloud for days. I didn't think I could work harder, but decided it was time to put every sport's cliché I knew into action: put up or shut up; leave it all on the floor. Out of fear and desire, I cranked up my energy into overdrive, determined to show my naysayers that I had the potential to dance on stage beside any of them. That jolt of fear may have helped. Soon after, one of my favourite teachers, Donald McKayle, gave me a big pat on the back.

Mr. McKayle began making dances in the late '50s with his own company, performing them on Broadway and around the U.S. He was the choreographer of a hit Broadway show that I had seen—*Golden Boy*—starring Sammy Davis Jr. He had briefly been a Graham Company member, and only taught occasionally. His classes were inspiring as he broke away from traditional sequences and created his own expressive phrases. He stayed honest to the ideas in the Graham technique, but used them as a means to an end, which involved coming up with movement that reflected his multifaceted background. The dynamics and vocabulary of both Broadway and jazz dance affected his sensibility. An African-American man whose parents had been Jamaican immigrants, he was wide-shouldered and tall. As he taught, he constantly wiped the sweat off the thick, black-framed eyeglasses he always wore.

I met him one morning while walking down 63rd Street towards the studio. He said, "I enjoy teaching you. I'm glad I'll be able to be a part of helping you realize your potential. Hopefully you'll dance in my company one day."

"I Get by with a Little Help from My Friends" (and with some quotes)

A Georgia Peach

Before Graham class one Monday morning, I began a conversation with a raven-haired woman with a turned-up nose. She drew my eye because of her daring movement quality and, not insignificantly, because her lavender leotard looked like it had been spray-painted on. Her name was Georgia and she was from Georgia (and I'm not making this up).

We left the studio together and continued our conversation. Georgia spoke about feminism, so I willingly listened, not only hoping to win favour, but also because I knew nothing about the movement and felt it was time to learn. She talked for two hours straight, as if she were reading from a political pamphlet: "Kenny, the National Organization of Women recently formed. Its members are questioning the unequal treatment of women. Do you have any idea how badly women are treated, even in America?"

Spoken with her soft southern accent, her jargon was warmly seductive. She used words new to me, such as chauvinism, sexism, patriarchy and misogyny. She loved saying "misogyny." Dragging it out for several seconds with her lazy southern drawl, she somehow made that word sound appealing. I began to realize what a jerk I could be (had been, would still be). "Promise me you'll read Betty Friedan's book *The Feminine Mystique* and Simone de Beauvoir's *The Second Sex*."

I bought both that night on my way home and kept them in my backpack, hoping to pull them out to impress her as soon as possible.

On Tuesday, during lunch, we talked about how dance was one of the only professions where women were stars and how, in the Graham repertoire, they were the greatest protagonists. Pretending to search for my wallet in my dance bag, I pulled out *The Feminine Mystique* and placed it cover-up on the table. I dared a look up to see if she was impressed. She nodded and I was sure I saw her eyes send out an extra bit of sparkle.

I invited her to my place, on Wednesday. She immediately began checking out my chipped dishes and cracked mugs. Instead of the free love I was hoping to experience, I found myself being pushed out the door and led to Azuma, the inexpensive Asian import store on 6th Avenue. Once there, Georgia introduced me to the bounties of '60s globalization; later that day, colourful Japanese ceramic mugs and plates, unlike anything in my parents' Wedgwood- and Corningware-filled cupboards, lined my orange-crate shelves. Bamboo blinds from China hung in the windows and bright, patterned bedspreads from India covered the bed and one of the walls.

On Thursday night, I went with her to a Buddhist meditation session. Georgia's hand brushed against my right knee as we sat on the floor and chanted, "Nam-myoho-renge-kyo" hundreds of times with a couple of dozen truth seekers. The sound filling the room was like a swarm of bees: it tickled my skin and seemed to lift me off the floor. The group leader told us we chanted to tap into the deepest levels of our existence, in which our lives and that of the universe were one. Tapping the deepest level of my existence hadn't given me the courage to make a pass at Georgia, so I was relieved when, on Thursday, *perhaps* noticing my hesitation, she began talking about free love: "You don't need to go out with someone a hundred times, you know, or spend a lot of money taking them out. You just have fun together." Always ready with a quote, she recited one from someone she identified as Joseph Campbell: "Follow your bliss and the universe will open doors where there were only walls." [10]

On Friday, she started talking about the safety of birth control pills: "They're totally legal, you know, for the last two years. My older sister couldn't use them because there were bad side effects, but they're fixed now. You can get them as easily as a bottle of aspirin."

I knew I'd better get over my shyness and follow my bliss pretty quickly or she'd be gone.

So I listened and learned. In my now exotic Asian-inspired apartment, we made love rolling in the waves of my water-bed. Without the fear of a boyfriend breaking the door down and stabbing me, my time together with a woman was finally uninhibited.

On Sunday, lazing around under my new bedspread, we talked about her moving in with me. I was in heaven and remained there for two more weeks.

During week number three, Georgia began saying, "I love you." Constantly. In bed, eating dinner, washing the dishes. A disturbing sensation overwhelmed me. I grew uncomfortable, fearful that someone who loved me would turn on me. I was not capable of giving Georgia an explanation because I didn't yet understand my feelings. I drifted away, feeling out of control, angry at myself for hurting someone I was crazy about, but unable to stop.

Fake Hippies Take Me on a Wild Ride

On October 21, as I was walking along St. Mark's Place early in the morning, a shiny new black Cadillac stopped beside me. A clean-shaven young guy with flowing golden locks and an exaggerated, toothy smile stuck his head out the window and asked, "Wanna come with us? We're going to Washington to the big Vietnam protest. We got room for one more."

I hopped in. And in a cloud of smoke—inside the van—("I get high with a little help from my friends"[11]), we headed for the Pentagon ("Power to the people"[12]).

My new friends were five New York University students, all wearing colourful headbands and love beads. They identified themselves with their hippie names: in the front seat were two men, Ziggy and Chakra, and one woman, sitting between them, Rainbow; to my left in the back seat were Serenity and beside her, Willow. With their fancy Cadillac, they reminded me of acquaintances back in Toronto who called their parents capitalist pigs, and then willingly accepted their money to finance post-university trips to Europe.

When they heard I was an aspiring dancer from Canada, with little knowledge about the war, they gave me a quick lesson. Ziggy, the golden-haired driver, started with a flourish: "Our criminal government is supporting South Vietnam, which is fighting North Vietnam, the Viet Cong and their communist friends."

A joint was quickly passed around, after which freckled Serenity, who was mellow like her name, continued slowly: "The U.S. is in it to stop a communist takeover of South Vietnam, but the North sees the South as a puppet state controlled by us."

Rainbow interrupted at a faster clip: "The point is, we're bombing them to bits from the air." Her voice grew louder: "And their guerillas, with a fraction of our firepower, are demolishing us."

The car sped up with Ziggy's next words: "Over 10,000 Americans have been killed, man. And who knows how many Vietnamese. Citizens too. Women. Little kids. Our president has become the enemy."

Everyone nodded vehemently. I realized I was nodding vehemently, too. Serenity, her head now relaxed on my shoulder, continued: "Now the government is talking about a draft lottery. Any of you guys could get enlisted."

That's when I thought: "Here I am, smart me, an illegal alien afraid of the draft, getting stoned and going to an anti-war demonstration in the U.S. capital."

As we drove past Philadelphia, with about two hours of our trip remaining, the spirit in the car brightened. My car-mates decided to give me a few lessons on how we, privileged sons and daughters of the Age of Youth, could create heaven on earth ("We've got to get ourselves back to the garden" [13]).

Ziggy told me I had to listen carefully to our music heroes, especially to Jim Morrison, lead singer of The Doors, who encouraged youth to work toward a personal transformation before struggling to change the world. Quoting him, Chakra said, "There can't be any large-scale revolution until there's a personal revolution, on an individual level. It's got to happen inside first."

And I had to pay attention at the movies. Serenity, her right leg now flipped over my left, between hacking inhalations of her joint, quoted from the film *Easy Rider*, a movie featuring two rebels on motorcycles travelling across the country: "What the hell is wrong with freedom?"

And then they all enthusiastically joined in: "That's what it's all about!"

After passing Baltimore, Rainbow, who had rainbows painted on her cheekbones, turned to face me so she could introduce me to her favourite book. It was *Silent Spring* by Rachel Carson. "This is my food bible, man. It's about how chemicals in agriculture, especially DDT, are destroying the planet."

For the entire trip, Willow had been silent. She had passed two hours gently waving patchouli incense over us. The word "chemicals" must have brought her back to life. With a surprising burst of energy, she exclaimed, "Yeah, but some chemicals we absolutely loooove." And she reached into her shirt pocket, took out a pill and swallowed it down. "LSD. Want one?" I declined. I was feeling happy enough.

They were all vegetarians, and talked to me about the purifying effects of an organic, vegetarian diet. But they obviously favoured the combo-pack of organics and drugs.

Chakra had a friend whose parents owned a house just outside the city centre. We parked there, and walked towards the Lincoln Memorial, the crowd getting thicker the closer we got. Almost everyone was young and in a festive mood. By the time we reached the D.C. Mall, we were shoulder to shoulder. Tens of thousands of us, smoking joints, chanting, waving signs: "Hell no, we won't go," "We must resist, we must resist," "Meet the new boss, same as the old boss," [14] "LBJ, pull out now, like your father should have done."

Through the distorted sound of speakers that were a 100 yards ahead of me, I heard only a bit of the speech by Dr. Benjamin Spock, a pediatrician, author and pacifist: something about feeling betrayed by President Johnson, who had pumped up the war machine after promising to cut it back. There were hundreds of armed soldiers around. Word spread that Beatle George Harrison was nearby, along with dozens of hippies, stuffing carnations into the barrels of bayonet-spiked M-14 rifles. Caught up in the excitement, I became convinced like everyone around me that world peace was just around the corner ("How many years can a people exist before they're allowed to be free?"[15]) and if we only meditated and/or took enough drugs, made love generously, led peaceful lives without greed ("Imagine no possessions"[16]) and ate organic food, we could change the world ("And the world will live as one"[17]). After all, we were experiencing the dawning of the *Age of Aquarius*. ("No more falsehoods or derisions/Golden living dreams of visions"[18]). A new sun was rising and we were its rays ("We are stardust, we are golden"[19]).

When we later arrived at the Pentagon, soldiers were lined up in front of the steps. Dozens of protestors rushed them, trying to get through. I wasn't sure what they were thinking they would do if they did break through, but it didn't seem to matter. Golden dreams and stardust quickly gave way to rifles and tear gas. I was back in the crowd, but I saw a few protestors beaten down with rifle butts; I heard screams; saw blood. A few protestors were arrested and taken away. The scent of tear gas made my nostrils quiver. Someone started singing "America the Beautiful," and everyone joined in, except the Canadian guy who didn't know the words and whose euphoria had turned to a gut-ripping fear. By this time it was getting dark. Cool night air moved in. Some protestors broke up their signs, using them to make bonfires. My pals and I, somehow still together, took off with the majority of the crowd.

New Choices

Soon after the Washington march, I got a new hairstyle. While riding the subway home one night with Robert Cohan, my Graham teacher, he convinced me to let him update my still parted-on-the-left-side *West Side Story* hair to a '60s look. We went up to his place where he just mussed it up and let the curls have their way. We jokingly called the new look a "Jewfro." Not surprisingly, the name did not catch on. But I liked the result: it was very Bob Dylan meets Jimi Hendrix.

My new look, by Robert Cohan.
Photograph: Kenn Duncan/©The New York Public Library

Ronald Reagan, the Governor of California, had described what he thought defined a hippie: someone who "dresses like Tarzan, walks like Jane and smells like Cheetah." Soon I was wearing beads, Birkenstock sandals and the widest bellbottoms in town. I dressed like Tarzan and wore my hair like Jane, but like most of my generation, I bathed and did not smell like Cheetah. However, I couldn't follow professor Timothy Leary's advice and "turn on, tune in and drop out." As a struggling-from-behind dancer, who needed to get to class several times a day, I knew I could not take heavy drugs.

"Live the life you've always imagined."[20] That's the hippie expression that inspired me the most.

My Scholarship Audition

I had believed every Martha Graham Company dancer was a superstar. Whenever possible, I arrived early for my 6:00 p.m. class so I could sit by the studio door and watch these company dancers leap and dive fearlessly across the floor as they took the top-of-the-ladder, advanced-level 4:30 class. I knew that if I were ever to join these dancers, my heroes, I would have to overcome personal challenges and sweat buckets over many years in my quest for excellence.

Sometimes, while hanging out with fellow dance students, someone would ask us what we did for a living. My friends usually answered, "I'm a dancer." I only felt comfortable saying, "I'm studying to one day be a dancer," which I felt was a long way off.

In December of my first autumn in New York, I auditioned, along with thirty others, for a scholarship to pay for intermediate-level classes. The audition comprised a dance class watched by all our teachers, including Ms. Graham. It was a nerve-wracking two hours for me, as I kept thinking of Ed the piano player's grim comment concerning the teachers who had said I didn't have what it took to be a professional dancer. I went to that audition determined to prove my naysayers wrong.

The next day, when the acceptance notice was posted, I was shocked and thrilled to see that my name was one of the five listed. And I was totally floored when, in February 1968, only two months later, I was invited by the school faculty to join the advanced class. Admission to this exalted territory was by invitation only. Three teachers had to recommend you.

Predictably, after feeling a moment of joy because I had succeeded, I became neurotically disappointed. Did I want to be in an advanced class that would accept me? Did these people understand the meaning of excellence? How could a person who had only recently been recommended as an intermediate dancer be ready to leap across the floor with the glorious beings of the advanced class?

After I joined the class, the answers to my questions became clear. I was just good enough to enter the advanced class—not nearly at the peak of my development as I always imagined I would have to be, but at the bottom of the ladder. Some teachers had decided that I was ready to begin a new phase of training alongside dancers who would inspire and challenge me in new ways.

I felt timid and apprehensive before my first advanced class. I tried to project a confident physicality through engaging in some visualization work. I filled my body with breath, directing it from my gut up through my spine into my upper back. My chest opened and my shoulders dropped. I imagined roots growing down through my feet into the floor, helping to ground me and connect me to the power that comes from the earth. In that moment of imagination, I felt like I grew six inches. No one treated me as if I didn't belong. By the end of class, moving through space, I realized I had the ability to keep up, if not in technique, at least in energy and commitment, with anyone in the room.

The Everyday

The Big Three

Bruises appear. They are mostly on and around my knees. In the Graham technique, some of the work is done "standing on the knees." There are drops to the knees, balances on one knee, crawls and spins on two. Until I learn to use the right muscles the right way and find the proper alignment, I often knock them into the floor. Splotches of blue are guaranteed. When the moves are done well, the knees are safe; but that achievement, like all good things in dance, takes time. At age twenty-two, I'm not thinking about how the intricate web of ligament and cartilage in and around my knees is twitching and straining.

When I began taking classes, my feet met the floor with skin that was soft and smooth. Now they look like I have just walked over a bed of hot coals. The friction created by turning on one foot has taken its toll. The skin on my soles is torn, and there are "splits" between and at the base of my toes. Imagine a sensitive paper-cut and then magnify it until it is an open, painful wound. I have developed calluses, but the skin still splits between them. Not all dancers' feet tear. I am told it's a question of the skin's texture: oily skin helps. Sometimes I soak my feet in black tea; the tannic acid is supposed to toughen the skin. Every night I use a pumice stone to smooth out calluses and rub a variety of oils, almond, olive or sunflower, into the moonlike surface of my deteriorating feet, going to bed smelling like the salad I had eaten for dinner. The artful application of tape is a helpful, but incomplete, defence.

The last of the big three daily pains is the predictable muscle ache. Just when I think I've finally understood a concept and am embodying that concept in my work, fresh information or understanding makes me work more deeply. Working with greater depth, muscles are used in new ways and soreness often results. Professional dancers tell me that in rehearsals, the muscle pain becomes more extreme. During the last half hour of class, when we dance physically challenging phrases that may last around a minute, there is always time to stop and rest, as I wait for my turn. But in rehearsal, lengthy sections of choreography are done over and over again, with only brief pauses in between when the director gives notes on how to make things better. Pushing through the soreness is the only way to rise above it. I am told that if I can't get through a couple of run-throughs of a difficult dance in rehearsal, dancing full out, holding back nothing, I will never make it through a single run in a performance when the adrenaline is flowing and I will have to rise to a level beyond what I have ever achieved in rehearsal.

The Big "One"

I show up for classes every day except Sunday, bruised and cut, tired and sore. But class always acts like a drug that enhances my mood and leads to euphoria. Optimism, joy and exhilaration wash over me during each sacred, sweaty hour-and-a-half session, even if it is the third one of the day, when I feel I have nothing left to give.

Late at night, however, feelings of jealousy often diminish my optimism. They are directed at guys who are more advanced than I am, who jump higher and turn more effortlessly. These feelings do not survive. In the heat of class, inspired by the passion and striving of like-minded beings, encouraged by a teacher I believe in, propelled by the flying hands of musicians on drums or piano keys improvising music never to be heard again, I indulge in emotion and sensuality through my striving physicality. I progress through heartening breakthroughs and disappointing setbacks, stepping an inch at a time towards my goals.

Work

Under the Table

Four months after my arrival in New York, the Graham School administrator did some research and discovered that having a student visa would not make me eligible for the military draft. The student visa allowed foreign students to be in the U.S. legally, but it did not allow them to work. I got a student visa, but even with my rent set at $36.50 a month, I still had to make money. Working "under the table" was my only option if I wanted to stay. Most of my dancer friends worked in restaurants and were always complaining about how wrecked their legs were after walking for hours on hard floors. I hoped I wouldn't have to join them.

One morning, I saw a flyer stuck to a lamp post, boldly advertising the Under the Table Agency. I visited their office that evening. It was a storefront on East 70th, close to the Graham School. Instead of a sign above the door, the window was papered with dozens of flyers. The office, a ten-by-twelve room lit by a single desk lamp, looked like it had been set up for business five minutes earlier. The shadows the minimal lighting created made the woman sitting at the desk look alluring and mysterious. "My name is Saundra," she said with a breathy whisper. "Not Sandra, but Saundra." With the slightest move of her hand, she invited me to sit down. I was ready to do whatever she might ask.

"The deal is, you join for $3. We have a list of temporary work opportunities, so you choose what suits you best. The fee we get is $1.60 an hour (the minimum wage in New York State in 1968). Out of that we pay you $1.25. Paying taxes is up to you. Do you want to sign up?"

I had no choice, so I nodded "yes."

My immediate work future involved walking dogs and cleaning several apartments.

One of the apartments I cleaned was the striking Central Park West home of Jett Raybourne, former resident of Raleigh, North Carolina. Ms. Raybourne was what Blanche duBois (from Tennessee Williams' play *A Streetcar Named Desire*) might have been like if she had married rich and moved to the Upper West Side. Apparently in her late fifties, she had a faded beauty, warm gray eyes and a demure smile. She always wore an artificial gardenia clipped into her hair, just in case anyone forgot she really was a lady from The South.

Every Monday night I worked away, vacuuming, washing dishes and cleaning mirrors. She kept to herself. Once in a while I felt her watching me, but when I returned her stare, she looked away. She was always polite.

After a few weeks, this routine changed and so did her reserved demeanour. One evening, she invited me to join her beside the bureau in her hallway. "Come here Kenny," she called out in a much-heightened Southern accent I had not previously heard. "I want to show you something."

She opened the top drawer. All I could see in it was a riot of coloured fabric. She reached inside and pulled out a scarf with a pastel floral design and waved it in front of me. Then she crumpled it in her hand and held it against her cheek. "My husband gave me this for my twenty-fifth birthday. I wore it during our honeymoon in Paris. We sat outside at a restaurant near Notre Dame."

She closed her eyes and smiled. Then she angrily threw the scarf down onto the pile where it gave up its identity, and yanked out another, this time one with a design of triangles in greens and pinks. She waved it just a little bit harder than the first. Her voice grew louder and I took in the smell of scotch. "He bought me this one at the Museum of Modern Art's gift shop five years later when we were living in New York. It was a make-up gift because we fought the day before over the Chicken Kiev I made for dinner. He said it was too salty, that I was trying to kill him, with his high blood pressure and all." She paused. "Maybe I was. He was having an affair. I'd seen the lipstick stains, smelled the perfume, waited up for him too many nights."

That was more information than I needed to vacuum carpets, so I smiled awkwardly at her, wondering how to make my getaway.

She flung the scarf down, and I realized as I followed its path that there were at least thirty scarves in that drawer and probably a story to go along with each one.

"They're beautiful," I said. "Thank you for showing me. Are you all right?"

She nodded a slow yes.

"I'll go back to my work now." I returned to my cleaning, aware that she remained hovering over that open drawer for another ten minutes, after which she disappeared, possibly to return to her bottle.

During the next two weeks, she showed me many of her scarves. Her marriages unfolded. There was a checked scarf from a cruise to Acapulco and one featuring blue sky and white clouds from a trip to Florida, both gifts from that same husband, a banker. Yellow roses and jungle foliage were birthday presents from her second husband, the owner of a landscaping company. Her third, an oil company executive, had shown his environmentally sensitive side with robins, canaries and bluebirds.

The week after the birds, only one scarf emerged. She seemed shocked after reaching deep into the drawer and pulling up a black piece of fabric covered with tiny golden Japanese characters. She held it straight out from her body, stretched between her two hands, which trembled from the fierceness of her grip. Then, with the most exaggerated Southern accent yet, she said, "I wore this to my son's funeral. My husband and I were in Japan when it happened. He was all alone here, only eighteen. A car did it." She stood there vibrating. I led her to a chair and made her sit.

The next week when the phone rang, Jett picked it up and called, "It's for you."

I had given her number to a few of my friends. As I walked towards the phone, she abruptly turned away, arched her back and in an aristocratic tone said, "Who is it please?"

There was a silence, and then, just as I was expecting her to hand the phone to me, she inhaled deeply and said sharply into the mouthpiece, "Well you can't talk to him. He's not available. He's mine right now and he will not come to the phone." Then she slammed the phone down and left the room, leaving a scented trail of lavender mixed with scotch.

I liked Jett a lot so I kept quiet, even though I was disturbed by the "He's mine" line. She was warm, smart and haunted by memories kept alive by coloured pieces of fabric. I was intrigued. I thought about her son. I vacuumed.

It was two visits later, after four more scarf stories and one more interrupted phone call, that I saw the photograph on her piano, framed and standing upright. I was sure it hadn't been there before. It must have been her son.

He looked around my age and had a curly head of hair like mine. I saw my smile on his happy face.

An hour later, mirrors sparkling, the scent of vinegar in the air, I said good-bye, knowing that this visit had to be my last. I thought of buying her a good-bye gift, a scarf of course. I had seen a nice one with Monet's water lilies at the Museum of Modern Art.

But then I imagined her showing it to her next apartment cleaner and saying, "Here is the scarf from that boy I was so good to, who left me all alone."

I bought her chocolates instead.

Respect

One day, the city sent a plumber to 69 East 4th Street to fix a leaky sink pipe. (One advantage of having a rent-controlled apartment was the provision of occasional free maintenance work.) The paradoxically muscular and pot-bellied Puerto Rican plumber arrived and introduced himself as Jamie. I was happy to have the chance to learn a little about his country, to talk about mine and to speak my few words of Spanish. "Me llamo Ken," I said, feeling so cool.

Jamie admired my sound system and little record collection. "I'll put on my favourite for you," I said. It was by Aretha Franklin.

While he twirled a wrench to the rhythms of "R-E-S-P-E-C-T," he told me he had been living in New York for five years but was returning home to Puerto Rico in a week. He was working overtime so he could buy gifts for his family. I proudly told him that I was training to be a dancer and was heading out for a weekend workshop at a university upstate. He nodded, looking very impressed. I offered him the Aretha album to take home for a gift, but he wouldn't accept it: "No, gracias, it's your favourite. You must keep it." After he left, I felt so pleased. What a good communicator I had become. My life was to share.

I came home after the workshop to see that the security bars had been pried out of one of the courtyard windows. My sound system and record collection were gone. Someone was working overtime all right to get gifts for his family.

In the sink, leaning against the repaired faucet, was the only album left behind, my favourite by Aretha Franklin.

My First Dance Job

After six months in New York, I got my first dance job offer and it wasn't what I had expected. I had thought that, before I, with luck, got into a company, I would follow the path of most young dancers, performing for a small fee in an independent production, in a tiny loft space with mainly friends in attendance.

But on February 15, 1968, a week after my first professional New York audition, I got a phone call that was short, surprising and deliciously sweet.

"Hello, is Kenneth Pearl there?" an unfamiliar man's voice asked.

"Yes, this is Kenneth." I was sure it was a call about a phone bill I hadn't paid.

"I'm calling from the New York City Opera Ballet. We'd like you to be one of six men to dance with the company." Then he gave me a number to call to arrange for my contract.

A week earlier, I had auditioned for a position with the company at the State Theater in the famous Lincoln Center. State Theater was the venue where George Balanchine's New York City Ballet performed. I was thrilled to think that, in exactly one month, I would be appearing on that majestic stage in two operas. The first was a new work called *Bomarzo*, to be choreographed by the legendary Jack Cole. The second was a return performance of John Butler's *Carmina Burana*, with a choir singing the music of Carl Orff. Aside from working in a great theatre with inspiring artists, I would have union work, which meant a salary that would save me from cleaning apartments.

I'd gone to the audition because I had heard that a great dancer from the Graham Company, Robert Powell, would be dancing one of the two male leads in *Carmina Burana*. The chance to perform in a production with him, to have the privilege of watching him rehearse every day, had made me put aside my I'm-not-ready-yet attitude and show up.

More than 200 dancers auditioned, including at least 50 men. The audition started with a ballet class and finished with a session of partnering, which involved doing complicated lifts. Never having done any partnering before and fumbling around trying to figure out the co-ordinations, I was sure I wouldn't get the job. I had therefore put the idea of dancing on stage with Mr. Powell right out of my head. So I was stunned to hear that, somehow, I was one of the six men chosen.

"Yes!" I shouted into the receiver, "I'll do it. I'll do it. Thank you so much."

"Don't thank me," replied the indifferent voice on the other end. "I only do the paperwork and I need your Social Security Number (SSN) so I can send you your contract."

Social Security Number! In my excitement I had forgotten that, without one, I couldn't dance at Lincoln Center. My student visa did not permit me to work, and getting the required number was impossible for a U.S. visitor without a Green Card or work visa. This was a union job in a renowned theatre, not illegal work cleaning apartments for the Under the Table Agency.

"I don't have it with me," I said, barely able to get the words out.

"Well, make sure you get it to me by the end of the week."

Becoming Oswald Clarke

The Dance Gods Smile – #1
My belief in the Dance Gods, entities whose presence I had felt but not paid much attention to, was confirmed two days later. I had first sensed their presence while watching *West Side Story* when I was sixteen and after discovering the one book about dance in my school library; they were there with me in Rochester, when I had felt a pull to go to New York; and they had rescued me, most recently, when I had given my "round-trip" ticket to the U.S. Immigration Officer at the border. The day after receiving the offer to dance at Lincoln Center, their existence for me became unquestionable.

After class, in the dressing room at the Graham School, I was telling my tale of woe to two Jamaican friends, Derrick and Patrick, fellow dancers of the past few months.

"Tough break, man," said Derrick, "You want to get in. We're getting out. Once the snow comes, that's our cue to go back home. We want to be on the beach for Christmas."

"Yeah, student visa's all we got, same as you," said Patrick. "No opportunity for us here in the land of opportunity."

We all laughed, shrugged and then got introspective as we changed. I said goodbye and headed home.

I was walking down the stairs, heading for the No. 6 subway a few blocks away from the school, when I realized I'd left my sunglasses on the changing-room windowsill. Exhausted, I wanted to get home and thought about leaving them, hoping they would still be there the next day. But I turned and ran back to the studio.

"Hey Kenny," said Derrick, who was drying off from his shower as I entered the changing-room, "Oswald here is going home next week and he's the only one of all of us who can stay and work legally. This superhero has a Green Card and a Social Security Number." He was referring to Oswald Clarke, another member of the Jamaican contingent.

"You're kidding," I said, surprised, turning toward him. "How'd you get that?"

"At the Caribbean restaurant where I was washing dishes, they needed a chef," replied Oswald.

"Yeah," said Patrick, patting his solid abs. "Oswald here makes the best shrimp curry and rum cake in New York. No American can cook like him, so they made him legal."

"But now I'm going home to be with my lady," Oswald said, a huge smile taking over his round face. "I'm going to eat a lot, get fat and have lots of kids."

"Hey, lover man," Patrick said laughing, "Kenny here got a big dance job. He needs a little social security. Why don't you give him your card?"

I laughed, thinking that was a big joke, but Oswald calmly got his wallet from his bag, took out a card, gave it to me and simply said, "Good idea."

"That's very generous," I said, holding that passport to heaven at arms' length, "but I'm not Oswald and it's totally illegal. I could be deported. And it's yours. You earned it, not me. I couldn't possibly use it."

At home later that afternoon, I called the Production Assistant of the New York City Opera Ballet. "Hello," I said nervously, "this is Kenneth Pearl. By the way, that's my stage name. My real name, the one on my Social Security Card, is Oswald Clarke. Here's the number."

Rehearsals

Dancers in Flight

My arrival each day at Lincoln Center for rehearsals was, for me, miraculous. I woke up in my rundown neighbourhood and three subway rides later, walked proud steps into the glamorous Lincoln Center Plaza. Completed only a few years earlier, it featured three architecturally stunning buildings. To the south was the State Theater, to the north, facing it, Philharmonic Hall and, in the centre facing east, greeting people as they entered the plaza, the Metropolitan Opera House. In the northwest corner was a Henry Moore sculpture bathing in a rectangular pond, surrounded by trees that blossomed with white flowers in the spring. Beside it were the Vivian Beaumont Theater and the New York Public Library for the Performing Arts. Some of the world's greatest performers in music, dance, acting and opera performed in those theatres almost every night.

Before going backstage, I always walked into the grand central plaza and stopped in front of the round fountain with its vertical plumes of water. At 9:00 a.m., tourists with their cameras were already sitting on its rim, snapping photos. My morning shot of inspiration came from standing in front of that fountain, feeling its spray and taking in the epic paintings by Marc Chagall that filled two of the five glassed-in arches, making up the facade of the Metropolitan Opera House. Informed by the artist's dreams and visions, the paintings are landscapes, populated with dancers, musicians, angels and smiling creatures, all overcoming gravity, hanging and flying in skies of red and gold. Staring at so much effortless airborne life, I always felt particularly earthbound, but knew that on a good rehearsal day, at certain moments, I could escape boundaries and soar. After admiring Chagall's work, I headed for the stage door, ready for a day of intense work and hopeful of experiencing flight.

In the mornings, we rehearsed *Bomarzo*. The music was written by Argentinean composer Alberto Ginastera, with lyrics by Manuel Majica Láinez. It had premiered less than a year earlier in Washington, D.C. We heard that the Argentinean government had banned a production in Argentina because of its sexual content. But here in New York, at this time, not much was censored.

We worked with the legendary musical theatre choreographer and performer Jack Cole. He is known to have been a prime innovator of theatrical jazz dance, choreographing such Broadway shows as *Kismet, A Funny Thing Happened on the Way to the Forum* and *Man of La Mancha,* as well as movies that included *Gentlemen Prefer Blondes* and *Some Like it Hot.* It was hard to believe that I was going to be rehearsing with a man who had worked with Marilyn Monroe and Rita Hayworth.

He was known to be a tyrannical, perfectionist taskmaster who lived in an apartment that was entirely black, carpets and ceiling included.

He *was* compact, intense and tightly wound. He was also a terrific director; he demanded that we open ourselves up and show how we felt during dramatic moments, even if we had to summon up feelings that were foreign to us. He wanted us to live big lives on stage to reflect the story in which the lead character, Pier Francesco Orsini, the Duke of Bomarzo, descends into a world of frustrated love, jealousy and betrayal. As a chorus member, I was involved in a number of court and battle scenes. During one, in which the Duke's father is killed, Mr. Cole directed me to rush to his side and show my concern. Focusing on the movement, I did it the first time, apparently, with too much indifference. Mr. Cole asked me to react to show that I cared. Trying to please, I evidently got much too melodramatic. He broke up everyone in the studio by coming over, putting an arm around me and telling me it was good to feel, but I didn't have to become Walt Whitman on the battlefield.

During the second half of the day, we worked with John Butler, a choreographer who created work for both stage and television, and who had been a dancer in the Graham Company. His dance-opera, *Carmina Burana,* was inspired by the writings of wandering medieval poets, which were discovered in 1803 in Bavaria. The poems are the greatest known collection of secular lyrics from the Middle Ages. The sections of poetry that had inspired Mr. Butler were those involving love in all its guises, from romantic ("See how I am faithful, with all my heart, and with all my soul; I am with you, even when I am far away"), to bawdy ("I am eager for the pleasures of the flesh, more than salvation. My soul is dead, so I shall look after the flesh").

Set to the lush, dramatic score by Carl Orff, the work had been a sensation when it opened in 1959. Critics later said it was the dance-opera world's answer to the musical *Hair* (though it was created earlier) because of its exploration of sensuality.

Carmina Burana is not like most operas in which the dance is sporadic; the choir sits off to the side and the dancers communicate all the action. The production involved two lead couples: one made up of two classically trained ballet dancers and the other of two modern dancers, the great Robert Powell and Carmen de Lavallade. Supporting the action was a chorus of twelve dancers, six men and six women.

Working on *Carmina Burana,* I learned to partner. We males balanced our female partners on our thighs and our shoulders. We dipped them, swung them and lifted them overhead for hours every day. My partner, a ballet dancer named Margot, was a great beauty, almost my height. She was an experienced dancer, used to being partnered by skilled hands. So she had to be patient as I figured out counterbalances, timing and proper placement of my hands, and as I gradually built up the strength to lift her five-foot-ten body into the air, over and over again.

On opening night, I felt focused as I waited in the wings to go out on stage in my first New York performance, in front of a sold-out crowd of 2,500. Margot turned to me an instant before our entrance and said, "I get really pumped up during performance, so watch out. I'm going to be jumping all over you with more energy than you've ever seen." She did, and I survived, my energy rising to meet hers. We had a ball and flew at times like the inhabitants of Chagall's visionary paintings.

I Get Lucky

The Dance Gods Smile – #2

I wasn't completely happy about my new false identity. The good part about becoming Oswald Clarke from Jamaica was having his SSN, which I could perhaps use indefinitely; it would allow me to go on working and paying taxes. I found it interesting how I redefined degrees of morality to justify my stay in New York: While I could live with my choice to sneak into the U.S. without a visa, I couldn't handle the idea of remaining there using someone else's papers. I decided that, if I was going to bend the rules, I wouldn't involve Oswald or anyone else. I tore up his card.

I heard about a number of interesting methods that would allow me to make my status legitimate. The first: marry an American friend. A Green Card would arrive in the mail shortly after a brief ceremony at City Hall. I decided not to take this route. I learned that a marriage of convenience could be risky business. I knew a Canadian woman who had made plans to marry a gay friend. On the steps leading up to City Hall before the ceremony, he had shocked her, saying he would not go through with the ceremony unless she gave him $2,000.

The most extreme strategy involved a trip to a local cemetery. *All* I had to do was search through the gravestones and find one with any male name and my birth date. The deceased could have died twenty years ago or yesterday. I was to take his name and then call the Social Security Department and say I had lost my own card. The officer wouldn't know the person had passed away, and so would send me a new one. Then I could legally make the name my own.

A third, and legal, method was to have an employer enthusiastically recommend me, saying that I was a dancer indispensable to the artistic life of the United States. I had danced at Lincoln Center, but unfortunately, being in a chorus of twelve didn't exactly make me visa-worthy. With the graveyard method as my best possibility, there appeared to be no hope.

So I made an off-the-wall choice. I decided to try and get my SSN in the most upfront way possible. I would be honest, something new for me. I would just call and ask for one. Other foreign artists told me it was impossible to get a number this way, but one morning I decided to give it a try. I called and told the truth: "I'm a Canadian citizen living in New York. I have a bank account here and would like a Social Security Number."

In a week, a card arrived in the mail. No one could believe it. A couple of friends tried my way and failed.

Maybe the official had put back a couple of drinks at lunch. Maybe he assumed I had a Green Card already. In any case, I now had a very real SSN. So, strange but true, even though I could still not work legally, as I didn't have a work visa or Green Card, I could get work with the SSN. I worked illegally but paid all my taxes legally!

Seeing the Alvin Ailey American Dance Theater

In September 1968, I had the life-changing experience of watching, for the first time, a performance by the Alvin Ailey American Dance Theater. The show took place at a theatre at the Fashion Institute of Technology at West 28th Street and Seventh Avenue. It was a trial run of the dances the company was to perform on an upcoming tour, and it was free, at least free for all those who could manage to get a seat. I knew a big crowd would show up, so I arrived at the theatre an hour early; I was still way at the back of a long line.

Though the Ailey Company had given its first performance in 1958, it was now known as THE hot company, the one to see, the one whose dancers had the most physical daring and passion. As the audience entered and packed the theatre, the noise was so high-decibel I thought I was at a rock concert.

The curtain rises. The dancers glide onto the stage two at a time, sleek and cool, wearing black pants, jazz shoes and white tank tops. The knowing audience gives out an actual cheer. The dance, choreographed by Louisiana-born Talley Beatty, is called *Toccata*. The choreography challenges the dancers to execute the most complex mix of modern, ballet and jazz styles I have ever seen. Their bold, sensual physicality excites me in the way I had been excited when I first saw *West Side Story*.

Watching, I also have a realization about my own work. I recognize that, as a dancer, I am concerned primarily with the shapes I am making, and always making certain that "the picture is right" is leading me to dance safely. In contrast, these dancers are taking big physical risks, dancing on the edge of danger and moving through shapes rather than making the forming of shapes their main purpose. Shapes serve dance, but dance is flow.

My knowledge of the company had led me to expect that all the dancers would be African American, but I see there is a powerful white woman on stage whom I identify from the program as Linda Kent. Also on stage is a sensual Japanese woman, Mari Kajiwara, whom I had met a year earlier at the Graham School.

Revelations closes the program. In an article in *The Village Voice*, I had recently read that Alvin Ailey choreographed *Revelations* in 1960, when he was twenty-nine. Inspired by African-American blues, work songs and spirituals, he explored his childhood recollections of people, places and experiences in and around his rural Texas church. Mr. Ailey described the memories that inspired the work as "blood memories," because they were so strong he felt they were as much a part of him as the blood that ran through his veins.

I have heard a lot about *Revelations*; everyone has called it a masterpiece, so I am on the edge of my seat, eager to watch this passionate company bring it to life.

The piece is sung by a live choir led by Brother John Sellers, an African-American gospel singer, who is dressed in a shimmering yellow gown and skullcap. It unfolds as a suite of seven dances set in three movements, using a true community of dancers to express feelings that range from despair to joy, from fear of damnation to hope for transcendence. The dance illuminates a journey through lives deeply felt. One movement flows into the next as naturally as successive heartbeats. There are no sets or props except for fans, poles, long pieces of silky fabric and stools.

Each of the seven sections has its own unique beauty, from the grounded opening, "I've Been Buked" (in which the dancers, dressed in earth tones, begin by evoking the sculpted figures of Rodin's *Burghers of Calais,* a masterpiece I have recently seen at the Metropolitan Museum of Art), to the work's mid-section, "Take Me to the Water," in which a group of seven dancers, led by long, leggy Judith Jamison, exuberantly enacts a baptism ritual, to the exultation of the piece's finale, "Rocka My Soul." From start to finish, I am riveted.

A section called "Sinner Man," in the final movement, is the one that makes my heart race. Set to a driving song that begins, "Oh Sinner Man, where you gonna run to?" three bare-chested men in black pants, led by a powerful, chiselled Miguel Godreau, flee from their inevitable damnation with sequences of ferocious virtuosic movement. I have seen New York audiences go wild for other dances and other dancers. But after "Sinner Man," there is pandemonium, an ovation that is more than a sign of great appreciation. It is an emotional release necessary for each audience member to experience before being able to witness more.

I know our screaming will only subside with a new section, strong enough in contrast to "Sinner Man" to quiet all of us down. And it comes. In the instant it takes for a new lighting cue, we are silent and expectant once more. A soft orange sun appears on a dark backdrop. We all take a deep breath. The singer begins, "The day is past and gone." It is dusk, the end of a hot day.

The finale starts, easygoing and funny. It is time for church. Eight women in yellow dresses, wearing floppy hats, enter one by one to share the news of the day, speaking through the agitated moves of their fluttering fans. Each one's unique character is immediately discernible.

Eight men, in black pants and gold and yellow vests and shirts, join in and have a dance-conversation with the women. Set to the rousing rhythms of "Rocka My Soul in the Bosom of Abraham," their dancing communicates an intense joy—call it ecstasy—that lifts us out of our seats and has us clapping and stomping along with the dancers.

After the standing ovation, multiple curtain calls and an extended encore, and after the audience members are gone, I sit in my seat unable to move until a building attendant appears and asks if I am okay. I realize I am crying. "Yeah, I'm fine thanks." He points to his watch and politely asks me to leave.

While I'm sitting on the subway, vivid pictures, in which I am dancing with the Ailey dancers with a velocity I have never before experienced, take over my imagination. Then there is a click, reason takes over and my home movie ends. The company clearly doesn't hire many dancers who aren't African American. It never holds auditions and there is no Ailey school. So I cannot imagine any possible route that will take me from where I am sitting to where I have just dreamed of being.

The Paradox

The Paradox was a restaurant that could only have existed in the Lower East Side of Manhattan during the late 1960s. Located on East 7th Street, it was frequented by a ragged bunch of artists, hippies and students.

The dining style was communal, with one long wooden plank table set at the centre of the room with benches along its sides. Filling out the rest of the space were a few round tables. Above them, light bulbs hung from the ceiling, each one covered by a brown paper bag—East Village chic. The kitchen and its two chefs were on view, separated from the public tables by a counter on which sat a broken cash register with a drawer that was always left open. At the long table, you sat beside anyone and anyone sat beside you. One day when I was there, a bald man with no eyebrows threw his backpack on the table, sat down and groaned, "Man, somebody spiked my canteen with LSD yesterday and I lost all my hair."

The Paradox's menu was strictly macrobiotic. Macrobiotic refers to a diet that promotes longevity. I learned at workshops given by the husband-and-wife team Aveline and Michio Kushi, leaders of the macrobiotic movement in New York, that the word was first used in the writings of Hippocrates, the father of Western medicine. Those who follow a macrobiotic diet try to balance the eating of different foods according to the Eastern principles of "yin" and "yang," which are complementary opposites. According to the macrobiotic way, yin foods are expansive and cool (sugar is an extreme yin food); yang foods are contractive and warm (red meat is an extreme yang food). The best food for you is what is grown in the immediate world that surrounds you. New Yorkers, who live in a temperate zone and who follow the diet, avoid extreme yin and yang foods; they eat mainly plant-based foods, including veggies, beans, whole grains, sea vegetables, and some fish, fruits and nuts.

The main reason we all ate at the Paradox so regularly was that "the macro special" cost ninety-five cents. And it was good! Even in 1968 this was an amazing deal. A minute after ordering, you were served a plate piled high with generous portions of brown rice, mixed veggies, bean of the day, hiziki seaweed and a salad made from cabbage, currants and walnuts. For an extra twenty-five cents you could have a small piece of fish, the least yang creature food. A very dense apple crumble was the most popular dessert, at thirty cents a bowl.

The owners of the Paradox were practitioners of Scientology, which I knew nothing about. They frequently came over to the tables and asked us customers to squeeze devices that resembled tin cans, while they checked a meter. Given the price and quality of the food, we willingly squeezed.

One night, the communal table was full, so I asked a woman at a side table if I could join her. As I sat down, and before she had lowered her gaze, I took in her amber eyes and saw that she was beautiful. Her long elegant neck, slim torso and hair tied up in a bun, an unusual style for someone eating at the Paradox, made me think that she might be a dancer. We didn't talk for almost the full meal. I was shy on occasions such as this and so was she, evidently, or else she was just giving me the cold shoulder because a lot of strangers had tried to pick her up.

We finally began talking. Her name was Brenda; she lived two blocks from me. We discovered that we were both in love with the theatre. She was an actor who had just made an appearance in the movie version of the musical *Camelot*. We spoke for hours that night and soon started hanging out together.

One day I got a note in my mailbox from Brenda saying she'd be away for a few months in Los Angeles, working on a film. That was it. Then, six months later, she called: "Kenny, I'm staying at the fabulous Plaza Hotel. The producers put me up here for the opening last night."

The movie was called *The Doves* and was playing at the Paris Cinema, right across from the hotel. She had one of three leading roles. "I have no money left, not a cent, but they gave me an expense account at the hotel. Come over and we can have the most amazing dinner." She told me to wear a suit and tie, neither of which I owned, so we decided that we would order room service, and then walk across the street and see her movie.

When I arrived, my beautiful Hollywood-star friend led me into her ornate hotel room, which offered an expansive view of Central Park. I noticed that Brenda's long hair had been permed into a wavy configuration, which seemed to have a life of its own, bouncing up every time she stepped forward and falling in slow motion between steps, flattening out before it swelled up once more into its new shape. She was a TV shampoo commercial.

We ordered enough food for a small village and soon a slim, vertical gent made his first entrance, pushing a cart piled high with our supper. An expensive bottle of wine started things off. Then we gorged on grapefruit-and-avocado salad, plates of glistening salmon and well-organized asparagus, just like all those meals we had shared at the Paradox!

For dessert, our waiter set down two huge bowls of strawberries topped with mounds of fresh whipped cream. Stuffed and drunk, abandoning all Plaza Hotel dignity, we spooned the whipped cream into each other's mouths, missing often, and then, just as the waiter began removing our plates, began a full-out pillow fight that, after a few soft whacks, felt like it might lead to a more personal encounter. It didn't, because the waiter, likely resisting the temptation to call security, was keeping an eye on us. Brenda used her expense account to tip him the equivalent of my rent.

Barely able to walk, we headed over to the cinema. The ushers at the entrance greeted Brenda with smiles so exaggerated I thought they would do serious damage to their facial muscles.

Watching the film, I thought about how, in those sexually permissive times, Brenda and I had never even touched each other, the pillows a couple of hours earlier providing the occasion for our most personal contact. But maybe because of the effects of the wine and the whipped cream, I felt and hoped that things might change. Leaving the theatre after the film, I put my arm around her shoulder. Nice.

Her body turned warmly towards mine. Nicer.

Puffing hard on a cigarette, her agent came running towards us. "Hey kiddo, there's a Red-Eye leaving for LA in two hours from Kennedy. Here's cab fare." He handed her a twenty. "I just got you an audition for a film at noon tomorrow."

Brenda called me two weeks later. No work had come from the audition, but she had decided to stay in Los Angeles.

A year later, during a hot July, she was back in New York for a family visit. She had driven across the country in her 1963 black Ford Mustang convertible. Driving with her along the beach in Long Island, I turned to observe my beautiful sun-glassed friend. Tossing her hair back as she laughed, she did look like a movie star. She told me she was now getting a lot of small roles in TV shows.

Brenda and I walked the streets of the East Village all night, arms wrapped around each other. We sat on a bench in Tomkins Square Park under trees, black against the pale early morning sky. We had a great time laughing a lot as always, talking about "old times" two years ago when we had both been poor. I was still poor, but laughed along with her anyway.

The first rays of the morning sun skimmed the tops of nearby tenement buildings. The light acted like a theatrical cue. We turned to each other and, as if we'd been rehearsing for months, dove into our first kiss.

An hour later, she hopped into her cool black convertible and drove away. I never saw her again.

In Demand but Still Poor

After my time with the New York City Opera Ballet, I was in demand as a dance professional, performing in non-union concerts that required a lot of rehearsal time, but paid little. Choreographers usually paid dancers an honorarium, whatever they could afford, for performances and months of rehearsals. It was considered a great privilege to perform, so we made do. A lot of my dancing friends had to take on outside work when necessary to get by. I was lucky: I never had extra money, but was able, largely because of that rent-controlled apartment and some money saved from the Lincoln Center performances, to support myself with dance work alone. Dancing with different artists was a blessing. They each had their own movement style, offered different kinds of instruction and challenged me in unique ways.

During the second half of 1968, Mary Anthony, a skilled choreographer and exceptional teacher, invited me to join her troupe. We gave performances around New York State and throughout New England. *Threnody* is her best known piece. It is set to music by Benjamin Britten and is based on the play *Riders to the Sea,* by Irish playwright J.M. Synge. The dance tells the story of a mother's struggles with the loss of her three sons in a shipwreck. I had great fun fighting the waves and drowning on stage with two terrific dancers, Ross Parkes and Daniel Maloney. As well, I performed in Joyce Trisler's robust *Dance for Six,* in a concert presented by a studio called The New Dance Group. Ms. Trisler had been an early member of the Ailey Company and her piece was later added to the Ailey repertoire. I also performed in a dance by Sophie Maslow, a former Graham Company member, as part of a celebration of Jewish culture at Madison Square Garden.

Preparing for these shows, I sometimes finished my day by 6:00 p.m., but rehearsals often went as late as 10:00. Occasionally, after an evening rehearsal, dancers would go out for drinks together to socialize, relax and blow off steam. Once in a while, we'd go to the theatre. Most of the time, we dragged ourselves back to our apartments.

Back home, I manoeuvred in slow motion, washing sweat-saturated dance clothes. Then, after dinner, I'd lie back in my kitchen bathtub, close my eyes and relax as Roberta Flack's soothing voice struggled through my new cheap speakers. I'd review, beat by beat, movement sequences that I had learned during the day. Come Saturday night I would always go out dancing or see a performance. Recovery day was Sunday. I'd visit the St. Mark's bookstore, go to a museum and usually visit Central Park.

The choreographers with whom I worked showed great patience dealing with their dancers' demanding schedules that often included classes and rehearsals with various companies.

My two main jobs during this period—both of them strength-, endurance- and character-building experiences—were with the companies of Donald McKayle and Pearl Lang.

Dancing with Donald McKayle

Older and Better

Donald McKayle (he liked to be called Donald) constantly challenged his dancers with intense, physically demanding movement. His work was also humane and emotive. He invited me to join his company in April 1968. I joyfully accepted and went on to perform many of his dances, including two that are now recognized as modern dance classics, *Games* and *Rainbow 'Round My Shoulder*. The former, an early McKayle work, juxtaposes the innocent imaginings of urban kids with the real dangers they face, through rhythms, chants and street games. The vocal score is provided on stage by two of the dancers (one of whom was Donald when I performed the piece). In the latter piece, the "rainbow 'round my shoulder" referenced in the dance's title is the light reflected off the imagined swinging pickaxes of men working on a chain gang. The piece communicates, through skilfully layered patterns that build from simple beginnings to a heart-wrenching and explosive finish, the labours, hopes and dreams of men who are confined, vulnerable and desperate. Aside from a solo done by a woman who represents both mother and lost lover, the men are in action all the time. The dance is gruelling.

Demanding and uncompromising, Donald was also consistently positive and generous. In rehearsals he would teach and run dances with more energy than any of us, and he was twenty years our senior. His dances were all cardio workouts of non-stop movement. We kept up because of the example he set and because there was no way we were going to let him show us up.

In the final solo of *Rainbow 'Round My Shoulder.*
Photograph: Kenn Duncan/©The New York Public Library

Panting and sweating alongside him, lungs bursting, we developed the stamina that allowed us to give everything every time, learning that there was more power and life in us than we had ever imagined.

He showed us that a big part of being a great teacher is never to merely indicate, gesticulate or talk through things; it is rather to set the best possible example by working full out, demonstrating the qualities and spirit required. Both the creative energy that infused his classes and the kind encouragement and strong work ethic that distinguished his rehearsals inspired all who were lucky enough to work with him.

Dancing with Pearl Lang

Dolphin or Shark

Pearl Lang (she liked to be called Pearl) had been a renowned soloist for ten years with the Graham Company. She had also danced in the Broadway musicals *Carousel* and *Finian's Rainbow*. In 1952, she formed her own company, the Pearl Lang Dance Theater. All of us dancers at the Graham School knew that a rite of passage, which might get us a step closer to being invited to join the Graham Company, was to perform for a period of time with her. I auditioned and she invited me to join her group.

I quickly saw why her company was considered a training ground. She used a vocabulary that was similar to Ms. Graham's. And, like Mr. McKayle, she had a great eye and was an outstanding mentor and coach. She demanded complete dedication from her dancers, while she painstakingly worked on every detail of her choreography.

However, she rarely danced alongside us, setting an example as Donald did; she preferred to rehearse privately. She did demonstrate movement, and would usually rehearse sections of a dance in which we partnered her. But other than that, she remained seated in her chair, dressed in her trademark rehearsal outfits, consisting of tights, skirt and top, all in matching navy blue. All through rehearsals, right up until the very evening of a performance, we often had to imagine where on stage she was going to be whenever she performed her solo movement.

And, while Donald led by example and through positive feedback, Pearl constantly berated us, no matter how hard we worked. After dancing for hours, giving everything we had, we rarely got thanked. Instead, what we usually heard was, "Dancers, you don't know what you're doing. What's the matter with you?" She would instruct and sometimes praise, but she would also blame and insult, often all in the same sentence. I saw many dancers leave her rehearsals in tears because of her insults. I managed to stay composed during her most antagonistic moments by heading downstairs to the bathroom with a few other dancers during rehearsal breaks. We then spent a necessary moment throwing ourselves against the metal walls of the stalls to dissipate our anger.

With Pearl, you never knew what you were going to get. You just had to jump into the water, prepared to meet dolphin or shark.

In the end, coached by her idiosyncratic mixture of instruction and bullying, everyone in the company appeared on stage well prepared and ready to do a lot of big, physical movement. In one piece, *Tongues of Fire*, Daniel Maloney and I had lead roles as fiery Old Testament prophets. (This was in the day when it was still popular for modern dance companies to create dances that told stories.) Our duet was a big break for each of us. We rehearsed for months, learning our sharp, aggressive movement, enduring the slings and arrows as Pearl coached, scolded and pushed us to be our best. During rehearsals, I danced my part downstage on stage right, at the same time as Daniel did his on stage left. We danced our hearts out, just the two of us, feeling proud of our achievement.

After our dress rehearsal for *Tongues of Fire*, Daniel and I met backstage really confused. We agreed that the designer must have gotten the lighting wrong, because we were dancing in darkness, while in the centre of the stage, right between us, was a bright circle of light. We mentioned it to Pearl and she told us she knew and not to worry.

That opening night, *Tongues of Fire* was scheduled to close the show. Our moment came and all the other members of the company cleared the stage leaving Daniel and me to move into place to begin our high-energy duet. As I started my movement, I noticed I was still in darkness. I looked over at Daniel and could hardly see him. Then that bright light appeared again, illuminating centre stage. "Darn, they forgot to fix it."

Suddenly, Pearl Lang entered, black hair gleaming, eyes flashing, and danced her way into that bright pool of light, where she began a dazzling solo. My jaw dropped and my eyes just about popped out of my head. Three months of rehearsal had passed, including the dress rehearsal that very day. Because we had not once seen Pearl dancing during those rehearsals, we had never imagined she would be onstage with us. Yet there she was, the only person dancing in light!

The piece ended and we lined up for bows, Daniel and I on either side of Pearl. I looked at Daniel, whose eyes had rolled back so far into his head I couldn't see his pupils. The audience applauded and we graciously bowed. I knew that, later that night, even though she was my boss, I was going to speak up, not just about her surprise appearance, but also about all of her intimidating tactics over the past months.

Moonways and Dark Tides, choreographed by Pearl Lang.
Lar Roberson, an unknown dancer, Daniel Maloney and myself.
Photographer: unknown

At the company reception, Pearl approached the two of us, soft, gentle and warm. I had forgotten that socially she was the most agreeable person in town. She seemed a foot shorter, frail and ten years older than she had appeared in the studio and on stage. Her eyes no longer flashed. She generously complimented the two of us on our performances. There was no hint of the fact that two days later, back at rehearsal, she would be a foot taller, a shark once more, letting us know that nothing we did was right. I didn't say a thing.

A Major Slip-Up

Six months after joining Pearl Lang's company, she asked me to do a big jump, known as a *tour jeté*. To perform this jump, you kick one leg out in front of you as you leap and, while suspended in the air, you flip your body to face the opposite direction, "kicking" your second leg back behind you. Pearl requested that I vary the way it was classically executed: she asked me to thrust one arm forward as I flipped around, and to keep my torso parallel to the floor, instead of upright.

I practiced this new move for Pearl until she finally gave me an okay. Then she asked me to add a roll to the floor as I landed. If I had taken the time to mark the movement, to do it carefully at first, everything would have been okay. But always eager to bash my way through things and to "muscle" every movement in my quest to prove myself worthy, I chose not to be careful.

Going full steam, in front of Pearl and the company of ten dancers, I took off into the air. As my body descended from the height of the jump, I tucked one leg under to begin my roll but angled my body badly. My hip hit the floor with the sound of a ripe pumpkin smashing into pavement.

I got up quickly, hoping no one had noticed. I saw everyone staring at me, horrified, but I gave a "no problem" shrug. (When I was starting out, dancers had to be almost dead before they would admit that anything had gone wrong.) After I had picked myself up off the floor, I just kept dancing. My hip in fact didn't hurt much while I was in motion.

Around 2:00 a.m., I woke up feeling like my whole body was on fire. I reached for my hip and felt a lump the size of a half grapefruit.

I had a guest staying with me: fellow Canadian David Hatch Walker, a dancer my age who had been a full-time student at the National Ballet School since childhood. He heard my groans and helped me out to the street. It was

3:00 a.m., but this was downtown Manhattan, so a cab was ready waiting. As we headed towards it, someone came up behind us, pushed us aside and jumped in. Downtown Manhattan, too.

Soon, I was lying in a yellow-curtained cubicle in the ER at St. Vincent's Hospital in Greenwich Village. One of the nurses recognized me from one of my stomach-cramp visits and joked: "Our favourite guest." The doctor's prognosis was severe bursitis. He gave me a cortisone shot and the swelling went down. He said I'd be out of commission for at least six months. Like most young dancers or athletes before the first big blow, I had believed I was indestructible.

I spent most of the next month at home, pulling myself around on crutches. I discovered Kurt Vonnegut, read books on nutrition and healing, and learned to crochet, making ankle length vests, popular at the time, for all my friends. Ahead of the doctor's schedule, after only a month, I willed myself to a Pilates studio and a beginners' dance class.

Two months and twelve crocheted vests after my fall, I was frail, but back in the studio for rehearsal. Pearl had no intention of taking it easy with me. She asked me to do a series of leaps across the floor, simpler though than the kamikaze leap that had finished me off two months earlier. Without my strength back, I was afraid of being boring; but I took it easy because I had to, doing just what was required and not forcing anything, not grinding every muscle in my body. I felt like I was doing nothing, projecting no energy at all.

Pearl flashed a rare smile and said, "You've never danced better."

At that moment I realized that I didn't have to "muscle" every move to be an interesting dancer.

Postcards Home #1

(1968 – 1970)

These are excerpts from a pile of postcards I discovered in my Mom's bureau after she had passed away. (My sister Toba was not living at home at the time that I had sent them.)

Dear Mom, Dad and Wendi,

"Hi! I'm fine. My cold is gone. My picture (of my back!) is in September's Dance Magazine. Rehearsals are hard. Going to Maine on Tuesday to perform for two days at a college with Pearl Lang."

"I waited ten hours in Central Park to see Barbra Streisand. She was wonderful and what a great crowd. 100,000. Other than her free concert and a few $2 movies at the St. Marks Cinema, I haven't done much in the way of show going. My finances are low, but will last me – thank God for the cheap apartment."

"All is well and moving quickly. Unfortunately the fridge broke down in this great heat and most of our food was ruined. Martha Graham taught us yesterday. She told stories about Helen Keller, John Gielgud and Marilyn Monroe and quoted more appropriate poetry and words from the Bible and Greek mythology than one could ever repeat."

The Lower East Side Mafia

Some stories I wouldn't likely have shared in a postcard to my family. My friendship with David Strattus—known as Elbows—and Dolores from London was one of them.

David Strattus only ate desserts. For lunch, he had three and for dinner, five. He was the sugar-rush man. Before eating a lunch of chocolate cake, lemon meringue pie and strawberry ice cream, he had a stooped back and dull, baggy eyes. After the five minutes he needed to inhale his food, his spine was erect and sparks shot out from clear blue eyes. Before a meal, he looked forty. During the sugar-rush, he looked the twenty-five he claimed to be.

I met him over apple crumble at the Paradox. One hot summer night, eating my macro special, I saw a crumpled trench coat appear at the door. Bobbing above it was a craggy face, topped by Bob Dylan hair that looked as though it had been disinterestedly dropped off-centre on top.

He approached and his six-foot-two body plummeted into the chair opposite me, a hungry pelican diving for fish. He barely got out a "Howzigoin' man? I'm David, but call me Elbows," before he slumped down over the table, his face almost in my food.

"I'm good. I'm Kenny," I answered, nudging my plate a bit closer to my end of the table.

He slowly unfurled and got three dishes of apple crumble. In spite of the heat, he kept his coat on. We ate without talking.

Then, one order of crumble down, he shot out, "Did you see *Rowan and Martin* last week? A riot."

"No, I don't have a TV."

"Hey, Kenny," he said, his eyes getting noticeably brighter as he tossed back an overflowing tablespoon, "you're missing some good laughs."

"I'd like to watch, but I can't afford a TV."

"Listen man, I have an uncle in the business. Can you pay $30?"

"Well, $20 tops," I answered, watching him finish off crumble number two.

"Okay, cash on delivery. Deal?"

He stuck out his left hand for the handshake as he finished off dessert number three with his right. "I'll see you here tomorrow night at 8:00." Then he got up and shot out the door. I couldn't help but notice that, in his excitement to give his uncle some business, he hadn't bothered to pay.

I was certain I'd never see him again. But the next night he appeared right on time with a box with one word on it: "Sony."

Over the next month I watched Elbows eat only desserts. During that time, I became the proud owner of the TV, plus a clock radio, a Walkman and a winter coat, all courtesy of Elbows and his uncle.

One night, I ran into him at the doorway of a health food store, Over the Moon, which was on 1st Avenue at 6th Street.

"Watch this. You'll be amazed," he said, with a staccato delivery, his super-erect posture making it clear he had just had his sugar fix.

Dolores, a fair-haired, smiling beauty from England, was at the cash register. Since she had arrived three months earlier, I had been going to the store most nights to buy tofu, organic carrots, whatever, hoping to win favour. (In fact, I largely attribute my conversion to organic foods to the presence of Dolores.) Arranging a rendezvous with her had taken ongoing organic food-buying dedication. Just the previous night, after she had closed the store, we had rolled around in the aisle for a while beside the rice cakes. I was back with a gift to impress her, and hopefully to roll around in a more exotic section.

As he moved up and down the aisles, Elbows began talking with Dolores in a melodious voice that made me wonder if he had also shared in after-hour pleasures. I watched him, waiting to see him do the amazing. I mean, what was he going to do in a health food store that was amazing? Make objects disappear? Exactly.

As he was telling Dolores how sexy she looked wearing her new headband, he was taking jars of jam and honey, bags of carob-covered almonds and boxes of cookies, and placing them, very casually, inside his trench coat. While flirting, he stashed and fitted a week's supply of sweets inside his coat, using his left elbow (thus the nickname) to somehow control the goods. The truly amazing thing was that I had to look really carefully to notice just the slightest bulge in his coat. "Elbows, did you find what you were looking for?" Dolores called out politely.

Meanwhile, Elbows slowly headed for the front door, grabbing a bag of chips and somehow finding room for it under his coat. I considered this last move to be decorative, a show-off gesture. "Yeah, but I forgot my money. I'll be back tomorrow."

Then I followed him out. "So I guess you stole the TV. Everything I own that costs more than $10 is stolen?"

He casually nodded yes. "Meet me tomorrow at noon at 5th and 57th and prepare to be amazed once more."

I figured my relationship with Elbows was about to end, but I couldn't resist the thought of being "amazed once more."

The next day, we headed down 5th Avenue and stopped in front of an exclusive bookstore window. Mounted on an easel was an expensive looking book on Monet. We waited and watched for a minute as well dressed people entered. My soon to be ex-friend wolfed back three Crispy Crunch bars, two bites for each, so I knew something big was about to happen. He walked into the shop, a scraggly vulture heading into a cage of peacocks. I saw his experienced forearm reach over a low partition and pick up the book. A moment later, he was beside me on the street, flipping through the pages.

"Elbows, don't you think we'd better move away from the store?"

Always confident, he replied, "Don't panic, man. Let's just look at the pictures before I give this to Dolores."

Dolores! So he was interested in her too. How could I compete with 5th Avenue art books? After our passionate interlude, I had scraped together just enough nickels and dimes to buy her a little address book, with pictures of flowers at the top of each page. Pansies versus Monet's water lilies. I didn't have a chance.

I left Elbows and hurried to Over the Moon. There she was, gorgeous in macramé.

"What happened to you last night?" she asked.

"I forgot a gift I bought for you, so I went home to get it," I lied. "Here it is." I handed her the crumpled pages of my sad gift. "I'm sorry about running out yesterday. Maybe we can go out after you finish tonight."

Before she could answer, Elbows exploded through the door. He handed the book to Dolores, who smiled at him adoringly. My heart sank.

"Thanks Elbows," she said as he bolted out of the store. "Oh he's not being rude, Kenny, he's just off to get another." Responding to my gaping mouth, she explained, "David and I do business together. He gets expensive books for me from capitalist pigs who should be sharing their abundance anyway, so it's no big deal. Then I sell them real cheap to a friend who has a bookstore. It's how I'm paying for my massage courses. He told me he's stealing stuff for you too, so I feel okay telling you."

"Are you worried that he might be taking food from the store?" I asked.

"No, Elbows would never do anything to get me into trouble."

The week before, I had been in make-out heaven with Dolores. But now, how could I possibly go out with someone who was half of the Lower East Side Mafia? The time had come to end the relationship.

She took out the store key, smiling at me. "Do you want to go out for a glass of wine now?"

I took a deep breath and sadly got ready to refuse and say goodbye.

She then put her hand on my shoulder. All it took was that one touch for my moral compass to spin from north to south. The illegal alien forgave the thief. We stuffed ourselves with dates and chocolate and rolled around in the aisles once more.

Late Night TV, 1968

One night in June 1968, I was having trouble sleeping. I turned on the TV that Elbows had stolen for me. Emerging through the snowy picture, broadcaster Walter Cronkite appeared stone-faced. He was in the middle of a sentence, talking about someone being gunned down at a hotel in California—someone who was forty-two, compassionate, an idealist. It took just a stunned minute for me to realize that this person was presidential candidate Robert Kennedy Jr. He had just won the California primary and was leaving the hotel through the kitchen. This was the man much of America believed was going to reconcile the country's differences regarding the war, poverty and segregation. I had hoped he would be elected, partly as an appropriate revenge on the zealots and their followers who had wiped out so much optimism just two months earlier: in Memphis, Tennessee, an assassin had shot dead another great messenger of hope, civil rights leader Martin Luther King Jr.

For a moment, in the darkness of my apartment, I questioned what I had chosen to do with my life. Why was I trying to dance while the world was burning?

I answered my own question: dance could lead to personal growth and communicate what was best about ourselves. It could break down walls, and challenge and inform audiences. Instead of joining another demonstration at the Pentagon, I would dance life-affirming work on a stage: my own tiny way of protesting the evils of the world; my own peace march.

Sundays in Central Park

After a week of sweaty studios, underground travel, walking on concrete and looking through my apartment windows at dirty walls, a visit to the lawns, rocky hills (said to be over 450 million years old) and lakes (150 acres of water) of Central Park helped me stop thinking about dance. My favourite approach was from the southeast corner by the Plaza Hotel. I'd walk around the pond, taking pictures of its paint-by-numbers bridge, and then head north to the sailboat pool and its Hans Christian Andersen statue. With a sculpted Alice and her Wonderland friends in front of me, I'd sit for a while, reading, looking up to watch excited kids sailing their boats. Then I'd walk west to the formal Literary Walk and follow it north under tall arching trees, my companions now the statues of authors Walter Scott and Robert Burns, who eyed each other across the path. On any warm day, the distant sounds of guitars and voices pulled me to the path's end, to the top of the grand staircase that rose above the Bethesda Terrace with its multi-tiered fountain and the always-unexpected expanse of the tree-lined lake.

Looking down, there was a scene of vibrant moving colours muted by wispy clouds of smoke. Hundreds of bead-wearing, tie-dyed, stoned young people sat on the ledges by the water and around the fountain, singing Bob Dylan, Joni Mitchell and Laura Nyro. The angel statue that stood at the centre serenely looked down over everyone, making me feel like I was about to descend into the world's most blessed place. The haze from marijuana and sticks of pungent coconut, frankincense and patchouli incense hung over everyone. That grand and serene angel appeared to have been inhaling deeply like everyone else. Her mouth turned up in a smile and her wings began to beat. If you were lucky, a good conversation, or just spaced-out grinning at your neighbour in this blissful space, could evolve into a friendship, or possibly into something romantic.

After soaking in all the harmony and love I could handle, reassured once more that world peace was indeed inevitable, I'd set out for quieter spaces. Following the path along the southern edge of the lake, I'd sometimes take a detour south to visit the 1907 hand-carved horses of the Carousel, where I'd ride my favourite white pony. Then I'd walk across the rhythmic Bow Bridge, one of the thirty-six bridges in the park, and take in the lake, with its icy white and blue covering in winter and, in warmer weather, tourists in boats, rowing through reflections of trees and towers.

The Angel, Central Park.
Photograph: Kenny Pearl

After walking north under vine-covered trellises, I'd turn northwest. Visible over the tops of trees along Central Park West, the Dakota Hotel, built between 1880 and 1884, always caught my eye. Its gables, balconies and niches set it apart from all the other more contemporary buildings in the area. It was where John Lennon would soon live and die.

My route took me east, up a hill to the Delacorte Theater. Sometimes, if my timing was right, I'd watch a free performance of dance or theatre. I saw Meryl Streep there in a play by Shakespeare, before she became Meryl Streep.

There were baseball games in the field opposite, but I loved to sit beside the theatre at Turtle Pond. The view of the small, stone Belvedere Castle up on a hill gave the impression of what I imagined to be a European vista.

The Metropolitan Museum of Art was close by on 5th Avenue. I'd visit the special exhibits, but would always return to the familiar Spanish courtyard and Asian collections, the water lilies of the Impressionists and shimmering white Greek and Roman heroes and beasts.

Afterwards, after completing the long walk up the east side of the Reservoir, a 106-acre "lake," I walked through the park's relatively unvisited northeast corner, the Harlem Meer, at 110th Street. Here, paths led visitors through English and French landscapes filled with fountains, statues and beds of multi-coloured flowers. This splendour was a gift of peace.

Mondays, the endurance test would begin once more.

Trial by Fire

At Last, I'm a Dancer

In mid-1968, a senior Graham Company member and one of my teachers, Helen McGehee, was rehearsing for her own show, to be performed at the Kaufmann Auditorium. The theatre was a famous showcase for the arts located in the YM & YWHA on West 92nd Street. Months earlier, she had asked me to be in it. Hard to believe, I had been too busy to accept.

At 7:00 p.m., on the night before her opening performance, my phone rang. "Kenny, this is Helen. One of my lead dancers just pulled a hamstring. I need you to replace him. You'll be performing the role of a Greek king who is the father of an ungrateful son."

"Helen, I'm honoured. But I look twenty years younger than a Greek king with a grown son."

"Poise and makeup, Kenny. I need you."

It's beyond nerve-wracking going into a piece at the very last minute after everyone else has been rehearsing for months. You don't get the chance to develop what dancers call "muscle-memory," which comes after in-depth rehearsals, when you cease to think about what you are doing and allow your body to respond automatically to the music. When dancers go on stage thinking too much, because of uncertainty or a lack of confidence, they rarely give a compelling performance. But if someone you respect is in trouble and asks for help, unless you're lying in bed with casts on both legs, you say yes.

We started rehearsing at 9:00 p.m. at the Graham studio, and worked late into the night. Helen and her husband, the sculptor Umaña, fed me chocolate Häagen-Dazs ice-cream non-stop to keep me going. I learned a long solo and some partnering work with Helen, who was cast as my wife in the piece. She told me to remember the intention of the movement and to make up steps while on stage if I forgot the ones she was now quickly giving to me. I got home around 2:00 a.m., didn't sleep, left at 8:30 for a class and, after only one full company rehearsal in the afternoon, during which I made plenty of mistakes, got ready for my entrance.

Waiting in the wings that night to perform my first solo work on a New York stage, my brain was numb. But I had learned to make aggressive, confident entrances by this time, no matter how shaky I felt. I hoped the music would grab me and carry me.

I entered the stage perched on a throne carried by four male dancers, with my hands holding onto its metal armrests, as the King of Somewhere in Greece. Just what I was used to. Even with extreme makeup—bags under my eyes and deep creases in my forehead—I looked much younger than Ross Parkes, my "son." In the next hour he would betray me, but through the cunning that comes with age, I would triumph.

The unfamiliar lights disoriented me. Onstage were dancers to whom I had to relate, who kept checking to see if I was heading for the right place at the right time. Afterwards I didn't remember much, but I did know that I hadn't dropped Helen from a lift and that I had finished my solo at the right point in the music.

After the dance, standing in the wings before running on for bows, I noticed there were bloody gashes on my hands. I had been so wound up making my entrance that I had gripped the throne's metal armrests with an intensity that had caused them to slice my skin.

I had already performed in New York and in places nearby; but it was only after this trial by fire that, when people asked me what I did for a living, I felt I had earned the right to reply, "I am a dancer."

Dancing with the Martha Graham Dance Company

From Graduation Gown to Loincloth

Shortly afterwards, Ms. Graham invited me to be an apprentice in her company. I briefly experienced a familiar neurotic moment, wondering if I wanted to be in this exalted company if I had been asked to join. Then I gratefully accepted.

There were a lot of men at the Graham School. I felt deeply honoured to be the one Ms. Graham had chosen. Actually, I was over the moon.

Part of my excitement came from thinking about how proud my dance friends and my parents in Toronto would be. Mom and Dad's response was warm; they had become willing and able to give me congratulations at a distance.

Being an apprentice meant I would be on probation. I would dance some small roles in the upcoming New York performances at the prestigious Brooklyn Academy of Music and then, if Ms. Graham thought I did well, she would invite me to join the company as a full member. No pressure!

In rehearsals, Ms. Graham enjoyed grabbing handfuls of my long hair and tugging it whenever she wanted to make a point. The dancers laughed and some told me they had experienced the same "hands-on" approach: it was a sign of good will. They said that Ms. Graham had a special affection for "the two J's," Japanese and Jews.

Some of the company men hovered over me as I rehearsed, very obviously checking me out, deciding if I belonged on stage with them. Maybe they thought I wasn't ready. *I* wasn't sure I was ready. One day, I was taught a short solo, a series of steps that had me moving across the front of the stage, in a piece called *Alcestis*. I practised the movements endlessly and, finally, following our dress rehearsal, my efforts received nods of satisfaction all around. After my appearances in those shows in late 1968, I was awarded full company membership.

The company was on stage less than in previous years. Ms. Graham, though still performing and creating at seventy-four, was suffering from arthritis and, I was told, drinking heavily. So, while employed by the Graham Company, I continued to rehearse and perform with Pearl Lang and Donald McKayle.

Because of its long history, celebrated status and accepted need for foreign artists (mostly Japanese women), the Graham Company was able to get me a work visa, and I finally and happily became a legal U.S. resident.

One year earlier, as a university graduate, aged twenty-one, I had marched down the aisle of Convocation Hall at the University of Toronto, a diploma tucked under my arm, wearing a bulky graduation gown. Now, as a warrior in a number of Ms. Graham's Greek stories, I was dancing on the stages of Broadway theatres with a spear under my arm, wearing much skimpier outfits.

Learning

In the late '60s, there were three tiers of dancers in Ms. Graham's company. At the bottom, looking way up, were newcomers like me. Inhabiting middle ground, performing the roles of supporting characters in the story dances and occasionally a leading role, were dancers like Robert Powell, who had been around for about five to ten years. At the top, looking down from the clouds and inspiring all of us to climb, were the steadfast, our teachers and the senior performers, including Bertram Ross, Robert Cohan and Helen McGehee. They had all remained devoted to the company for around twenty years. Some had been leaping and turning before I was born.

These senior artists each possessed a rare mix of perseverance, passion, ambition, pain tolerance and talent. And these qualities had enabled them to last long enough in the injury-filled, low-paying world of modern dance to gain the depth required to perform convincingly the company's leading dramatic roles. They were able to keep working as mature artists in the Graham Company because, unlike most other western modern dance companies, it had a repertoire that actually required the qualities that only "senior" artists could bring to the work.

Watching these seasoned dancers I admired, as they performed the same material night after night, helped me to understand that excellence is not static or absolute. It comes in many guises. A fine performance one night will likely be different from a fine performance of the same piece a week later, even though all the steps are the same. During the intervening period, a performer has lived, reflected and changed. She has made adjustments because of feedback, injuries and fresh self-knowledge.

During this time, I often watched Bertram Ross (he liked to be called Bert) as he danced the role of the priest in *Appalachian Spring*, a 1936 piece set to the Shaker-inspired music of Aaron Copeland. In this dance, a frontier couple is to be married. Bert played the role of a dignified priest, who bursts into a demonic, frenzied solo before the marriage, warning the couple about the torments of hell that would await them should they break the rules. The steps Bert danced were the same in each run-through of the piece; but he often gave a different emphasis to certain moves. He danced to the music as required, but phrased it in personal ways. The resulting subtle differences kept the role fresh and spontaneous; they allowed him to be continuously evolving, to be constantly creative.

A newer company member whose artistry I admired and learned from was Yuriko Kimura. Slender and long-legged, she had a small round face with dark eyes that really did sparkle.

Yuriko had been cast in a small role in *Deaths and Entrances*, a dance Ms. Graham had choreographed in 1943, which explores the inner lives of the Brontë sisters, Charlotte, Emily and Anne. Some critics argue that the dance is the most ambitious of her psychological cycle, filled as it is with tense, physical movement that represents tortured repression. In the piece, one of the elegantly dressed sisters falls to the ground when she sees the man she loves walk into her room. When the work was first performed, many audience members found it scandalous that a woman, dressed in formal evening wear, would fall to the ground. I heard Ms. Graham defend her choreographic choice in a rehearsal: "When someone you love walks into the room, you fall inside." So why not depict the inner psychological state physically?

Cast as one of the "remembered children," who were younger versions of the adult Brontë sisters, Yuriko had to bring a goblet onto the stage and place it on one of the set pieces. This prop served to trigger memories in the lead characters. I had seen two other dancers in other casts do exactly that: put the goblet on the set and leave. But Yuriko expressed concern about that goblet. She set it down with care, adjusting it so it looked just right. Then, as she turned to leave, she showed the audience with the hint of a smile how pleased she was that she had got it right. She accomplished all this in the brief moment that her music allowed and, in this way, she made her minor character come alive. She was no ordinary performer.

The man who came to my aid just after I joined the Graham Company was a true acrobat of God named William Louther. He was a mid-tier dancer, but was given prominent roles. He was only four years older than I, but because he was so worldly, never had such a small age difference seemed so vast. A Juilliard graduate before joining the Graham Company, an accomplished singer and pianist, Bill had already performed with the Donald McKayle and Alvin Ailey companies, as well as in Broadway musicals. He had the ability not only to jump very high with an incredibly quick trigger, but also to miraculously suspend his body in space at the peak of each jump. He was the only person I had ever seen who regularly got an ovation from fellow dancers after executing a jump combination in class.

Our friendship developed out of chaos. During a rehearsal for Ms. Graham's new piece, *The Archaic Hours*, she asked the men to divide into groups of two. We were instructed to make up short dances in which we stayed physically connected to one another. Bill kindly asked me, the youngest company dancer, to work with him. Ms. Graham gave us twenty minutes to compose our dances.

Bill choreographed and I followed.

Our turn came to perform. The rehearsal pianist's fingers flew across the keyboard, sending Bill and me into our duet. As we moved, a startled look took over his face. When we finished, everyone was howling. Even Ms. Graham had a mischievous twinkle in her eye. Pumped up to the point of oblivion, I had performed our sequence a lot faster than rehearsed and, in doing so, had forced Bill to valiantly keep up. Apparently we had looked like two squirrels fighting over the world's only remaining nut.

Bill was an amazing dancer, and I was sure he felt embarrassed because of my nerve-driven hyper-performance. A lot of dancers would have made some audible comments to make sure that those watching realized that I alone had been at fault, and that they were innocent. But Bill simply said, "Kenny, take a deep breath. You can do this." Then he asked for the music to be played again. We danced and the big whoops of approval from fellow company members were the sign that I had come through.

After that incident, we became pals. He taught me how to put on makeup so I didn't look like a Broadway showgirl, introduced me to fresh movement ideas and, through his assessments of various dances, began to shape my critical eye. He took me home to his mom's house in New Jersey once in a while, where she fed me stacks of her "best-in-the-world" pancakes.

Bill left New York for London in the early 1970s. He choreographed and performed a hit solo show, with music for cello written by Peter Maxwell Davies, called *Vesalii Icones*. He sent me an envelope stuffed with rave reviews of his performance. He had been hailed by London's critics, becoming a celebrity there.

New York Times dance critic Jennifer Dunning wrote words of praise that summed up his brilliance. He was "a virtuoso dancer of rare physical and personal qualities, dancing with the tautness and tension of a coiled spring and the elegant softness of a cat."[21]

The Dance Gods and Their Grip

I was having trouble getting through the hard rehearsals with all my aches and pains. Yet every day I saw dancers who had been passionately involved for many years come to the studio and work full out, in spite of injuries and exhaustion, holding back nothing.

I sat down beside Bertram Ross during a break from a rehearsal one afternoon. I asked him how he had managed to stay so deeply involved in such an obstacle-filled profession. He responded, telling me that once he had discovered dance, he had no choice but to be involved: dance had grabbed him and had not let him go.

I then told him that I had felt something similar many times, including while watching him perform in Rochester, dancing in *Seraphic Dialogue*. Expecting him to laugh at me, I said that I was certain that there were Dance Gods out there who supported and guided us.

But he nodded seriously and told me that the Dance Gods were very real; that they had helped him many times. "They are fierce beings, Kenny, with tight grips, who will not let you go if they feel you are deserving. This is how I see it: Dancers are risk-takers who dare to walk across a chasm on a thin wire. Most aspiring dancers step out onto that wire and fall. The relatively few who stay on balance would all have been lost without the steadying hand of those Dance Gods."

Sweat Leads to My First Broadway Solo

A Time of Snow is Ms. Graham's exploration of the doomed love affair between student and teacher, Eloise and Abelard, in eleventh century France. The piece featured Ms. Graham as the elderly Eloise, who mainly sat on a chair, remembering her life; Argentinean dancer, Noemi Lapzeson, as the young Eloise; Bertram Ross as her teacher and lover, Abelard; and Robert Cohan as Eloise's avenging uncle, who kills Abelard. Each of the other five male dancers in the piece played a variety of roles. At one point, I stood centre stage on a podium.

My task was to announce, with a gesture of my outstretched arm, that the assassinated Abelard was about to be carried on stage.

During a Saturday night performance of my second New York season with the company, Ms. Graham sat to my left and, offstage to my right, four of my fellow male dancers were preparing to quickly hoist Abelard straight up over their heads and bring him to her.

However, that night, Bertram Ross as Abelard, costumed only in briefs, was so wet with sweat that the guys couldn't grip his body to lift him. I watched from my podium as the music played on, and saw Ms. Graham become increasingly confused as Bert kept slipping and sliding down out of the men's hands.

Nothing was happening on stage, so I took it upon myself to jump down from the podium and start making up a solo to fill the time, dancing every step I knew. I leapt to stage right, where the men were still struggling, to show the audience I was looking for someone. Following that came quick knee turns to Ms. Graham, who was so shocked as I rushed towards her, she almost fell off her chair. Then, seeing Bert finally airborne, I didn't waste a minute to execute a series of big jumps that took me back to the podium.

Having finally located a towel, the men had quickly dried Bert off and then easily lifted him. Without much music left, everyone went on improvising and somehow we finished our section at the right time.

I had hoped Ms. Graham would be so impressed she would call me to her dressing room to inform me she would be adding my solo to the dance each night. But she remained happy with her version of the piece.

Powell and Takako

Plain of Prayer, one of Ms. Graham's most challenging works for men, was the dance I was most looking forward to performing during my second New York season. Ms. Graham had created the piece to showcase the physical and dramatic talents of two of her young stars, Robert Powell and Takako Asakawa. In *Plain of Prayer,* they enacted a ritual, a rite of passage, exciting in its physicality, with a quartet of men serving as a chorus, framing and focusing the drama.

I had auditioned for the operas at Lincoln Center in order to have the chance to watch Robert Powell (he liked to be called Powell) in rehearsals. And now I was lucky to be on stage with him once more. Five years older than me, Powell had fair hair that he usually combed straight down over his forehead. With his strong cheekbones and eyes that suggested an Asian ances-tor, he had a commanding presence. Straight out of high school, he had been invited to join the Ailey, McKayle and Graham companies.

He was remarkable even in stillness: I once watched him sitting on the floor putting a band-aid on his big toe, amazed at the harmonious shape his body made. In motion, he was the embodiment of sensual athleticism.

Powell became a friend. When I was down he let me know that he believed in me. He did his best to make sure I didn't take the studio home with me, encouraging me to live a big life outside of dance.

One of the greatest compliments I ever received was from the wife of one of the company members. After a performance, she told me that during one piece she had thought I was Robert Powell.

Takako Asakawa, his partner in *Plain of Prayer*, had a wide, dazzling smile. She possessed an unlimited storehouse of physical virtuosity, and was humble, generous and kind. She often invited me to her apartment for nourishing dinners of miso soup, rice and fish so I would stay healthy. I had no trouble staying healthy on my own, but welcomed her home-cooked meals.

One Pill Makes You Taller and One Pill Makes You Dance

I always felt that I needed to keep both improving and proving myself. So I regularly put in extra time after rehearsals, practising on my own. On a Friday night, less than a week before a Broadway opening, after everyone else had gone home, I stayed to work on a short solo in *Plain of Prayer* that Ms. Graham had asked me to create. One sequence involved a leap that connected to a double turn on my left leg. After the turn, I had to bring my right leg forward and slide to the floor. Not knowing the meaning of the word "enough," I prac-tised the phrase over and over again, dozens of times, striving for the necessary clarity and power. Finally, exhausted and satisfied, I headed out of the studio; but just as I got to the door, my perfectionist self ordered, "One more time. Do it again. It's not good enough yet." So I returned and started practising the solo again: leap, preparation, turn, slide; leap, preparation, turn . . . As I turned aggressively, my foot stuck on a sticky patch on the floor. It locked in position, but my leg kept turning. Something strained deep inside my knee; I felt it rip.

The next day, the physiotherapist suspected I had damaged my cartilage and advised me to stop dancing for several weeks. Saturday and Sunday I stayed home, lying on my back with my leg elevated and icing my knee into numbness, hoping for a miracle, hoping that the physiotherapist had been wrong.

By Monday, patient young man that I was, I decided that I could not accept the diagnosis and stay home. After all, I had taken two days off, which to me was more than enough. I went back to rehearsal but was only fit to watch. And it wasn't fun watching a rehearsal of a dance that I had dreamed of doing and worked so hard to learn, being danced by someone else, even if that someone else was a friend. Of course I did my best to help, giving notes. It was my job to help him be the best he could be, because his challenge was great.

I did what I was supposed to do with a big smile on my face, but inside I was in despair.

After the rehearsal, I talked to Linda Hodes, our rehearsal director, about my disappointment: "What do I have to do to make you believe that I'll be ready for opening night? I will do anything to dance this piece."

Not knowing the physiotherapist's diagnosis, she made the appropriate response: "If you can dance full out during tomorrow's rehearsal at 4:00 p.m., I will consider keeping you involved. That's my deadline, because the cast has to be consistent so everyone has the chance to bring their performance together to the level of excellence required."

Her words made total sense.

I knew I wasn't able to dance, but still hoped something strange and wonderful might happen. While in the changing room, I shared my story with a senior member of the company. He told me he had a powerful prescription pill for pain and inflammation.

"But I don't have time to go to a doctor," I said. "I don't even have a doctor."

And then he made me an offer: "I'll give you some of the pills. Lots of dancers take them and besides, this is a big moment in your life."

"I don't think you're supposed to do that, share prescriptions," I weakly responded, knowing full well that I was going to go to his apartment immediately and gulp down as many pills as I needed to feel better.

The next day, I walked with manageable pain from the subway to the studio. I did my own warm-up and at 4:00 p.m. took my place for a run-through of

Plain of Prayer. I flew through it feeling light and strong, springing high above the floor on all my jumps, turning and sliding to the floor as if I had never missed a rehearsal.

I kept swallowing those little orange and white capsules throughout our two weeks of performances and I (almost) painlessly danced my way through opening night and a successful Broadway season.

Twenty years later, I was watching the TV show *60 Minutes.* There was a segment on racehorses with an exposé on drugs that were used to keep injured horses on the track. The drug the show focused on was the very one that came in that orange and white capsule: Butazolidin.

Butazolidin was powerful and toxic, suitable only for racehorses and other mammals much larger than me. A British surgeon, interviewed for the show, said that taking it was tantamount to killing a gnat with an atomic bomb. By the time the *60 Minutes* show aired, the drug had been banned for human use.

Scotch and Roses

In December 1969, just over a year after joining the Graham Company, I was invited to be a guest artist with the London Contemporary Dance Theatre. I told Ms. Graham about my invitation (which I eventually declined due to performance conflicts). Strangely, she wanted to have a talk with me about my possible departure and, even more strangely, she wanted the talk to be, not at the studio, but in her apartment. She set the time for the next day at 3:00 p.m.

Ms. Graham lived in an elegant yellow-brick apartment building, a short walk east of her studio. Right on time, I pressed the buzzer and, without asking who it was, she buzzed me up. I knocked and, a long moment later, a sad, dishevelled woman answered. Wearing a faded white nightgown, she made me think of the aged Miss Havisham from Charles Dickens' *Great Expectations.* The body filling the flimsy fabric was round and lumpy, and the hair, streaked gray and black, exploded from her head in ragged tassels. The pale, sallow face registered shock. I was shocked, too. "Sorry, miss. I have the wrong apartment."

It took me one stunned moment to realize my mistake. "Ms. Graham," I said, forcing a smile, "how nice to see you." I had only seen Ms. Graham at her studio, at the theatre or at company receptions. She was always immaculately groomed, makeup perfect, hair sleek and pulled tightly back, always wearing well-tailored, loose rehearsal clothes or evening wear. As I entered, I quickly realized how much preparation it must have taken on each public occasion to turn Miss Havisham into Martha Graham.

The scent of booze was in the air. A bottle of scotch and a half-filled glass were on a coffee table beside a vase of red roses. It was no secret that Ms. Graham indulged. I figured she had been drinking and had forgotten about our meeting. I figured she would be embarrassed and self-conscious about letting me see her as few had, and would ask for a moment to tie her hair back and to put on a robe. Actually, I was hoping she would tie her hair back and put on a robe. But she headed straight for a sofa, and the usually immaculately groomed Ms. Graham lay back on it, a frazzled, rumpled version of the woman in Manet's Odalisque.

"How are you Terry?" she drawled, getting two out of the five letters in my name right.

"I'm fine, Ms. Graham. How are you?" I replied, wondering about all the possibilities that lay ahead.

"I'm just fine too," she answered, now with an aristocratic, kind of British accent. "Would you like to look at my collections, Kerry?" (She was getting closer.) She pointed to a wall of shelves.

I got up, happy to be distracted and looked with appreciation at the Martha Graham museum. On display were dozens of stunning carved artefacts that included Buddhas, Shivas, sacred cats, elephants and frogs. Frozen in little frames were brightly coloured butterflies and beetles. "They're from my trips to the Orient," she said.

"Nice," was my educated response.

A long moment passed because I had no idea what to say, and I figured she was trying to remember what I was doing in her apartment. Finally I said, "Ms. Graham, you wanted to talk with me about my trip to London."

"Yes, London," she responded, eyeing the scotch but resisting reaching for it. "I'm not happy that you'll be leaving us." I reminded her that I would be returning after six months, and she seemed genuinely pleased that I would be doing so.

"Now Kenny (she got it), you're very young. How old are you?"

"I'm twenty-three Miss Graham."

"Goodness, I thought you were eighteen," she replied.

With that, the twenty-three-year-old novice in bellbottoms and the rumpled seventy-five-year-old genius in nightclothes, with a vase of roses and a bottle of scotch separating them, enjoyed an hour of conversation. Gone was the imperious tone she often used. Gone were the dramatic gestures that always sculpted the space around her as she directed life in her studio. At one point, she asked me if I was straight or gay; but other than that, she didn't get too personal.

She led the conversation. I did my best to keep up as we discussed the ongoing dilemmas of Israel's recent occupation of the West Bank and Gaza, and expressed relief that the assassins of both Dr. Martin Luther King Jr. and presidential hopeful Robert Kennedy Jr. had recently been sentenced.

Given the amount of scotch she had likely imbibed before my arrival, her clarity amazed me. She had insights that helped make sense of events and was patient with my rudimentary knowledge. Discussing the Woodstock music festival which had taken place four months earlier, I told her that I was sure its success meant that '60s culture would live on forever. She disagreed, pointing out a couple of impossible to dismiss events: Charles Manson, an American criminal and aspiring songwriter, along with his "family" of hippie followers, had brutally murdered seven people a week before Woodstock in an exclusive California neighbourhood, claiming that he had been inspired by lyrics in the Beatles' *White Album* ("what they need's a damn good whacking" [22]). She also reminded me that, just the previous week, during a Rolling Stones concert at the Altamont Speedway in California, the Hell's Angels, hired to protect the band, had stabbed to death a concertgoer who had been aiming a gun at the stage. "The '60s are doomed, Kenny. Trust me. They are doooomed!"

On my way out of the apartment, she directed me to a bookshelf and told me I could borrow a book. I chose *Lives of the Saints*, by Alban Butler, imagining there might be a story told in its pages that would one day become a subject of Ms. Graham's choreography. Then, for a brief moment, she was transformed back into the goddess on the mountaintop, the Martha Graham I had known. She raised herself up, arched her back and, with just enough ferocity, proclaimed, "Make sure you return it!"

Life is Good

During my almost three years with the Graham Company, I had been given the opportunity to perform in twelve of Ms. Graham's dances. As the youngest company member, I was often a spear-carrier and chorus member. Two of the pieces I performed in were new creations, *Lady of the House of Sleep* and Ms. Graham's 144th piece, *The Archaic Hours*. Neither of them became classics; in fact, neither one was performed for more than one season. Following the opening of *The Archaic Hours, New York Times* critic Clive Barnes wrote: "Productivity on a massive scale is no guarantee of genius, but it is a very frequent symptom."[23]

But I did get an opportunity to dance in two popular pieces. One was the aforementioned *Plain of Prayer*. The other was the classic 1948 work, *Diversion of Angels*, which I had watched in Rochester a few years earlier. Ms. Graham told us she had seen the structure for it while lying under a tree at Connecticut College, looking up into the pattern of its branches. The choreography for the four men is powerful and, at the same time, lush, lyrical and joyful. It gave all of us a chance to shine.

I assumed I would spend the rest of my dance days working my way up the ladder with the Graham Company, taking occasional side trips to work with other groups. Life was good.

A Door Closes; A Garden Gate Opens

"Everyone, it's important," our company manager shouted from the wings. "Please stay on stage." The curtain had just come down following our closing night performance of *Cortege of Eagles* at the American Dance Festival in New London, Connecticut. It was late August 1970. As calmly as he could, he said these unimaginable words: "Dancers, this will be your last performance until further notice. Ms. Graham is closing the company down. We don't yet know what will happen. There will be a meeting next week."

We took off to our dressing rooms and later to the New London bars for a night of frantic discussion. "Why," we asked ourselves, "had she made this decision?" Yes, there had been rumours about Ms. Graham not performing any more, because of her age, injuries and her arthritis. Still, even if she had decided never to step out on another stage, why would she choose to shut her company down? Most of her roles, in fact, were being performed brilliantly by senior dancers whom she had selected.

After almost fifty years, the oldest existing dance company in North America was closing its doors. I couldn't have known that Martha Graham's performance that night in *Cortege of Eagles,* a piece in which I had performed, would turn out to be her last.

The Dance Gods Stop By Once More

After a sleepless night, the next morning twenty dancers sat on a train, homeward bound and unemployed. I stared in silence out the train window. I thought about the fact that auditions for established modern dance companies were rare. Usually, artistic directors like Ms. Graham and Merce Cunningham recruited new members from their advanced classes. And I hadn't heard about any auditions recently. I had already lined up, for later in November, some part-time, low-paying work with Pearl Lang, to fill in the time that was supposed to have been a scheduled Graham Company break. I dejectedly thought about all the roles in the Graham Company repertoire that I had danced for the last time and the more challenging roles that I could no longer aspire to perform. I also thought about my return to apartment cleaning for the Under the Table Agency.

Billboards, trees, poles flashed by, creating a rhythm that was fortunately putting me to sleep. As my eyes were closing, I felt a tap on my shoulder. "Can I sit down?" It was my favourite dancer of all time, Robert Powell.

"I forgot all about it until right now as I was walking past you," he began, "but Alvin Ailey is having an audition tomorrow. He's looking for two male dancers." My heart started pounding. I became alert.

"I don't think many people know about it." Powell knew because, as a former Ailey Company dancer, he had friends who were currently performing with the company. "Only invited dancers can go."

My excitement level suddenly dropped. "Yeah, great, but I haven't been invited. And anyway, the company is mostly black and I have no jazz training so I don't have a chance." I was an expert at coming up with reasons why I would fail at undertakings.

Powell ignored my arguments and calmly said, "Kenny, look at me. I danced with Ailey. I'm very white and I never studied jazz. You have to go. Tell them that you've been dancing with the Graham Company. Tell them I told you to show up."

He took me by the shoulders, looked into my eyes and said, "Promise me you'll go."

I had no choice. "I promise."

3

REACHING

September 1970

Alvin Ailey's Humanism

"I am trying to show the world that we are all human beings and that color is not important. What is important is the quality of our work." [24]

Alvin Ailey was born in Depression-era Texas in 1931 in the town of Rogers, population less than 1,000. His father abandoned the family when Ailey was six months old, so he was raised solely by his mother, Lula Elizabeth Ailey, who moved her family often as she struggled to find work. Early experiences in the Southern Baptist church and local jook joints, places where black workers socialized, gave the young Alvin Ailey a sense of black pride. Growing up in a strictly segregated world hostile to African Americans, he learned to have a mistrust of whites. "I heard about lynchings. Having that kind of experience as a child left a feeling of rage in me that I think pervades my work." [25] In 1942, he and his mother moved to Los Angeles, where he got his first taste of multiracial life. He matriculated at George Washington Carver Junior High School and later attended the Thomas Jefferson High School. While in school, he showed talent for singing, writing and learning languages. He also began attending shows at the Lincoln Theater and the Orpheum Theater. In 1949, he found his way to the Lester Horton Dance Theater. Lester Horton, a white man, had established one of America's first integrated dance companies, one in which membership was based on talent alone. He became the young Ailey's great mentor.

In 1954, Ailey and his friend Carmen de Lavallade (the dancer who would later dance a lead role in *Carmina Burana*) moved to New York and performed in the Broadway show *House of Flowers*. Performances in other Broadway shows followed.

Alvin Ailey
Photograph: Kenny Pearl

Alvin Ailey formed his own company in 1958, calling it the Alvin Ailey American Dance Theater. Its first performance was held at the Kaufmann Auditorium, in the YM & YWHA. The fledgling Ailey Company featured two minority groups, one racial and one artistic: at that time, white artistic directors dominated the not terribly popular art form of modern dance (in which most dancers were also white). In Ailey's new company, all seven dancers were African American. He said, "I started out . . . to create a black folkloric company, to present to the public what black artists had created in music and dance."[26]

This vision quickly grew into something larger and more controversial: an integrated dance company that was primarily made up of African Americans. In deciding to create a multiracial company in a still predominantly racially segregated world, Ailey said, "This country has a multiracial society. I believe in black pride and a black renaissance but I do feel that we need to learn to come together."[27] He also said, "My dancers must be able to do anything, and I don't care if they're black or white or purple or green."[28] By 1960, he had introduced into his repertoire the dances of two white choreographers, Lester Horton, his mentor, and John Butler. To put matters into perspective: 1962 was the year in which a U.S. federal appeals court ordered the all-white University of Mississippi to admit James Meredith, an African-American student. Upon his arrival a mob of more than 2,000 white people rioted. In 1963, a survey showed that only sixty-two percent of Americans (twenty-seven percent in the southern states) believed that black and white students should attend the same schools.[29] It was perhaps an understatement when dance historian Deborah Obalil wrote: "An integrated dance company glorifying southern African-American culture would not be easily accepted in a society wrought with racial tension."[30]

Speaking of Ailey and his courage, the dance critic Clive Barnes wrote in a New York Times article entitled "A Great Lesson in Race Relations": "Ailey is an equal opportunity employer in a field and at a time when equal opportunity is not that fashionable . . . It would be easier—more acceptable—for Ailey to form an all-Black company . . . as the obvious Black leader in American dance, guilty foundations would have to beat a path to his door. But Ailey goes the hard way of his conscience."[31]

Ailey's conscience reflected the ideals of the early civil rights movement, under the leadership of Dr. Martin Luther King Jr. On a more personal level, he had been inspired by his original mentor, Lester Horton: "My master was an American choreographer named Lester Horton. Horton discovered me, he taught me everything I know, and he left his mark on my technique and my ideas. In everything I am and everything I do, there is, I hope, the lifeblood of his message."[32]

He was also moved by audience reaction to his work, especially the reception his company received during a 1962 overseas tour to Asia and Australia. He said, "The dirt and grit of (the African-American inspired) *Revelations* and *Blues Suite* and the power of Brother John's (Black gospel) singing had a profound impact on audiences all over Southeast Asia, but especially so in Japan."[33] In Australia, "They screamed from beginning to end; there was thunderous applause that went on and on, people throwing flowers, people crying."[34]

That tour confirmed what Ailey had intuited: "I discovered as we travelled through Asia that there were blues in all cultures, that there were these feelings in all cultures and that the people of any culture can express them."[35]

Ailey wanted dance to be held up as a mirror to his audiences. He wanted people to see in his dances the possibilities in humanity of generosity, joy and beauty, all conveyed through a dense and challenging physicality. Whatever the content of an Ailey dance, whether it was the literal telling of a story, an exploration of a piece of American culture, or a purely abstract work, it was performed with the dignity and power that would involve audiences and take them into a world of feelings and athleticism they may never before have experienced.

Writing in New York's *Village Voice*, dance critic Deborah Jowitt noted that the Ailey Company is "loved for its rapid attack and luxuriant strength . . . There is always something thrilling about the company's dancing in Ailey pieces. They throw every ounce of power and litheness into every step . . . they use the natural swing, thrust, weight of their bodies. Perhaps this is why—both in Ailey's best and worst dances—the audience responds so empathically. A jolt of energy comes from the stage, but it comes in a warm and joyful pulse that deftly aligns itself with their own heartbeat."[36]

I knew that if I were going to dance with Mr. Ailey's company, I was going to have to fly.

The Alvin Ailey Audition

Lost in the Crowd

The night before my audition, I didn't sleep much. The fear of failing tangled with excitement about possibilities. At 8:00 a.m. I loaded my backpack with my lucky bellbottom purple dance pants, a bottle of water and a bag of trail mix, prepared for what I figured would be a two- or three-hour audition. The Ailey studio was on East 59th Street, just a few blocks south of the Martha Graham building.

I arrived an hour early to warm up. The woman who responded to my knocking on the locked door was small and looked elfish in her green head-band. She took a long look at her watch and gave me a suspicious stare. "Sorry, I'm just always early," I said.

Then she gave me a smile, introducing herself as Ivy Clarke, Alvin Ailey's manager. I had come at 9:00; by 9:30, only a few other dancers had turned up. The audition was by invitation only, so maybe there would only be a few of us.

At 9:45, the crowd arrived. We were given numbers to pin onto our tops. I was given number 53. The last number to be handed out was 82. That number was surprisingly high. In Toronto, if ten capable men show up at an audition, that's considered a lot. I knew only one other dancer in the crowd: Mark Daniels, with whom I had danced in Donald McKayle's company. Almost all the men were African American.

At exactly 10:00, the procession of people who were about to watch and judge filed onto the small stage that rose at one end of the studio. A few wore brightly coloured dance clothes that revealed sleek, muscular bodies. These were the company members who would teach class and demonstrate move-ment. Others came in wearing headbands and scarves, leather jackets and bellbottom jeans. Their relaxed demeanour noticeably contrasted with that of the nervous eighty-two awaiting their judgment. Mark pointed out Sarah Yarborough. She was a stunning, long-legged woman dressed for the day in black leather. She had been a member of the Harkness Ballet and was now joining the company without an audition. Maybe she was there to check out possible future partners. The tall, majestic Judith Jamison, Mr. Ailey's muse, entered last.

Only after taking in this theatrical parade did I notice Alvin Ailey. I noticed him last, not because he was not physically powerful or handsome. He was both. But in that sea of elegance and bravado, his look was so understated. I thought of the first time I had seen Martha Graham swooping through the intermediate level class, makeup, outfit and attitude all giving her the look of royalty. With his hair trimmed to a modest Afro, a small beard and casual clothes, Mr. Ailey slipped into his chair as if he didn't want to be noticed. When Ms. Graham spoke, she had let all of us know she was, and always would be, Clytemnestra. Mr. Ailey said nothing.

The members of the Ailey group sat stretched across the stage from which they could look down upon us, already beginning to write notes down on their pads. I felt my adrenaline kick in. Whatever happened, I was having a chance I never thought I would have. I was going to dance for Alvin Ailey and, at that moment, I knew I was about to dance my heart out, for at least as long as I lasted in the audition. And I had no doubt that all the stunning people who had shown up to the audition were going to dance their hearts out right along with me.

A small, muscular dancer with tight, curly hair and an olive complexion hopped down from the stage. He introduced himself as Ramon Segarra. I had seen him dance a few years earlier as a guest artist with the National Ballet of Canada in Toronto. "I'm the rehearsal director and company teacher," he announced. "We will begin with a two-hour ballet class."

I was surprised; as a kind of hybrid jazz-modern company, the Ailey company was not where I expected to find dancers taking a ballet class.

"Then we will ask some of you to leave. After that, company dancers will teach five sections from our repertoire. Each one will be in a different style. After each section we will call out the numbers of the people who are to leave. I repeat, who are to leave. We're looking for two dancers to take on our tour to Russia, Paris and London, which will begin in four weeks." The restless eighty-two gave out a collective gasp, cutting off his speech.

"So," he said, as he waited for us to quiet down, "dance well, good luck and thanks to all of you for coming. Let's begin."

All of us positioned ourselves beside one of the *barres,* supporting handrails, lining the walls and arranged in lines on the floor. A typical New York class comprised a maximum of thirty dancers. Now we were packed, like rows of dominoes, with little room to move and not much possibility of even being seen. The sweet and spicy smells of eighty-two brands of deodorant, mixed with the throat-tightening stench of car exhaust spilling through the studio windows from the nearby Queensboro Bridge, were overwhelming.

The pianist entered and was introduced. Mr. Segarra gave us our first movements, a set of *pliés* with four different positions of the legs and feet. We all concentrated on the phrasing and physicality. Then Mr. Segarra set the tempo, counting out a slow four. The pianist's fingers picked up his rhythm and together we began a journey, moving as one.

The Audition

Right from the very start, I was prepared to be cut. My glass-is-half-empty thinking, the one I often started with, took hold as I reminded myself that I hadn't studied ballet since joining the Graham Company. Any feel I had for that form had likely vanished, and my rustiness with ballet's quick footwork would surely show as an obvious weakness. But as we progressed, my glass-is-half-full better self asserted itself, with the recognition that my legs were high in all directions and my jumps were, as I had been told, courageous.

For the first hour of the audition, we remained standing at the *barre*, executing a series of warm-up exercises that awaken and strengthen the body, beginning with the feet connected to the floor. We were then led steadily through a series of exercises, developing in complexity until we were performing large sweeping movements balancing on one leg while raising the other high above the ground. After this hour-long *barre* we were well warmed up, the sauna effect of so much physical effort in a relatively enclosed space leaving us all dripping with sweat, our hair matted and skin glistening.

For the second section of class, we were divided into small groups for centre-of-the-floor combinations, made up of a variety of phrases emphasizing jumps and turns. To finish, we danced in pairs coming across the floor on a diagonal, executing the most energetic, space-covering and challenging movements of the class. By this time, each of us was visible and exposed, dancing full out. There was a feeling of friendly competition in the room: we were sizing up one another as each did his best to jump the highest, while at the same time we all cheered and applauded everyone's efforts.

By the end of the two hours, there was a feeling of shared joy. We felt as though we had accomplished what we had set out to do. But as we applauded wildly in appreciation for our teacher and accompanist, we remembered why we were there and what was about to happen. The cut. Some of us were about to go home.

"Take five minutes," Ivy shouted from the stage. We collapsed to the floor, mopped up our sweat, drank our beverages and waited. All eyes looked everywhere except at the stage from which we could hear fifteen overlapping voices talking about us. Some choices, pro or con, would be unanimous. There would inevitably be disagreements about others.

Silence made us all look up. Ivy announced, "Thank you everyone. You did very well. However, you know we're only looking for two dancers, so we must begin the process of thinning out this crowd. If your number is called you will not, I repeat, *not*, be going on." She read about twenty numbers. Mine was not called.

Sixty of us began learning the first section of repertoire. Ten minutes into it, Ivy stopped us: "Hold on a minute. One of you is still here whose number was called. Number 26, you are not supposed to be here."

Number 26 looked flat-out shocked. "But you called my number."

He had gotten the information backwards and was embarrassed and apologetic. He was so sincere in fact that the powers that be decided to let him stay. He was cut shortly afterwards. My number wasn't announced after performing the first dance. It wasn't called after the second. Four hours into the audition, forty of us remained. There were some great dancers present, so although I didn't believe I'd make it through to the end, I was genuinely excited; by this time Alvin Ailey was most likely noticing I was out there and dancing well, or at least well enough to be one of forty.

Among the remaining dancers was a handsome Latino man named Hector, who moved with power. He kept breaking the rules, doing flashy turns in the centre of the studio, which no one had asked him to do. He was showing off, acting as if he was already in the company, and getting noticed. In spite of his brash attitude, and possibly because of it, it seemed like he would be one of the two final choices.

The fourth sequence was modern, with a Graham feel, a fast-moving section from a new Ailey dance that I had never seen, called *Streams*. Afterwards, ten more dancers were cut. I was not one of them.

Into our sixth hour, only five dancers remained, Hector, Mark and myself among them. In less than an hour, after one more sequence, three of us would be out the door. Hours before, I had been thrilled just to have made the cut following the class. Now that wasn't enough. I wanted it all. The five of us wanted it all.

The final, fifth sequence came from Talley Beatty's *Toccata*, one of the pieces I had seen two years ago at that first free concert. Mr. Ailey had saved the hardest sequence for last: it was a high velocity mix of modern, ballet and jazz. We danced together, feeding off each other's energy, though perhaps not feeling as supportive of one another as we had been earlier in the day. Exhausted, we willed ourselves through the movement, spinning and diving to the floor, leaping with our legs as split as we could make them and our torsos arching up. I wondered if what we were experiencing was like a typical day in the life of an Ailey dancer.

Then it was over.

Decisions had been made quickly all afternoon, but this time we waited for a half hour. Now that the audition was over, muscle-numbing fatigue caught up to me. My feet were newly torn, my knees bruised and floor burns covered my arms. Then Ivy came forward.

"You guys were amazing. We loved watching all of you. However, Alvin wants to see you do the last combination again, one at a time."

We were stunned. Couldn't believe it. After seven hours, they wanted more. We peeled ourselves off the floor. Hector danced first. Mark second. I was third. I had seen some great dancing that afternoon, but the four other remaining guys really inspired me. Everyone deserved the job.

"This time I will announce the numbers of the two dancers who *will* be joining the company tomorrow morning. Number 13."

That was Hector.

"And, number 47."

Number 47 was not Mark. And it was not me.

Toronto – New York City

Mark and I headed directly to a familiar bar around the corner. We lined up a row of Singapore Slings—the sweet-treat cocktail of the day that included gin, cherry brandy and grenadine syrup—and drank our way to closing time. Dehydration, fatigue, disappointment, plus alcohol. It was not a good night. I went home, happy about what I had achieved being a member of the top five, but angry at myself for not being good enough to get the job.

In the morning, the only thought just barely managing to work its way through my hangover was how close I had been to a job with the company whose work I loved and whose dancers inspired me. But I knew that whether it was because of a look, or technique, or both, Alvin Ailey had simply chosen the two people he felt fit his company best.

That afternoon, I decided to leave New York for a couple of weeks. I took a bus upstate to Lake Placid, where a friend from the Graham School, Monica Morris, was performing with Paul Taylor's company. I wanted a quiet place to think about what would come next, as well as someone to stroke my wounded ego. In a couple more months, I would begin a project with Pearl Lang and maybe some Graham dancers would produce their own concerts. Donald McKayle had recently moved to Los Angeles and was creating acts for celebrities, including Tina Turner. I had thoughts of moving to LA to work again with him and of becoming a show-biz guy. Who knew what could happen? Except for not being an Ailey dancer, everything was going to be good.

While my friend Monica rehearsed, I picked an isolated spot on an outcropping of rocks by the lake under a tall fir tree and reviewed the audition. I imagined every sequence over and over again, especially the last one when the group had been cut to five. I drove myself crazy rerunning every jump and turn until my hangover finally forced me into a deep sleep.

I watched Monica's high-spirited performance later that night, feeling proud of her for somehow managing to dance with a great company while dealing with challenges I couldn't imagine. She was the only twenty-two-year-old I knew who had not only been married, but was also divorced. And she had full custody of a two-year-old daughter. My audition problems felt trivial beside her challenges—but I discussed them endlessly anyway.

The next morning, low on cash, I decided to hitchhike to Toronto to visit my family, a 500-kilometre trip. Two rides later, I was there.

I stayed with my parents, who, while sympathetic about the outcome of my audition, used it as a bargaining tool to convince me to stay in Toronto: "These disappointments can be very hard and you know how your stomach reacts to stress."

I immediately called David Earle, my former teacher, and he invited me to give some classes at Toronto Dance Theatre, the company he had recently co-founded. I was inexperienced as a teacher so the invitation was a wonderful opportunity.

I enjoyed the teaching. I also felt safer north of the border, because the Vietnam War was ongoing. In fact, a year earlier, a draft lottery had been introduced for the random selection of draftees. I remembered the newspaper article about the German man who possessed a similar work visa to mine who had been called up for a military hearing. My Graham work visa made me all too visible.

But after two weeks, I was missing New York. While Toronto had become more dynamic during my time away, nothing could compare to the chaos and passion on the streets of the East Village. I felt I had no choice but to return.

From the subway at Astor Place, I walked along St. Mark's Place, anxious to feel the buzz of East Village energy. But the street was unusually quiet. No guitars were being strummed; no animated conversations were happening. I asked a guy slouched over on a doorstep what was going on and he told me that the rock star Jimi Hendrix had died. He was twenty-seven. Taped onto lamp posts were fliers covered with his quotes: "Music is a safe kind of high;" "I've been imitated so well, I've heard people copy my mistakes;" "Excuse me while I kiss the sky."

It was September 18th, 1970.

Back on East 4th Street, I stood across from number 69, the "Bowery Hotel," and took a long look at the building where I had spent the first three years of my New York life. Staring at rusted fire escapes zigzagging across the sooty brick of my tenement, I felt a rush of happiness. There was the window, occupied by the ever-present round head of my dragon-slayer. The super slouched against the wall with his Bud, the scraggly trees held onto their few struggling leaves and garbage overflowed. It was great to be home.

Do or Die

Fifteen minutes after getting into my apartment, the phone rang: "Kenny, it's Mari. Where have you been?" Mari Kajiwara was the dancer in the Ailey Company whom I had met when we were both students at the Graham School. "The office has been calling you all week." (The personal answering machine was not yet in use.)

"What office?" I asked.

"One of the guys Alvin hired from the audition didn't work out and he wants you to audition again."

"I can't believe it!" I had felt so relaxed returning home, at peace with my dance life for the immediate future, but in an instant, my adrenaline started pumping and I felt panic. "What do I have to do? Is the position still open? Who else is going?"

"Kenny, shut up. Call the office . . . NOW!"

The next morning at 9:00, Ivy Clarke let me into the building once again. I did my own warm-up in a small studio, upstairs from the big one where the eighty-two of us had danced our hearts out two weeks earlier and where the company would be beginning its class at 10:00. I didn't have a clue what to expect. Who would be there? What would I have to do? I stretched, focused on taking deep breaths, did Graham floor exercises and a ballet *barre*. I said a prayer: "Dance Gods, I would love your support again; I would be so grateful for a little assistance picking up material quickly; and for help getting my stomach to drop down from my throat for a few minutes. I will work beyond fatigue to show you I am worthy."

A little after 10:00, Mr. Ailey entered with Judith Jamison. I was instantly star-struck. Mr. Ailey, his brow furrowed, nodded a hello. He was all business. Judith smiled, said hi and put a tape into the sound system. Then she simply walked out into the centre of the studio and began demonstrating a sequence of movements. At first I stood there staring, forgetting that this was not a performance she was giving especially for me but an audition. She was just so riveting that it was hard for me to even contemplate dancing alongside her, just the two of us. Her attack, daring, spirit and confidence just hypnotized me. I recognized the movement as a jazz sequence I had performed during the first audition.

I ran behind her and surprised myself by remembering the movement. Then she stepped away and, as I danced solo, she gave me corrections—lots of them—referencing quality and technique. After a half-dozen run-throughs, Mr. Ailey quietly said something to her. Then Judith got up and put on another tape.

This time it was a sequence from *Revelations*, from the closing section, the one that never failed to fill the audience with joy and wonder. It had not been part of the audition, so I hoped I would be able to pick up the movement quickly enough to get beyond the steps and project its spirit. Alvin Ailey and Judith Jamison sat five feet in front of me. I danced, tentatively at first, with Alvin still frowning, and Judith giving me an encouraging smile, her head nodding up and down and not side to side, thank goodness.

As I rocked, spun and swung my torso to the high-voltage gospel sound of Brother John Sellers singing "Rocka My Soul," I realized that, as well as getting through the steps with some degree of accuracy, I was actually having a good time. The sound and movement came together in a unique way, the music leading the dance, then the dance seeming to inspire the music. I felt like it would be impossible to perform that movement without happiness taking over one's being.

Then Judith turned off the tape and I knew that my good time could be about to end with their soon-to-be delivered decision. They whispered; I waited. Had I made a fool of myself? Would this be another big blow? I stood in front of them, arms at my sides as Martha Graham had once instructed, letting them see "that place from which my heart beat."

Mr. Ailey stepped towards me. He was a bear of a man. I thought he could probably lift me over his head with one arm. But he didn't. A huge smile took over his face. His eyes sparkled, his brow unfurled and he extended his arm towards me. We shook hands firmly, him taking the lead: a light breath of a lift up, followed by one solid downward motion. No wasted energy.

Then he said his only words of the morning: "You're very musical. You're in."

I went downstairs and joined the company rehearsal, heart bursting.

An Unexpected Result

Was I completely out of my mind? I telephoned Martha Graham at her home on a Sunday morning in mid-September 1970 and told her I was leaving her company. (Yes, the company had officially folded, but we were advised by its manager to stay close by, so we could teach at the school.)

"Are you certain you want to do this, Kenny?"

"Yes," I replied. "I had to look for work elsewhere because of what's happening with the company. I auditioned for Alvin Ailey and he offered me a contract."

"Well, I don't think you should accept it. You've been a member of our family for many years."

"I know, and I've loved it and learned so much and I feel terrible. But, I have to move on. I really want to keep performing."

Then she shocked me: "Well, Kenny, if you stay, I will give you the lead roles in two of my most popular dances, *Appalachian Spring* and *Night Journey*."

I was the youngest member of the company. Those roles belonged to senior dancers, like Bertram Ross and Robert Cohan. I knew, beyond a doubt, that they would not be given to me. Anyway, it was doubtful that there would be performances of these or any of her other works for a long while, if ever.

"Thank you, Ms. Graham, but I've made up my mind."

"You'll be sorry. These are great roles and they're yours."

I could hear her getting tense. After all, she was the director, the source of light. I was supposed to follow her commands, bask in her rays. Still, I tried one last time to soften my leaving: "I feel really bad and I want you to know how grateful I am for everything you've . . ."

"Well then . . ." she interrupted. Her voice dropped, sounding like distant thunder.

There was a long pause, which I felt was definitely the calm before a storm that would knock me down. She shouted, and I mean shouted, six more words into the phone. Unforgettable. ". . . YOU CAN JUST GO TO HELL!" Then she slammed down the phone. I was demolished.

Later, I ran into a Graham Company dancer who was a representative on the company's board of directors. She told me Ms. Graham had come to their meeting the night before in a rage. She told everyone that I had called her to blackmail her; that I had demanded she give me leading roles in her best dances, or I would leave the company. "How dare he!" So she had fired me. *She had fired me!*

I didn't know until decades later what was really going on with Ms. Graham at the time. In her memoir, *Blood Memory,* she wrote: "A dancer, more than any other being, dies two deaths: the first, the physical, when the powerfully trained body will no longer respond as one would wish. After all, I choreographed for myself. I never choreographed what I could not do. I changed steps in *Medea* and other ballets to accommodate that change. But I knew and it haunted me. I only wanted to dance. Without dancing, I wanted to die."[37]

With the best intentions, I had called Ms. Graham to share my news and get her blessing. But I had called just one month after what she believed would be her last performance, at a time when she was "haunted" and "wanted to die;" at a time when she was drinking herself into oblivion; when she was living with the pain of closing down her company and facing the terrifying fact that, after almost fifty years as a giant on stage, she would likely never perform again; during a period of profound self-destruction that would lead her to a long stay in the hospital, where she lapsed into a coma.

Determined, tough and strong-willed as always, Ms. Graham did return to her studio, to her *Plain of Prayer.* Her Dance Gods had not yet let her go. Almost three whole years would pass, but in 1973, at the age of seventy-nine, she was back with her company creating a new work. There would be ten more.

4

DIGGING IN

September 1970 – October 1975

Learning to be a Panther

The climb began. The upcoming two-month tour to Russia, then Paris and London, was set to begin in two weeks. Mr. Ailey (he liked to be called Alvin) cast me in three pieces and told me to learn as much of the repertoire as possible on my own. With the schedule jam-packed with performances, there would be little time to rehearse on the road. So I stayed every night after rehearsals, loading clunky reel-to-reel tapes onto a massive playback machine to learn several dances, including one section of Alvin's *Blues Suite*, which featured a muscle-flexing, hard-driving male quintet called "Mean Ol' Frisco."

Rehearsing it with four seasoned dancers, including dance wizard Miguel Godreau, I found I couldn't keep up. By the end of every long diagonal phrase, my fellow dancers were across the floor, ten feet ahead of me, and I was wondering, "How did you guys cover all that space with so few steps?"

I had learned precisely the physical shapes the body had to make, but was apparently not covering, or "eating up," space with the urgency that the piece demanded. Miguel gave me a quick lesson in shifting my weight. Then Alvin got me laughing, telling me to stop trying to be a Greek hero (my Graham training), and to bend my knees and "get down" closer to the earth. Following their advice, I felt more natural doing the movement. In the next run-through, I was fine.

In Alvin Ailey's choreography, the shapes the body makes are a means to an end. And that end is big, bold movement that projects the daring and urgency that are the hallmark of his style. It's trendy at times in dance, and sometimes appropriate, for performers to project cynicism and ultra cool attitudes. Ailey's dancers, however, always project a love for what they do. I realized that, if I didn't project the required desire and love in my dancing, I would be mowed down, and not just by the men. The women in Ailey's company were fierce, and dancers like Judith Jamison, Consuelo Atlas, Michelle Murray, Sylvia Waters, Mari Kajiwara and Linda Kent could make us guys look like puff pastry.

Alvin said he didn't want us to dance politely. He wanted us to be like panthers. So I watched, listened and tried to learn quickly how to paw the ground and take the long, urgent strides required.

Draft Fears Emerge Once More

With my Graham work visa no longer valid, Ailey Company manager Ivy Clarke asked me for my passport. She was required to send it to the State Department in Washington, D.C. for approval. Our company's upcoming tour behind the Iron Curtain, to Russia, the heartland of the dreaded Communist Soviet Union, was the first of its kind. And it was taking place during the increasingly aggressive Vietnam War, which was to some degree a proxy war fought between the U.S. and the Communist East. According to Ivy, we were going to be closely monitored. Watching my passport disappear into Ivy's purse, I became nervous. I was going to be very visible.

Adding to my general anxiety was the infamous draft lottery. The government had devised a scheme that involved writing down numbers from 1 to 366 on slips of paper, each number standing for a day of the year, taking into account a possible leap year. Each number was put into a blue plastic capsule and then the capsules were placed in a glass container. The capsules were pulled out one at a time. If number thirty-three was drawn first, and your date of birth was February 2 (the thirty-third day of the year), you would be in the first group to be called to serve with the U.S. army. Capsules were drawn until the required number of men was attained. In 1969, in the first year that the draft lottery was put into place, over 283,000 young men, aged eighteen to twenty-six, had been inducted.

As I was twenty-four years old, there was a possibility that I would qualify for the draft. My eligibility depended on what list government agents were consulting to call up men. Were they consulting lists of those young men who held U.S. birth certificates, or Social Security Cards? Obtaining my card, which I had seen as a blessing, might now lead to disaster. And to help me lose just a little more sleep, my passport was now in government hands.

It wasn't possible for me to get a new work visa. The long-established Graham Company had hired foreign dancers for many years, and had obtained work visas for them by making the case to the government that no U.S. citizens could perform the job. The much younger Ailey Company hadn't yet acquired the status necessary to obtain work visas for the few foreign artists it had employed. There would not have been time anyways to obtain a new one for me. I told Ivy that, if caught without the proper papers, I would claim responsibility and tell the officials that the company didn't know a thing about my status. She didn't seem concerned, saying everything would be all right. I wasn't so sure.

In the back of my mind over the next ten days was the thought that government officials would see my passport as a flashing red light. My career with the Ailey Company would be finished before it had even started. My nerves were not good.

The day before our departure for Russia, somehow, my passport came back stamped and approved. The Dance Gods had smiled at me once more.

Our Pre-Tour Free Concert

No Business Like Shoe Business

In September 1968, I had sat in the packed theatre at the Fashion Institute of Technology, watching the Ailey dancers as they performed a free concert before leaving on a tour. In September 1970, I was about to look in the opposite direction, this time out from that same stage into a full house, two days before the company left for another overseas tour. This date was three years less a month after I had graduated with a B.A. in English Literature from the University of Toronto. My insides were jumping with so much joy, I felt that instead of making an entrance moving straight ahead onto the stage, I might just take off vertically and fly.

On that night and for the next two months, I would be performing in three sections of *Revelations*, as a member of the male quintet from *Blues Suite*, and in the show opener, *Toccata*.

Just before our 8:00 p.m. curtain time, my body was vibrating so noticeably that I wasn't sure how I was going to dance with the physical prowess required. I knew my fellow dancers would all turn their energy levels up a few notches once they got in front of the audience. I had to rise to their level.

As much as you have rehearsed and performed a piece, there is always an element of the unknown. Dancers live on a tightrope on which they've been trained to balance. But there is always danger.

Standing in the wings, I waited along with eleven other dancers for the breeze that would blow in after the curtain rose. It came, and the music began. I let two up-tempo phrases of eight pass, the time I had before entering. I knew that, in spite of fears, the music would guide me. As a dancer, you have no choice. The rhythm grabs you, your muscle memory kicks in and, caught up in the shared energy of fellow dancers, you go.

As pumped up as I had ever been, I flew onstage for the opening group section. Duets and trios followed, all done in typical Talley Beatty style at close to the speed of light. My body stopped shaking. I was into it.

We were wearing jazz shoes performing in *Toccata*. A barefoot modern dancer, I had never worn shoes onstage before. Halfway through the piece, the choreography required me to step back on my left leg with my torso leaning forward and pull back with my right heel along the floor. Overwhelmed by the energy of the live performance, I did something I had never done in rehearsal. In spite of all the preparation, I fell off my tightrope. As I pulled my heel back, dragging it along the floor, I put so much pressure down into the floor that I pulled my shoe halfway off my foot. The unknown had crept in for a visit.

I instinctively curled my toes under so I could grip the shoe better and keep it on, but that action locked my ankle and made it impossible to dance the steps properly. I executed my next move, a turn on my right foot and almost fell over. Then I had to swing my right leg up high, but couldn't because I knew the shoe would fly off.

Deciding to take my chances, I kicked the shoe off and watched it somersault into the wings. Dancing with a shoe on one foot that gripped the floor and only a sock on the other that made me slip and slide, I was one person doing two dances.

When the piece ended and the company took its bows, I was too embarrassed to look out at the cheering audience. I performed *Revelations* with accuracy, but disappointment in myself kept me from feeling its joy.

I left the stage devastated. I knew that both Ramon Segarra and Alvin Ailey must have watched with disbelief, putting a big X beside my name. Would they fire me immediately, or wait until the tour was over?

The next morning after class, Misters Ailey and Segarra gave performance notes to their company of sixteen dancers, fifteen of whom had danced with ferocious commitment, and one of whom, a loser, had lost his shoe in his first-ever company appearance.

Looking down at the floor, waiting for the axe to fall, I heard Mr. Segarra praise the company. Then he said, "I want to congratulate Kenny for his performance. He only had ten days to learn the dances and he performed beautifully." I looked up. Alvin nodded in agreement. The dancers applauded.

You never know.

Recollections of Our Tour to Russia

Our tour of the Soviet Union included scheduled performances in six cities, from the most illustrious—Moscow, Leningrad and Kiev—to the lesser known. (It took us a while to learn to pronounce Voroshilovgrad, Donetsk and Zaporozhe.) We heard that Donetsk had not been visited by outsiders, even by people living in other regions of the Soviet Union, for fifteen years, but none of us could find out why. Following the Russian tour, we had also been booked for a week at the Sadler's Wells Theatre in London and at the Théâtre des Champs Elysées in Paris for an international dance competition.

A week before our departure, representatives from the Soviet government visited rehearsals to check out the suitability of our repertoire. They okayed most pieces, but wouldn't allow a solo created by Geoffrey Holder, *Monument for a Dead Soldier*, because a prop used in the piece was a military jacket. We had to be careful not to send any wrong signals.

On the bus to the airport, Diana Ross belted out "Ain't No Mountain High Enough" from dancer Miguel Godreau's boom box. She had just left the Supremes and gone solo. Her new album would become the background music for the tour.

In 1963, the company had consisted of six dancers who toured the U.S. in a station wagon, props and costumes included. Now, along with Alvin and Ivy, we were a group of sixteen dancers and eight technicians—plus four thousand pounds of sets, costumes and lighting equipment.

Our First Look at Moscow

We flew into Moscow and, upon landing, were subjected to a prolonged luggage search by stern-faced customs officials. They confiscated my soy protein powder, and it was only through intense pleading, aided by an interpreter, that they let me keep my bottles of vitamins and jars of peanut butter.

Buses took us to the Hotel Rossiya in the centre of Moscow. We were to spend two days there before flying, at 6:30 a.m., to little-known Zaporozhe, our first performance stop.

The hotel was a massive, twenty-one-storey rectangular complex built for tourists and visiting government officials. With its 3,200 rooms, movie theatre and 2,500-seat concert hall, it was, at the time, the largest hotel in the world. The grand lobby was surrounded by glittering gift shops; all items, such as luxury fur coats and premium brands of vodka, had to be purchased with "hard currency" and were thus unavailable to most Russian citizens. I expected the rooms to be palatial, but they were smaller and plainer than the U.S. highway motel rooms I had stayed in; they had open shelves and only a few hooks on which to hang clothes. When I came back to my room after a rehearsal on the day after arriving, I saw that it had been searched, and whoever had done the searching had not been subtle. My belongings, which I had stacked relatively neatly on shelves, were all jumbled. Cassette tapes, removed from their cases, were lying on the floor. A quick tally revealed that nothing had been taken.

The Ailey Company in Russia.
Clive Thompson, Renee Rose, Dudley Williams, Consuelo Atlas, Miguel Godreau, Michelle Murray (peeking) Sarah Yarborough, Sylvia Waters, Hector Mercado, Linda Kent, myself, Kelvin Rotardier, Alfonso Figuero, Mari Kajiwara. Absent: Judith Jamison, Leland Schwantes.
Author's personal collection

The hotel was situated in a spectacular location: right in Red Square, the heart of Moscow. Just outside our windows were the red-brick walls of the Kremlin with its towers, palaces and churches, and the Russian Orthodox St. Basil's Cathedral. Soldiers in brown coats paraded back and forth.

Before arriving, I had expected only blandness and monotony. The unexpected dazzle of Russia's multi-domed cathedrals took me by surprise. Most of them no longer hosted services, as Communists considered religion to be, in the words of Karl Marx, "the opiate of the masses." Of all these architectural wonders, St. Basil's was the star: bright, extroverted and dazzling. Its red-brick towers were crowned by a fanciful assortment of domes with a wild mix of patterns and colours: blue and white verticals, a honeycomb of deep green and yellow, red and beige twisting spirals, horizontal lines of red and white.

Walking the streets after rehearsals with Mari and Hector, I saw dozens of women sweeping the pavement with brooms made of bundled twigs. In their plain, ankle-length skirts and white aprons they looked as if they had stepped out of a Hans Christian Andersen fairy-tale. The brooms worked; the streets were immaculate. There were no Times-Square-style billboards, neon signs or product advertising anywhere. There were, however, posters filled with neo-constructivist type and graphics depicting muscular men and kerchief-wrapped women with sharp cheekbones, fists raised defiantly into the air. Their style appeared to me to be the Russian version of our Pop Art.

As we explored, less intimidating real-life local residents showed us their curiosity. Western tourists were a rarity, especially people of colour. Three drunk men approached us. One of them wanted to run off with Mari. Another told us he had slept with every woman in Russia. Fifty people surrounded us in a department store. A young man told us how upset he was that Jimi Hendrix had died. He loved Led Zeppelin, Simon and Garfunkel, Jefferson Airplane and Chicago. A woman gave us candies. People begged us for our blue jeans.

The Real Chainsaw Massacre

As the newest company member, I had not been able to have my choice of roommate for the tour. All the longer-standing company members had already hooked up. There was only one person available to room with me from the entire cast and crew—our wardrobe designer, Lester. He was a nice guy, so I had no concerns.

The first night on tour, however, after turning out the lights, I realized why he had been unpopular. Loud snoring does not begin to describe the sound that came from Lester's bed. I felt like I was lying in the middle of a lumberyard, saws spinning, wood chips flying.

Stuffing Kleenex in my ears and hiding under the covers didn't help. Nothing could stop what was now my own *Texas Chainsaw Massacre*. I grabbed my blanket and pillow, went to the bathroom and made my bed in the bathtub. In the morning, Lester couldn't understand why I was in the tub, because of course he had never snored in his entire life.

The next day, knowing I would hurt Lester's feelings, but having no choice, I asked two of the other dancers, Hector and Alfonso Figuero, about the possibility of sharing their room for the rest of the tour. Lester may have felt hurt, but he ended up being the only one, except Alvin, to get a room to himself.

Things We Do in Bed

Zaporozhe was the first performance stop of our tour. It is an industrial city in southeastern Ukraine. Situated on the banks of the Dnieper River, the centre of the city is an island connected to the mainland by two concrete bridges. On the road from our hotel to the theatre, we passed by a massive hydroelectric dam; a statue of Lenin hovered over it, so authoritative in expression that he seemed to be giving the water permission to flow.

We could have used his powers on opening night, because despite being in a city renowned for its electrical generating capacity, during Act Two, the power failed and the sound and lighting equipment shut down. The audience was confused, we dancers were devastated and Alvin was distraught. Frequent breakdowns plagued our entire first week of performances. As well, theatres and studios were cold, and the food was awful. Several dancers, including Miguel and Hector, got injuries; everyone was sniffling and coughing. We believed our tour was doomed. In her autobiography, *Dancing Spirit*, Judith Jamison writes: "It was what the blues were about. You think we didn't know how to dance *Blues Suite* after all the things we went through? It was as if we were being treated like a bunch of cattle."[38]

Most upsetting was the fact that the Soviet audience did not seem comfortable with the company's presentation. After all, the tradition of ballet was firmly embedded in Russian culture; many of the great dances, such as *The Nutcracker* and *Swan Lake,* originated there. Ballet was taught in every Russian town and city, so audiences had become accustomed to the bravura performances of classical ballet companies, with their live orchestras, decorative costumes and abundant scenery. We were told we startled them with our sparse set designs, consisting of only a few chairs and ladders, our simple costumes and, especially, with the naturalness and spontaneity of our dancing.

Mari Kajiwara and Alfonso Figuero with
employees in a Donetsk "factory."
Photograph: Kenny Pearl

However, during our second stop in another industrial town, Donetsk, the sun started to shine. We arrived on a day off and went to an afternoon performance of the local circus, which featured daredevil jugglers, clowns and acrobats who thrilled us. We met the cast following the show. After the musicians told us how much they loved American jazz, Alvin invited them to the theatre where we would be performing, to listen to his jazz recordings.

Later, as we walked the streets, workers invited us into their "factories": barren rooms, furnished only with essentials such as sewing machines that looked as though they belonged to an earlier century. The scowling face of

Lenin, with his pointed beard, looked down at us from a photograph placed high on every wall; but he did not dampen our enthusiasm as we shook hands and grinned wordlessly at our hosts.

Then, following our opening night show, a clown from the circus came backstage with a bottle of champagne. Local classical ballet dancers started visiting our company classes and rehearsals. Their warmth and enthusiasm began to make us feel that we *were* in the right place for the best of reasons. (One ballerina, after watching a steamy company duet, said something like, "These are things we do in bed.")

By the time we got to Kiev, our performances were sold out and, halfway through the tour, in Voroshilovgrad, the cultural Iron Curtain finally fell. At the end of shows, audiences were chanting "Alvin Ailey! Alvin Ailey!" Out on the streets, people shouted "vodka!" at us, assuming it was the one Russian word we would all understand. We were told it was their way of saying thank you.

Siberia?

There were, however, strict limits as to how much friendly contact we were allowed to have with the people.

In Zaporozhe, for example, a Russian man named Ivan helped Lester with our costume maintenance. (There was a lot of cleaning and ironing to do, as we were performing up to six dances a night, some with all sixteen of us.) Midweek, Ivan invited Lester to his family's home for dinner. The next day, Ivan was not at the theatre. He had been fired.

Then a pretty, red-haired Russian woman, who had been watching our rehearsals every day, got hooked on Hector. She followed him wherever we went and had begun to ride our bus as we travelled to the theatre. One day, a soldier in a long brown coat, rifle slung over his shoulder, stopped us as we were pulling away from the hotel. He arrested her, led her off the bus and we never saw her again. We were all stunned and worried she would be sent off to the Gulag in Siberia.

Despite these events, I longed for contact with locals. In Kiev, I met a red-faced, paunchy middle-aged man named Boris outside the theatre. He had seen a performance and asked if I wanted a walking tour. He spoke good English, which he had learned at the local university. I was excited to get a private tour of the city, a beautiful cultural centre whose population was close to 2,000,000. I knew by then that the Soviet military police would not favour my being in such close unsupervised contact with a local citizen; curious to have a personal guide, I slipped out of our hotel early one morning.

Boris led me on a tour of the hilly, chestnut-tree-lined streets of Kiev. As we passed through grand public squares, I took pictures as he proudly pointed out the nineteenth-century museum and opera house and the blue National Theatre. Here, as elsewhere, the multi-domed cathedrals fascinated me, especially the gold and blue ones of St. Michael's and St. Andrew's.

What I loved most about Kiev was the water. Like Zaporozhe, the city was built on the Dnieper River. Here, streams branched off the river; ponds and little lakes appeared everywhere, softening and humanizing the urban landscape. I felt as if I could hang out there for a while.

My tour with Boris went undetected. I gave him my blue jeans.

Learning Quickly

In Kiev, on opening night, one of our male dancers injured his ankle and was out of action. At that point, I was performing in only one section of *Blues Suite*. As I was leaving the theatre, rehearsal director Ramon Segarra called me aside: "Alvin wants you to perform all of *Blues Suite* tomorrow night. There's no time for extra rehearsals at the theatre, so ask someone to teach you at the hotel."

Judith and Mari, though exhausted, graciously put in the hours rehearsing the entire piece with me late into the night in our hotel lobby, on a scruffy carpet beside the front desk. With each of our moves and between gulps of vodka, the concierge broke into applause, which cheered us up.

Alvin had choreographed *Blues Suite* in 1958, and many critics consider it to be his first masterwork. The dance is set in the jook joints and on the lamp-lit streets and deserted railroad tracks of a southern town—the kind of place where Alvin had grown up—on a sultry summer night. It suggests the sadness, humanity and humour of the blues, which Alvin had told the company were, to him, "hymns to the secular regions of the soul."

Particularly challenging for me was the second-last section called "Sham," which conveys the high spirits of the characters before the sun rises and the sadness of their no-hope-for-the-future reality sets in. The "Sham" was challenging because I had to learn on my own quick sequences of steps that were meant to be done in a large group. I practised those steps a hundred times. During a full-company run-through two hours before the show, however, I still messed up. I felt terrified.

There is no postponing the rising of the curtain. If the ticket to a show says it will begin at 8:00 p.m., the curtain will go up by 8:10. The audience members aren't worrying that someone on stage might be frightened or unprepared: they simply expect a great show. As we waited for the curtain to rise, I saw all my colleagues who were not in the piece standing in the wings, fingers crossed, watching me make my debut.

I made it through without a glitch. The new guy made good. As we took our bows, the big smiles of my fellow performers and the applause from the wings made me feel great. As more of the men were sidelined with injuries, I learned other dances, including Talley Beatty's *Congo Tango Palace*, in airports and even in the tiny space outside the restroom of an airplane. Halfway through the tour, Alvin asked me to perform in "Sinner Man" from *Revelations*. I felt like I was in heaven.

Sweet Inspiration

In the course of this intimate tour, I got to know my fellow dancers quickly. Here are some short takes of a few of the many who moved me.

Judith Jamison, Alvin's muse, felt every moment deeply, and was equally comfortable with high drama and comedy. She left absolutely everything on the stage in every performance. The joy she communicated in "Wadin' in the Water," a section of *Revelations*, lifted people out of their seats. Her personal qualities were as memorable as her spectacular dancing. Even after becoming a famous modern-dance superstar, unprecedented at the time, she remained humble and generous. I never partnered her on stage, but in a lecture-demonstration at a university, Alvin had us doing a duet. I thought she might be dismissive of me, but she surprised me in rehearsal by being helpful and open. Lifting and supporting her as we performed later, I felt the determination and focus in her every move.

Dudley Williams' dancing made me appreciate the value of simplicity and economy in movement: he danced sequences of steps with elegance and power, and never added flourishes or unnecessary gestures. The lines and angles his body made were always balanced and pleasing to look at. Moving with fluidity and a clear variety of dynamics, he drew the eyes of every audience member to him. He danced with soul in pieces like "I Wanna Be Ready" and could express humour as well as any dancer I had ever seen, playing such roles as a downtrodden loser in the "Sham" section of *Blues Suite*.

John Parks had a personal technique, meaning he had his own way of doing things. And he got them done. He was statuesque, with a wingspan like basketball star Michael Jordan's. With his shaved head, unusual at a time when most African Americans wore an Afro, no one was more charismatic, physical and exciting. He could power himself into movement with great velocity, and there was no risk that he didn't love taking.

Linda Kent's pretty, blonde looks could give the impression that she was a gentle, lyrical dancer. But she danced as if she were on fire. Few could tear into a movement phrase as she did. When we were all exhausted in rehearsal in the middle of the tour, it was always Linda who picked up my energy because she never did anything less than full out.

Sylvia Waters brought dignity and vulnerability to her work. Offstage she was no-nonsense, and kept me in line when I veered. Whenever I went into a jag of complaining about how tired and sore I was, it was always Sylvia who told me to "chill out and be grateful."

Becoming Macroneurotic

No matter the city in which we were performing, we didn't get back to our hotel until after 11 p.m. In spite of this, the hotel's kitchen staff workers were ordered to prepare our dinners and serve them at a specific time—three hours before our return! Furthermore, the strict Soviet authorities did not allow us to go out to eat at restaurants. So, every night, the food that was left for us was cold, and either soggy or dried out. It was only by means of great exertion that we could saw through the stiff substance on our plates that was supposed to be edible meat. The energy spent chewing it seemed about equal to what we regularly expended performing a stamina-challenging Ailey dance. Our usual dessert, at one time likely identifiable as ice cream, had also been left out with the main course; by the time we sat down to eat, it was a warm puddle. Though served fresh, our breakfasts were no culinary treat. Our rubbery fried eggs folded in half when we cut into them.

I decided to give up eating meat. I had been reading books on nutrition since arriving in New York. I had been juicing vegetables and, because I had enjoyed the food at the Paradox so much, ate a mostly macrobiotic diet. I had also read about the factory farming of animals and the unnatural corn and antibiotic-laced diets they were being forced to eat. In 1969, there had been a widely reported story about how, because of the excessive dumping of industrial waste, the Cuyahoga River, at Cleveland, Ohio had caught fire. Learning about how chemicals were infiltrating food and water, I had begun making the switch to organic foods.

On each floor of our hotels, there was a security desk, beside which stood a little fridge. I discovered that from it, the security guard sold hard-boiled eggs and very good yogurt. I also found nearby stores that sold dried fruit and nuts. These new items, along with kasha, soggy vegetables and melted ice cream, formed my new diet.

Filled with excitement about my new commitment to vegetarianism, I began to annoy as many fellow dancers as possible, letting them know how their lives would be vastly improved if they would only follow my path. But they were having too much fun to pay much attention to me, teasing me with lines like, "Enjoy your bird-food." So I quickly gave up on the preaching. But I became so obsessed with gathering my food every day that, when other dancers asked me what my diet was, I answered, "macroneurotic."

Forbidden Art

Everywhere, the combination of cultural wealth and ordinary poverty of the Soviet Union took me by surprise. Following our performances in Kiev, on a day off at our next stop, Leningrad, I went to the Hermitage. Located on a canal and surrounded by courtyards and gardens, its six historic buildings, including two palaces, were said to house the largest collection of paintings in the world. Masters such as Matisse and Picasso were featured in the collection. The works of art were barely visible, however, because the rooms were lit by only a couple of forty-watt light bulbs.

Clive Thompson at the Hermitage Museum,
with a painting by Henri Matisse.
Photograph: Kenny Pearl

They Like Us, They Really Like Us

Our week-long run in Leningrad was sold out before we arrived. On opening
night, so many students were clamouring for tickets that the box-office people
finally let them in. They filled every available space, breaking the fire regulations as they packed the aisles. After *Revelations* and our bows, no one would
leave. Alvin went down into the orchestra pit and signed programs, bits of
paper, even people's arms.

On our final stop in Moscow, which we called the Big Cabbage, we got a
twenty-three minute standing ovation at the end of our performance. Having
finished our complete repertoire of bows and encores, we finally ran to the
front of the stage and spent another twenty minutes shaking all the eager
hands that extended towards us.

Dancers Who Sparkle; Dancers Who Fizzle

In Moscow the company was invited to visit the palatial school of the Bolshoi Ballet, one of the world's most renowned ballet companies, and we had the opportunity to observe a number of classes. The first was for young boys, around ten years old. They sparkled. They all danced with joy and without inhibition, not seeming to care if their moves were perfectly executed. They also appeared to love their teacher, who demanded a lot as he praised and encouraged them. All were captivating because they were so involved and natural.

Then we watched a seniors class made up of eighteen-year-old women. These dancers were physically talented, capable of doing all the jumps, turns and high leg extensions with precision and strength. They were also physically beautiful, hand-picked as small children to be future Bolshoi company dancers.

But the qualities of the boys that had captivated us were absent. As these female dancers moved, their faces were stone, their eyes dull, and we grew weary watching them. They appeared to derive no enjoyment from the incredible feats they could perform. Many looked at themselves in the mirror with apparent discontent, probably thinking they were not good enough or thin enough or as talented as the dancer who stood beside them. I was sure that on stage many would rise above their sorrowful state and be exuberant and poetic, but I wondered how they felt about themselves day to day. How did they get through the incredibly demanding hours without, apparently, loving what they were doing?

I had often wished I had started dancing when I was a child, but after watching those classes, I wasn't sure. I didn't have the technique of those girls, but what I did have was some of the exuberance of the boys.

Family

The November day we left Russia, the first thick snows of winter fell. It was during our tour that my life-long interest in indigenous arts and crafts began, and I left the country with my suitcase packed with gifts of Russian matryoshka[39] dolls and black cloisonné boxes covered with colourful national heroes and nature scenes.

As we sat on the plane getting ready for takeoff, I knew that we would be arriving in Paris for the Paris International Dance Competition as a tight, supportive group.

1971 — Broadway and Beyond

Shortly after returning from overseas, on January 18, 1971, the Ailey Company performed at Broadway's ANTA Theatre (American National Theatre and Academy) with a two-week run. Fresh from the successes of Russia and Europe, which included our Gold Star Awards in Paris for Best Company and Best Choreographer, we were glowing, moving with a sense of well-earned pride. There was a combination of gratefulness and swagger in our bows as the curtain came down opening night to a wild ovation. Anna Kisselgoff, dance critic for *The New York Times*, wrote: "Something of the excitement of a bullfight prevails lately at the ANTA Theatre . . . a sold-out house shouts its encouragement to the dancers and requires an encore."[40] Don McDonagh, another *Times* writer, wondered "whether it matters what the company is doing as long as it promises not to stop."[41]

During the first week of our run, the company was also asked to perform on NBC's *Today Show*. That ten-minute television appearance benefited the company beyond all expectations: every ticket to the remaining shows sold.

The night before our television appearance, Alvin had asked me to dance "Sinner Man." I felt great afterwards, when former classmates from university, who just happened to be watching the show and would likely never see me on stage, called to give congratulations. My parents had sincerely wished me luck before the show, but didn't call afterwards. I was sure they felt that their congratulations would create the false impression that they approved of my chosen career. When I called them a few days later, they did surprise me by saying, "We're curious. We're coming to New York to see you dance next year."

Four days after closing, we left on an eight-week U.S. tour. Then, in the spring, there was a three-week season at New York's renowned City Center, a 2,700-seat theatre on West 55th Street, just east of Broadway, followed by another cross-country national tour. In September, the company performed in Leonard Bernstein's *Mass* in Philadelphia and in Washington, D.C. Following that, in December 1971, we were booked for three more weeks at City Center.

Before arriving in New York, I had privately tempted the fates, daring to imagine performing in a great company, touring to exotic places and performing in Broadway theatres. On New Year's Eve, 1971, when I finally had time to catch my breath, I stared at myself in the mirror that hung over the kitchen sink beside my bathtub and asked, "What just happened?" All my dreams, as over-the-top as they had seemed, had turned out to be tame when put beside the reality of that first year with the Ailey Company. But in spite of all the successes, the anxiety I had always felt when my parents denied my creativity remained. I had a deeply rooted sense that if my dance life was too good to be true, if my creative spirit was being nurtured and allowed to flourish, then something or someone would swoop down, catch me by surprise, and make all my good fortune come to a screeching halt.

The Leonard Bernstein Mass

Meeting Mr. Bernstein

The Kennedy Center is a theatre complex on the banks of the Potomac River in Washington, D.C., built as a memorial to the assassinated President John F. Kennedy. Leonard Bernstein had been commissioned to write the music for *Mass*, an opera that had been scheduled to open the Center in 1971. Mr. Bernstein was most renowned for composing the music for *West Side Story*, the musical that eight years earlier had inspired me to become a dancer. He was also known as the composer of other musicals, such as *Candide* and *On the Town*, and as an orchestra conductor who often appeared on TV, wielding his baton as if he were channelling thunder and lightning.

As conceived by Mr. Bernstein, *Mass* was to be "A Theater Piece for Singers, Players and Dancers," and a 1970's reinvention of a formal religious ceremony. Stephen Schwartz, of *Godspell* fame (and since, *Wicked*), was hired to write the libretto to be set to Mr. Bernstein's music. Gordon Davidson, Artistic Director of the Mark Taper Theater in Los Angeles, was chosen to direct. Word on the dance grapevine was that Jerome Robbins, Broadway and film dance legend, and often Mr. Bernstein's collaborator, had turned down the offer to choreograph. So Alvin Ailey was honoured with an invitation to create the dances on his company members. The cast of dancers, actors, singers and musicians, numbering nearly 200, included many of the most talented young performers in America's musical theatre scene, as well as the Norman Scribner Choir and a full orchestra.

The structure of the opera followed the form of a Catholic mass. It used rock, blues and folk music to tell the story of a young guitarist who becomes a priest, but turns his back on his unappreciative congregation after they express doubts about the necessity of God in their lives and the role of the mass itself. Much later, I learned that Mr. Bernstein had written *Mass* as an implicit attack on President Richard Nixon and the war in Vietnam (perhaps one reason why the President never showed up to see it).

We began rehearsals in a large ballroom in the Astoria Hotel, at 72nd Street and Broadway. Most of the dancers were chosen to play pedestrians, as part of a chorus. Alvin chose seven of us, including Judith Jamison, Sylvia Waters, Dudley Williams, Estelle Spurlock, Ramon Segarra, Lee Harper and me, to play acolytes. At first, we acolytes were disappointed with our roles, as we thought that most of the dance movement would be performed by the chorus dancers. They would be freewheeling in street clothes, while we would be wearing bulky layers of robes. As it turned out, we priests got to rock, dancing themes of celebration and condemnation centre stage.

The first day we arrived at rehearsal, Mr. Bernstein was sitting at a piano, playing for a handsome, fair-haired man, actor-singer Alan Titus, the guitar-playing priest who was the show's protagonist.

Sixteen of us sat a few yards away, watching and listening. The melody flowed and Mr. Titus sang softly and with power: "Sing like you'd like to sing. God loves all simple things. For God is the simplest of all." We applauded as Mr. Bernstein got up and turned towards us. Our stage manager announced proudly, "Mr. Bernstein, this is the Ailey Company." I was thrilled about meeting him. He was a fellow Jew and, other than Robert Cohan and Bertram Ross, I did not know other Jewish men working in the arts.

As he walked towards us, we stood up to greet him. He was smaller than I had imagined, but just as suave, with a head of wavy gray hair that made him look like a biblical patriarch. He reached the outer edge of our circle of bodies and then, without stopping, he started walking through us, almost pushing everyone aside.

Confused, we all turned to see where he was going. He marched straight to the back of our group where our star, Judith Jamison, was standing, put out his hand and said, "Hi Judith, I'm Lennie."

I went on loving his music and his hair, but for me, he had fallen off his pedestal.

Process

Mr. Bernstein (he liked to be called Lennie) and Steven Schwartz composed music and wrote lyrics as we rehearsed. We thus had the opportunity to hear melodies and lyrics being developed and altered. Sometimes the two creators made slight changes, adjusting only a few notes or words. Other times they tossed out everything they had done. We, too, participated in the process, once Lennie passed his music to Alvin, who set the movement.

Director Gordon Davidson then intelligently and patiently brought the music, lyrics, and staged and choreographed movement together, moving the drama forward and giving it coherence.

Revelations and West Side Story

Alvin had just finished an upbeat and energetic section of choreography for the priests, set to the "Gloria" portion of the *Mass*, a celebratory passage praising God—"*Gloria in excelsis Deo*; Glory to God in the highest." It was filled with some of his trademark moves, including torso rotations and reaching arms. Alvin called Lennie over to take a look at the completed piece.

After dancing, we got our water bottles. The two men sat down to talk. Lennie said to Alvin, "What I just saw looks a lot like *Revelations*."

Choreographers do not enjoy being told that their new creations look like old creations. Even though there was a physicality in the piece that referenced the opening of *Revelations*, it was in fact a very different dance.

Alvin glowered and met Lennie's critique with a beat of silence. He was usually a man of few words, but definitely not a man of silence, so I wondered if a little skirmish was about to begin.

Then Alvin's eyes started to twinkle and his face broke out into a big smile. He began singing Bernstein's "America" from *West Side Story*—"Life can be bright in America." I gagged on my water. While "America" and "Gloria" were two different pieces of music, they seemed to share the same signature rhythms.

Was this encounter going to get ugly?

They had called each other out and, acknowledging that, slapped each other on the back, as if all that had just happened had been good-natured in spirit. They began talking excitedly and walked away.

The Opening Night Reception in Washington, D.C.

We played in Philadelphia for a week before opening at the Kennedy Center. Following the opening night performance, there was an epic reception. We dancers walked down a receiving line of Kennedy family members, all wearing gowns and tuxedos. The Kennedy charisma was undeniable, in the sparkling eyes of Senator Ted Kennedy and in the sweet smile and delicate beauty of former First Lady Jacqueline Kennedy. At the food table I stood beside Gregory Peck (even more handsome in person than he was on film), who generously told the lead singer, Allen Titus, how much he had enjoyed his performance.

Controversy

During our performances of *Mass* in Philadelphia and Washington, I hadn't been aware of any public controversy. I didn't read the reviews, but the audiences seemed consistently positive. The climate changed, however, during our August shows in New York, at the Metropolitan Opera House in Lincoln Center. On the opening night of a four-week run, as we priests, dressed in bright pink robes, rolled on the floor as if possessed, a Catholic nun in the audience stood up and shouted, "This is sacrilege!"

I thought that possibly someone involved with the production had placed her there, because her words stirred up some interesting public debate that likely encouraged ticket sales.

In fact, many critics, mainly from the classical music world, thought the music was sacrilegious. They wrote that its mix of classical and popular styles—not unusual today—came across as too self-consciously hip, too obviously written by a resolute liberal after the assassination of a beloved president during an unpopular war. A review of the music, written after a 2010 revival of the piece at the Royal Festival Hall in London, reflects much of what the critics had to say back in 1971: "It remains a paradox that the composer of a work of genius like *West Side Story* should have plummeted so low while aiming so ambitiously high."[42]

There were also supporters: "On one level *Mass* is a brilliant piece of the-atrical entertainment—the original dramatic conception, the dazzling musical variety, and the sheer creative exuberance of it all literally leaves one's head spinning."[43]

Why I Loved *Mass*

I loved performing in *Mass*. I enjoyed its emotional score and the height-ened drama. I loved being a priest who at times calmly enacted rituals, and at other times lost control and tore up the stage. (For a year after the show, Alvin insisted on calling me "Father Pearl." Every time he said the name, he would break up laughing. In his piece, *Feast of Ashes*, based on the story, "The House of Bernardo Alba" by the Spanish writer, Frederico García Lorca, there is a priest who carries a massive cross. I was chosen to play the role—the one Jewish guy in the company! I loved it.) It felt special to be a part of a unique celebration in honour of a beloved president, and working on something new with Alvin was always inspiring. It was also a treat, in spite of the fact that he had singled out Judith for attention while ignoring the rest of the company during the first rehearsal, to work in a room with Mr. Bernstein. As dancers who worked non-stop and had limited chances to meet performers outside our enclosed, intimate world, it was also unique to have the chance to meet performing artists in so many other fields.

Two Sultry Singers and a Pink Priest

During rehearsals for *Mass* I got the word that one of the musical theatre per-formers was interested in me. Marion was beautiful, funny and riveting singing the one sultry song in the score: "If you ask me to love you on a bed of spice/ Now that might be nice/Once or twice./But don't look for sacraments of sacrifice./They're not worth the price." She was an African-American woman who had the most engaging smile. I was intrigued. By the closing-night recep-tion in Washington, we were finally a couple. We went out for only a short while, because show-biz people in Hollywood soon recognized her big talent and, before I knew it, she was gone.

When *Mass* opened at the Metropolitan Opera House two months after our Washington run, Linda had taken Marion's place in the cast. She, too, was African American and sultry when singing her solo. I never thought of myself as a priest in a pink robe to whom African-American women singing sultry songs would become attracted. But before the run was over, Linda and I were also a couple.

Smashed

My love life was progressing erratically, with exciting but short-lived relationships, as I celebrated my fourth anniversary of living at 69 East 4th Street. My apartment's orange-crate decor was still intact, but my art prints were no longer scotch-taped to the wall. They now had frames, do-it-yourself ones from Azuma. I had acquired my second sound system and a slowly expanding new record collection, a cassette recorder, Le Creuset pots and pans from Bloomingdale's, a vegetable juicer and a three-piece suit from Barneys. I had also collected photos, letters and theatre programs, items connected to special moments that told the story of my four years in New York. I had safely stored them in a woven straw box.

A modern dancer lucky enough to be in a great company, I was doing what was almost impossible: earning a salary on a full-year contract, which, after taxes, came to $204 a week, more than enough to cover all my costs and build some savings.

Returning to 4th Street on a hot August evening after a performance of *Mass* at Lincoln Center, I was feeling confident and happy. Alarm bells started going off the moment I entered the building. My nose instantly picked up the smell of rotting food, and then, walking down the hall, I saw that my front door, police lock and all, was open.

It looked like an Oklahoma tornado had blown around my three little rooms for a couple of hours. The stacks of orange crates had been smashed to pieces and were mixed with what appeared to be the fragments of my Japanese mugs and plates, glasses and lots of wall plaster. As I stepped inside, the debris crunched discouragingly under my feet. Above the kitchen bathtub was a hole in the wall large enough for a body to squeeze through. Someone from the next-door apartment had smashed through the adjoining wall! He or she had then carted off all my clothing, my juicer, and the pots and pans. The framed posters and the sofa were gone. Once again, I no longer had a sound system or collection of record albums. There was no parting gift left in the sink this time. I had an Indonesian puppet: its head was ripped off. A kitchen knife was stuck into its little batik-covered chest. Beside the front door were two intact orange crates loaded with books, ready for pickup. It seemed that reading material was low on the priority list of whomever was still leisurely cleaning me out.

The smell of rot came from my bedroom. The waterbed had been slashed, but it had a liner so the water hadn't flowed out. In the water, now sludge, was what had once been all the fridge food. Islands of eggshells bobbed around between what might have been rotting pieces of bread and carrots. But it was a huge water beetle enjoying a float on a corner of paper sticking out of the muck that made me freeze. The thief had found my box of precious letters and photos, four years of memorabilia, personal treasures connecting me to friendships, family and tours, and had dumped them into the water.

Most irreplaceable were almost all of my photos from the Ailey Company's tour of the Soviet Union and a funny letter from my dad. I immediately made a clothesline, clipping on to it all the photos and letters that looked like they had a chance of being saved. (Few survived.)

All I owned in July 1971, after four years of hard work and careful saving, were the clothes I was wearing, my suitcase with its contents and two boxes of books. Did I have insurance? No. No legitimate company had agreed to give me insurance for a rent-controlled, Lower East Side, orange-crate-filled firetrap, whose hallway was often inhabited by Bowery drunks.

I took a look out the door. The next-door neighbours had moved out before I had left town, and the building manager had put a small padlock on the front door. The idea, I thought, was that management was going to gradually clear out all the present tenants, renovate and then charge high rents.

The door to the vacated apartment was unlocked. Inside were a small table and two chairs. Scattered around were dozens of Budweiser cans and syringes.

Given that part of a wall had been smashed, the robbery must have been noisy; as well, my door was open and the apartment was in plain view. Why then hadn't the police been called? Where were my neighbours, the super and his wife? I believed she was honest, but what about him? What about all those cans of Bud in the next door apartment? My guess was, once he realized I was away, he had given some pals the all-clear in exchange for a cut of the prize.

I phoned a friend, a potter in Greenwich Village, and slept in her studio that night. In the morning I returned to ask questions. There was the super, the stick with a belly, leaning against the front door, Bud in hand, eyes staring at overflowing garbage. Naturally, he knew nothing. But the head resting on crossed hands watching the world go by wasn't there. I visited the building every morning for the next ten days, but my dragon-slayer, the guardian of the Bowery Hotel who had protected me with her frying pan, never appeared.

I knew that I had to leave the apartment "broom clean" before the city would return the deposit I had paid four years earlier. The worst part was that I had to clean out the waterbed by hand, as the rented pump kept getting clogged. What days of contrast: I started each morning at 7:00 a.m., scooping reeking sludge into a bucket; I finished at 10:30 p.m., taking a bow at the end of *Mass* on the stage of one of the most majestic theatres in Manhattan.

For the two weeks that it took me to clean out my apartment, I slept cross-town in my friend's pottery studio. Lying in bed after hectic days and nights, I focused my gaze along shelves filled with her creamy glazed pitchers and bowls, everything reassuringly intact, until I fell asleep.

One Monday evening, a few days after I had made the apartment broom clean, I was back in my old neighbourhood to catch a $2 double bill at the St. Marks cinema. Lining up to get my ticket, I saw her, my superintendent's wife, walking quickly down 2nd Avenue. I ran across the road, not to ask her about the robbery, but to say hello. I didn't even know her name, so I touched her on the shoulder. She turned around for an instant, looking terrified, and rushed away, but not before I had spotted a black eye and a dark purple bruise along her cheekbone.

My only thought was that her husband, a wimp she could have taken out easily with her frying pan, had beaten her. I felt with certainty that she had been assaulted because of the robbery. I imagined she had threatened to tell me or had resisted the robbery and had paid the price. I went to a police station to file a report; the police said they couldn't do anything because there were no witnesses and because she had not come to them.

A Meltdown

Two weeks after the robbery, I had a minor meltdown. It took place during one of those short periods of anxiety when you think you're in control but you're not, and you act with the greatest certainty, making choices that a week later you cannot believe you made.

I moved to Brooklyn, got two cats and began to steal. These choices were surprising because I had only rarely been to Brooklyn, was allergic to cats and did not consider stealing to be an appropriate pastime.

Following the break-in, I decided that I not only had to vacate my East Village apartment but all of Manhattan. I had been to Brooklyn to visit some of its major sites: the stunning Botanical Gardens, the grand Brooklyn Museum and the Brooklyn Academy of Music, where I had performed with the Graham Company. The good feelings I had about those places, which were close to Manhattan, but not too close, made me feel that I would be safe.

Park Slope, which was near the sites I had visited, is now an expensive and much sought-after Brooklyn address. Back in 1972, it was an up-and-coming part of New York, a place where you could still get a great deal on a large space. Louise, the owner of a five-storey brownstone building, led me through the fourth-floor apartment. While chewing vigorously on a huge wad off gum, she pointed out its many highlights. The apartment was bright, had hardwood floors and consisted of five good-sized rooms. And, finally, there was a toilet inside the apartment! The rent was $250.00, a lot more than I had been paying, but half of what I would have paid for a much smaller place in Manhattan. I immediately signed the lease.

Two days later, I sat on my new doorstep looking out on a quiet street, nodding hellos to moms pushing baby strollers and people walking designer dogs, and realized I had made a mistake. I had thought that I wanted peace and quiet, feeling I needed to be far away from the scene of the crime, but I didn't. I missed the Lower East Side with its never-ending action, work, restaurants I loved and, most of all, my friends.

Possibly because I felt isolated, I got two cats. I love cats, but when I turned twenty-one, I developed serious allergies to them. I got cats anyway, Lisa and Coconut. Companions. And, having just been robbed, I inexplicably began doing a little robbing myself. This was not planned shoplifting. I just reached out and grabbed, without thinking about what I was doing or why. I only stole from one store, the local health food store, owned by a couple that I liked a lot.

My thefts were small, not the hefty stash my old friend Elbows had manoeuvred into his baggy trench coat. One day I grabbed a bag of almonds; a few days later, a bottle of Vitamin C. I would chat with the husband or wife at the counter, then buy a few things and steal something else, then say goodbye, feeling utterly confused by my own behaviour.

After a month, as I was leaving with a bag of cashews in my pocket, the husband stopped me. "Before you go, you should leave those cashews on the counter."

I felt both horrified and strangely relieved. I apologized for a while and said, honestly, that I didn't have a clue why I had been stealing, that I liked him and his wife a lot. He wasn't impressed.

He then acted like the priest from *Les Miserables* who tells the authorities that the silver candlesticks that Jean Valjean has stolen are really a gift. He took me by the shoulders and said, "If you were starving, I would have given you something to eat. I could call the police right now, but I won't. We actually like you. Just don't do it again."

Then he one-upped the priest in *Les Miserables* and offered me a job. Anytime on weekends, when I wasn't rehearsing or on tour, he wanted me to be a chef in the veggie restaurant he was about to open. Without having any idea whether I could actually cook, he put me in charge of making the soup of the day.

I didn't know the value of what I had taken, but gave him what I could spare: about $200. I made many pots of soup of the day.

I have never forgotten the generosity of that man and his wife. I hope they are happy, with beautiful grandchildren and a summer house in the Hamptons.

A week after I had been caught stealing, I hired a couple of teenagers from the neighbourhood to help me paint my apartment. They painted well, but after they left, I noticed that many of my belongings were missing: some cash, a few records, a six-pack of beer, a sweatshirt. I was glad to see Lisa and Coconut were still around.

After tallying up the damage, I sat there sniffling beside my cats, and wondered at the logic of instant karma.

Alvin Ailey and His Company

1970 – 1975

Though my life outside of dance was unstable, my life onstage was flourishing. During the period in which I danced with the Ailey Company, its popularity and fame grew. It has now been so popular for so many years that people often think that from the moment it came into being, with its first New York performance on January 31, 1960 at the YM & YWHA in the Kaufmann Auditorium, it was a runaway sensation. The truth is that it struggled on the fringes of the artistic scene for more than five years, with the mainstream press paying little attention. The first mention of the company in the *New York Times* had only come in 1963, and it was concerning shows not at home, but in Rio de Janeiro.[44]

One day in late December 1971, Ivy Clarke showed me a glowing article about the company in the *New York Times*. She told me that in 1968, there had only been five articles in that paper about the company, and that this year there had already been twenty-five. Perhaps influenced by the Civil Rights Movement and then by the "Age of Aquarius" hippie movement, mainstream America had gradually embraced a predominantly African-American, but mixed-race, dance company.

During 1971, no other American troupe performed and toured more. In 1972, the *New York Times* reported that the Ailey Company's New York season opened at City Center "with what the management says is the biggest advance sale for any event, dance or nondance, in that theater's history."[45] As the Center's first resident dance group, the company gave two sets of performances every year, each three weeks in length. Then a two-week summer engagement at the State Theater in Lincoln Center was added. Performing for eight weeks a year in New York City, giving eight shows a week in theatres with over 2,500 seats, was a historic first for a modern dance company. All in all, we were giving around 150 full performances a year, at home and on tour.

Alvin told us that in the 1950s, he never imagined he would have a company of his own, let alone one that, by the 1960s, was already spending most of its time touring. And in the '60s, the thought that he would lead his company to become one of the world's greatest dance organizations was, perhaps, not even a sidebar in his imagination.[46]

Alvin believed that dance came from the people and he wanted to give it back to the people. So, no matter how popular the company became in the big cities, we continued to perform and to give master classes and lecture-demonstrations in small towns and on college campuses.

All of us dancers were fortunate to be with the company during this time when it was on a dramatic upswing. We weren't the New York Yankees, but because of all the exposure, we were often recognized on the street. Many times, strangers would say to me, "I know who you are," and then offer me whatever they were carrying, such as magazines and fruit. Once, a woman on a bus reached into her shopping bag and handed me a cantaloupe (I hoped that that was a good thing). On another occasion, while walking down the street, I heard someone singing lyrics from *Revelations*. I turned around to see a smiling man who shook my hand and said, "Thank you."

The landmark musical *Hair* had opened on Broadway in 1969. With its focus on youth, individual expression, sexual freedom and hedonism, it was an unlikely candidate for approval by mainstream America. But the unimaginable happened.

At the end of Act One, cast members of every colour stood and faced the audience as a closely-knit group, naked. Audiences gasped and applauded. Yet, years before *Hair*, Alvin Ailey had already presented the same mix of humanity to audiences; he had showcased people of all colours dancing together sensuously and harmoniously (not nude, but in some pretty skimpy outfits), celebrating their beauty as individuals and as a collective. And he had been doing it for a decade.

Alvin's Gifts

Alvin's role within his rising company evolved over time. During its early years, he choreographed, rehearsed dances, performed, chose fabric, sewed costumes, made bookings and did fundraising. By the time I joined, there was a small staff that handled a lot of this work, though Alvin was still involved in making every decision. At the age of thirty-three, he quit performing: he realized that he needed time to choreograph, nurture his dancers and attend to the business of running his organization, by now a true enterprise.

Alvin always knew how best to publicize his company. He knew which photos or images to use on posters and which to send to newspapers. His interviews with the media conveyed the energy, high spirits and uniqueness of the company. He always sounded so very "cool" and so completely in and of the moment.

And he was prolific. In 1971 alone, he choreographed an astonishing six pieces: four for the full company, a quartet called *Myth*, in which he chose me to perform and the solo *Cry*, for Judith Jamison. The latter, dedicated to "all black women everywhere—especially our mothers"[47]—is a fifteen-minute endurance test set in three sections. Judith, wearing a white leotard and skirt, and using a long piece of white fabric as a prop that changes from a scrub cloth to an elegant turban, took audiences on a journey through bitter sorrow and brutal hardship to ecstatic joy. It was her brilliant performance of *Cry* that made Judith a dance superstar.

We often heard that living with the pressure to create another *Revelations* drove Alvin nuts. But as an artist, he was too curious not to explore and too brave to settle down. *Streams,* for instance, was a piece that one could only barely identify with Alvin. It was set to a percussion score by Miloslaw Kabelac and was Alvin's first full piece with no narrative. Built mainly on diagonal lines, its solos, duets and group sections evoke the dynamics of bodies of water, from gentle streams to turbulent seas, relating them to emotional states.

Different ways of moving influenced him at different times. He liked to play with fresh dance ideas until he made them his own. I loved watching him at work, transfixed by the way he put steps together and by the way he moved. This grounded, earthy, sensual man, the true panther, made dance look rich, natural and accessible.

The sum total of a particular dance work is always greater than its parts. Its music can be engaging, its vision powerful, its dancers generous and gifted. The idea for the piece can sound plausible when discussed and can appear to hold up in studio rehearsals. But the "truth" is never known until the dance is unleashed before an audience. It's only then that the power of the work as an instrument of communication can be known. If a dance didn't connect with the audience, Alvin knew it. He had a quick hook. He didn't often spend time reworking a piece that had an awkward first run.

As well, one of Alvin's greatest gifts was that he knew how to put five or six dances together to make a program that captured an audience from the instant the curtain rose to the encore-inspiring finish of the final piece, which was usually *Revelations*. During the years I was with the company, we sometimes closed with *Carmina Burana* or Canadian Brian MacDonald's *Time Out of Mind*. But we dancers knew that the audience had missed something special when Alvin's signature piece wasn't performed.

Alvin set an encore when we closed with *Revelations*, a repeat of "Rocka' My Soul," which was the piece's finale. All of us would act pleasantly surprised as Judith Jamison, standing centre stage, signalled us to our places to begin again. Once, in Budapest, dozens of people rushed onto the stage before we finished and started dancing with us.

Variety is the Spice

A bold leader, Alvin also generously recognized the gifts of others. One of his unique accomplishments was that, during an era dominated by choreographer-driven companies, he was the first of the modern dance leaders to develop a repertory company, one that performed the work of a variety of choreographers presenting a broad range of dynamics and personal visions. His belief in presenting many voices was not only generous, but wise. The company had too many New York City performances to rely on the work of only one choreographer. As well, having time away from the studio, while guest artists worked with his dancers, gave him opportunities to attend to other company needs; it also allowed him to be a guest choreographer elsewhere, which helped him earn necessary funds.[48]

To add to his own work, he selected dances by colleagues that he felt would harmonize with, or give balance to, his vision and that would challenge his dancers. The company's repertoire included dances by well-known choreographers such as Donald McKayle, Pearl Primus, Talley Beatty and Paul Sanasardo, as well as by up-and-coming artists like Louis Falco and Elisa Monte. One of my favourite pieces was choreographed by Mexican-born, American artist José Limón: *Missa Brevis*, a full-company work depicting an indomitable humanity rising up from the near destruction brought on by the Second World War. I also loved dancing again in John Butler's *Carmina Burana*. I performed in the ensemble, but was also given a lead role in the second cast, the same one that my idol Robert Powell had danced.

Wednesday Matinee, June 30

BLUES SUITE

Music: Traditional

Choreography by Alvin Ailey
Decor and Costumes by Ves Harper, Lonnie Dann
Lighting by Nicola Cernovitch

GOOD MORNING BLUES .... THE COMPANY
LONG TIME .... JOHN PARKS and THE COMPANY
MEAN OL' FRISCO .... JOHN PARKS, HECTOR MERCADO,
FREDDY ROMERO, LELAND SCHWANTES, KENNETH PEARL
HOUSE OF THE RISING SUN .... LEE HARPER, ROSAMOND LYNN, GAIL REESE
BACKWATER BLUES .... SYLVIA WATERS, MORTON WINSTON
IN THE EVENING .... HECTOR MERCADO, CLIVE THOMPSON,
RONALD DUNHAM, KENNETH PEARL
YANCEY SPECIAL .... THE COMPANY
SLOW DRAG — GOING TO CHICAGO .... THE COMPANY
SHAM .... MORTON WINSTON and THE COMPANY
GOOD MORNING BLUES .... THE COMPANY

INTERMISSION

DANCE FOR SIX

Music by Vivaldi (Le Cetra)

Choreography by Joyce Trisler

RAMOND SEGARRA	**MORTON WINSTON**	**KENNETH PEARL**
LINDA KENT	**MARI KAJIWARA**	**SYLVIA WATERS**

"Dance for Six" is set to Vivaldi's Concerto #9 in B Flat major and Concerto #12 in B minor.

INTERMISSION

REVELATIONS

Music: Traditional

Choreography: Alvin Ailey
Decor and Costumes by Ves Harper
Lighting by Nicola Cernovitch

PILGRIM OF SORROW

I Been Buked .... THE COMPANY
arranged by Hall Johnson
Daniel .... JOHN PARKS, MARI KAJIWARA, LINDA KENT
arranged by James Miller
Fix Me, Jesus .... JUDITH JAMISON, CLIVE THOMPSON
arranged by Hall Johnson

TAKE ME TO THE WATER

Processional .... MARI KAJIWARA, JOHN PARKS, CONSUELO ATLAS, FREDDY ROMERO,
ROSAMOND LYNN, RONALD DUNHAM, KENNETH PEARL
Wading in the Water .... MARI KAJIWARA, JOHN PARKS, CONSUELO ATLAS
"Wading in the Water" sequenced by Ella Jenkins.
"A Man Went Down to the River" is an original composition of Ella Jenkins.
Soloist: BROTHER JOHN SELLERS
I Want to be Ready .... RAMON SEGARRA
arranged by James Miller

MOVE, MEMBERS, MOVE

Soloist: BROTHER JOHN SELLERS

Sinner Man .... FREDDY ROMERO, KENNETH PEARL, HECTOR MERCADO
The Day is Past and Gone .... THE COMPANY
You May Run Home .... THE COMPANY
arranged by Brother John Sellers and Howard Roberts
Rocka My Soul in the Bosom of Abraham .... THE COMPANY

A typical Ailey touring program.

Alvin Ailey and His Dancers

Alvin wanted us to dance with urgency and with the control that allows for abandon; with heart-on-your-sleeve emotion, fearlessness and enough intensity to allow energy to move past the places where the body ends. Dancing for him required moving in a way musician Wynton Marsalis, writing about the company, called, "a 'die-for-the-moment' intensity."[49] Alvin knew, personally, what it was to be totally committed, to dance with heart and soul to the edge of fatigue and then come back night after night to do it again. He demanded the same from each of his dancers. This is not the only way to dance, but it's what Alvin believed in and he asked his dancers to reflect his belief. I loved it.

We all soared because Alvin gave us challenges that we didn't expect, that forced us to grow. He rarely gave us technical corrections, leaving that task to his rehearsal director, or to senior dancers. But there were times right before a show, while I'd be on stage practising a solo variation from one of his dances, when he'd hover over me, watching. Then, moments before the curtain rose, he'd make a change (always something much more difficult), coaching me with great intensity until the stage manager called, "Places please."

A man of few words, he was always to the point. After a performance, he didn't often shower you with verbal praise. He could put a smile on your face with a quick comment, such as, "Nice second variation," or keep you on edge, striving for more even after you had just been dancing your heart out, with a dismissive, "What was that?"

The "call-board," a square of cork hanging on a wall, was a magnet that drew us to it the moment we walked into our rehearsal or performing space, whether at home or on tour. On it was pinned the information that shaped our dance lives. Ever-changing, it gave us information about upcoming tours and daily schedules. Most dramatic were the notices about casting. No matter where or when, you might come to rehearsal and discover your name on the call-board beside a new role that Alvin had decided he wanted you to try, a role that you thought was way out of your range. Nervous, but accepting the challenge, you'd push hard to learn it quickly, because inevitably he'd schedule you to perform the part only a week or two later. Sink or swim, there you'd be in the spotlight, in a small town or on a New York stage, proving by the success of your performance that Alvin's instincts regarding his dancers' abilities were usually right.

Once in a while he did the opposite and, without explanation, took a role away. He did this even with the company greats. Perhaps he just wanted to see someone else dancing the role in a way that would inevitably offer changes that he was curious to see. Or, maybe he thought you couldn't cut it. No one was ever told why he or she was removed from a role. Moreover, dancers that didn't work out for him as company members were often quickly and quietly let go. Sometimes the reasons for the dismissals were inexplicable to the rest of us. A senior company member told me his hasty decisions were often a result of his wicked mood swings, which I did not witness until I had been dancing with the company for a while. Someone else always did his dirty work. He could be scary that way and hurtful.

Alvin wanted dancers who expressed themselves with dignity. Dance technique was the means through which his company members could perform the steps he had choreographed, but he knew it was our conviction that would convey his vision, communicate what would really grab an audience. He wanted to see who you were when you performed. "I always tell my dancers: don't look like a dancer; be a vessel for human emotions; try to look like a human being."[50]

We believed in his vision, in the communication it offered, in the hearts it opened. He had grand expectations and we were determined to meet and go beyond them.

Poor Reviews for White

Alvin said that he "got a lot of flak during the 1960s"[51] when he chose to make his company multiracial. As a visible minority in a group that was mainly African American, I had moments of self-doubt in which I questioned why Alvin had chosen me. I once asked him if I was out of place performing in dances that had African-American themes, such as *Blues Suite* and *Revelations*. Alvin looked at me intently and said, "The feelings expressed in those dances belong to everyone, so I don't care what colour your skin is; what matters is what you feel inside. And you feel it, so don't worry."

There was, however, one role that Alvin cast me in that I asked him to take me out of: the role of a Congolese priest in Pearl Primus' *The Congolese Wedding*. Ms. Primus was an artist with an MA in education from New York University. She purposely created work featuring African dance to raise the consciousness of Western audiences and to give them, with dignity, a view of another way of life. After Alvin's supportive words to me, I felt fine dancing to the blues or to jazz in American-themed work, but playing a Congolese prince? I just couldn't do it.

I did learn, on several occasions, about the "flak" that Alvin had experienced. For example, after an opening night performance in London, England, I arrived at Sadler's Wells theatre at noon for company class and read the review that was posted backstage. We had performed a piece called *Dance for Six* by Joyce Trisler. Three men and three women performed it, each wearing only a white leotard. I was one of the dancers in the piece, who, along with Linda Kent, represented the cast's white contingent.

The reviewer said something about how well the piece had been danced (thank you very much). He then went on to say how glorious the skin of the black dancers looked against the white leotards, and how disappointing the leotard looked beside the pale skin of the white dancers. I could see how this might be true. However, had we been wearing black leotards, and had the critic written the opposite, he might have ended up in court.

As I was reading the review, Alvin walked in. He must have already read the paper because he headed directly for the review and ripped it off the wall. He then shrugged, crumbled it up and tossed it into a garbage pail.

Though troubling, I knew that this incident was insignificant when compared to the intolerance that my African-American friends often experienced. I remember how, at the front door of a Detroit hotel, security agents looking for weapons frisked only our African-American male dancers, while allowing all the women, as well as the white and Asian men, to pass through without concern. Checking into a hotel in Kentucky, the desk clerk quickly handed me my room key. But he humiliated our African-Americans dancers by not giving them their keys until they had paid in advance.

Too bad that the desk clerk didn't come to see our performance, which got a standing ovation from an integrated audience. As Clive Barnes wrote in "A Great Lesson in Race Relations": ". . . he (Alvin) understands that the African culture is as much a part of American life as European culture . . . Today his non-black dancers can keep up in his company's idiom, which, for the most part is Afro-American. As a result—and I wouldn't stress this but rather take it as it comes—every performance he gives is the greatest lesson in race relations you are going to get in a month of Sundays."[52]

Gene Kelly and Body Paint

I didn't pay much attention to the London reviewer who had disparaged the look of my pale skin. But shortly after the review appeared, following a New York performance, a friend came backstage, stared at me intently, and said, "You look like Snow White on stage. I mean you're white, but do you have to be *that* white?"

Talking to our lighting designer, Chenault Spense, I mentioned the comment and asked him what he thought. "Yeah, sorry about that. When I do lighting, the skin tones I have to relate to are the ones of the African-American dancers. So it's a bit bright out there for you white guys."

As well, I realized that we Ailey men often danced bare-chested, which likely increased the glow.

I began to wonder if audience members had to put on sunglasses while watching me perform. I decided to invest in some new makeup. This was not the shoe-polish variety I had been forced to wear imitating Al Jolson in black-face when I was seven. It was a colour only a bit darker than my own skin tone that would keep me from looking washed out under bright lights. I tried it and was happy with the results. The down side was that, before performances, while everyone else was relaxing for a few moments, I had to take an extra half-hour to cover my body with it, or as much of my body as would be seen in that performance. A company member finished off the parts of my back I couldn't reach. I also had to take extra time to wash it off after each show.

Following a New York performance, I was scrubbing away as always and about half done, when one of the dancers, already dressed, ran into the shower room. "Kenny, you'd better get out here now. It's an emergency!'"

As I ran into the dressing room, towel wrapped around my waist, a man in a blue suit was leaving the room.

"That was Gene Kelly," everyone shouted. "He came in to say how much he loved the show. He said we were terrific."

"Oh man, I can't believe I missed him," I said, water dripping. His crisp, athletic moves had always inspired me. I ran to the door and saw him down the hall talking with Alvin. He must have sensed I was staring, because he quickly turned to me. I gave him an enthusiastic thumbs up, which he returned with that sparkling *American in Paris* smile and a wave of his hand. Then he started to laugh.

But it took the howls of laughter from my fellow dancers to make me realize that I was at the door greeting a dance legend with a towel around my waist, looking slightly mad, two toned and standing in a puddle as opposed to "singing in the rain."

"Sinner Man" — *Three Stories*

Doing

Each of the seven sections of *Revelations* has its own unique beauty. The sixth section, performed by three men, is "Sinner Man." It has a raw power and velocity.

Halfway through *Revelations*, Dudley Williams is dancing the meditative solo, "I Want to be Ready." The three of us "sinner men" are waiting in the wings. We have all performed the trio a hundred times, but it is always new, always personal. Tonight I am dancing the second of three variations—a new assignment Alvin had given me to push me further. Usually I perform the first.

The song's opening words, "Oh sinner man, where you gonna run to?" repeated slowly three times, have lots of spaces between them for our emotional lives to fill. We run onstage one at a time, chased by our fears, but stop as if the land has dropped away in front of us, because we are no longer on a stage, but in a hostile world.

Rooted to our places on a diagonal as the music slows down briefly, we three sinner men prepare to face the unknown. Then the music takes off into a driving tempo that pushes each of us into our own solo variations. We are men trying to escape from our worst demons. We catapult ourselves through high-velocity movement variations, with the wildness and urgency of men looking for a safe place, but never finding it.

My first performance of "Sinner Man" in Moscow.
Photograph: Vladimir Bliokh

On the last phrase of the third man's solo, the two of us who have been waiting, panting in the wings, race onstage to join him. We arrive on a diagonal, arms reaching sharply up to the balcony.

"Satan, Satan, won't you hide me?" The demands of the last section after a hard night of dancing are wicked, but so satisfying. A furious canon section begins. We dive to the floor and crawl frantically for a moment, then rise and dive to the floor again. Breaking the momentum, adding suspense, there is a much needed pause in the music. Facing the audience, fists clasped in front of us, we take four slow-motion beats to revolve our torsos in a muscle-flexed moment of introspection.

Finally, the last burst of energy: we leap upstage in unison away from the audience, airborne, legs reaching, and then earthbound towards it, spinning quickly to our knees, finishing sharply, arms stretched out to the audience. The moment is a startling acceptance of our fate, which is a descent into hell.

Blackout.

Upside Down

Dizziness and nausea hit me during class before a New York performance. I suspect food poisoning. At half-hour call, I feel so ill I think I should tell our rehearsal director that I can't perform. Other dancers know my roles and can easily cover for me at the last minute. But hating the idea of appearing weak and inconveniencing others, I fight through my discomfort.

The first piece on the program is *Streams*. Following a diagonal crossover by the full company, I dance a duet with Sylvia Waters. It is up-tempo, involving a lot of partnering. In the final moment, I prepare to take Sylvia, hands on her waist, and to lift her straight-armed over my head and run off into the wings. This is of course a reckless choice, because if the nausea returns, I risk putting Sylvia into danger.

I do feel dizzy, but hold on and make it through the lift. Success makes me feel in control, so I perform *Blues Suite* and, later, get off to a good start dancing the first solo of "Sinner Man."

Near the end of my solo, I do a quick slide fall to the floor. But as I make my move to spring up, the ceiling of the theatre, which has been right above me up till that moment, becomes the floor. The whole stage begins to spin and, as I go into my final turns, I fall on my face. Yes, I fall directly on my face. In front of 2,000 people. In New York. There is no way that the audience is thinking that my fall is part of the choreography. I can't get up, so I crawl offstage with as much dramatic flair as I can manage.

Transformation

One night, dressed for the finale of *Revelations,* wearing black pants, a yellow shirt and gold vest, I'm watching the show from backstage, waiting for the finale. "Sinner Man" is about to begin. I am not scheduled to perform in it that night. Before the entrance of the three men, Warren Spears, who is dancing the second variation, limps towards me and, punctuated with some distressing groans, says, "I can't do this. My hip is really in pain. I just can't do it."

There is only a half-minute to go before it starts, so I tell him, "If you want I can do it for you."

"No," Warren responds, grimacing with pain, "I should do it. I'll be okay." He is just like me.

He runs onstage and dances his solo beautifully. Racing offstage as the third variation begins, he falls onto me. "I can't go back out there. I can't! Please go out there for me and finish." He is due back for the closing trio in just a few seconds.

As Warren falls to the floor in pain, I rip off my vest and shirt, buttons flying, Superman in a phone booth, and tear out onto the stage getting into place right on the beat.

I finish the dance for him and, afterwards, wonder what the audience has thought about the transformation.

The Visits

Now that I was performing regularly in New York theatres, my parents began showing excitement for my dancing for the first time. "It's fantastic!!" Mom would proclaim, with at least two exclamation marks, in conversations over the phone. Her enthusiasm made me feel fantastic, too.

Then I got a letter from Dad in which he congratulated me on the achievement, and ended with the news that he and Mom would be coming to New York to see our next opening night performance. I was filled with happiness and pride.

The night they watched the show, I performed in three dances. I felt great on stage. It seemed that Mom and Dad would be more accepting of my chosen path after seeing, firsthand, how hard we dancers worked and how much joy we gave to our audiences.

Backstage afterwards, waiting for them to arrive, I saw my fellow dancers being greeted by friends and family with bouquets of flowers and enthusiastic hugs. Everyone was smiling. I couldn't wait for my turn. Then I caught sight of Mom and Dad. No flowers. "That was okay," I thought. "They didn't know where to buy them." I looked forward to the hugs; but they kept a cool distance, rooted in place. "Well, they're smiling," I said to myself. "That's a good sign."

Dad was the first to speak: "Son, we loved the music and the theatre is beautiful."

Mom continued: "We thought Judith was incredible and what a great closing number."

It was as if I hadn't appeared on stage at all.

During that first visit to New York, and on two visits afterwards, a pattern emerged. It began with big good-luck wishes expressed over the phone, followed by excited words about how fantastic my dance life really was. That expression of enthusiasm was the decoy, a promise of good things to come. Then, after I'd taken the bait and was feeling hopeful, in person, backstage, they'd pop me off. All my parents' positive comments would be about the friends I had danced with, the music, or the beauty of the theatre.

I packed a bottle of tranquilizers into my dance bag before their visits. And I would drop a couple just before greeting them, to be safe.

I trusted myself more and didn't allow their lack of positive feedback to shake my day-to-day confidence. I had accomplished enough to know that I was good. I also realized my parents were trying; but the sadness I experienced after their visits, and the regrets I had about the distance that kept growing between us, affected me. I said nothing to them, but carried what I felt inside. And I realized that there is often nothing more disturbing than what we learn to live with.

During each of their visits, after saying goodnight, I would walk the streets until I was too tired to stand. Then, disciplined young man that I was, I would make sure that I was the first to arrive for class the next morning.

My Own Personal Cheerleader

One day, during my third year with the company, I woke up feeling good and realized I had been waking up feeling good for months. The severe abdominal cramps that had been sniping at me for ten years, disrupting the flow of my life, were gone. Gone! It was a miracle.

I believed that there were three reasons for their departure. The first was my new practice of meditation. My sister Toba, almost three years younger than me, had become a teacher of Transcendental Meditation (TM), an ancient form of meditation that was brought to the West by the South Asian guru Maharishi Mahesh Yogi in the mid-1960s and, soon after, was made popular by the Beatles. Toba had graduated as a physiotherapist from the University of Toronto. However, while taking a year off to travel, she had learned about TM and had ended up saying goodbye to physiotherapy and becoming a devout TM practitioner and teacher.

Toba gave me a book describing studies on the positive effects of TM, most of which involved stress reduction. I figured that, even if all it did was help me to sleep better, TM would be worth a try. TM required little effort. It could be done anywhere: at home, on a tour bus, or in an airport. All you had to do was meditate morning and evening, repeating a specific mantra, or sound, for twenty minutes at a time.

Toba taught me TM. My cramps rarely returned.

My sister Toba, around 1975.
Author's personal collection

My role models were also a supremely positive influence: male artists such as Robert Cohan, Donald McKayle, William Louther, Robert Powell, David Earle and Alvin Ailey, had all supported me. They lived the dancer's life full out, without (to my knowledge) questioning its validity.

The final reason for my release from abdominal pain lay, I was certain, in the act of dancing itself. Rehearsing and performing the emotional repertoire of the Ailey Company allowed me to be expressive, which helped release pressure. On stage I loved, murdered, celebrated sacred events, and expressed alienation, joy and anger. I was even lucky enough to have the deliciously dramatic opportunity to be shot and to die on a regular basis as a soloist in the final moments of *Rainbow 'Round my Shoulder*.

While my parents' disapproving voices were never completely subdued, they did quiet down as my own inner voice became more approving, a kind of personal cheerleader.

A friend who had not seen me perform for over a year came backstage during this time. She gave me an enthusiastic hug and said, "Kenny, I didn't recognize you out there. You are completely transformed."

I was relieved to learn that change is really possible.

The Martha Graham Reunion

Feeling strong and confident, three years after resigning from the Graham Company, I returned to the Graham school to take a class. I needed to make peace with the place. Ms. Graham's false accusation, that I had tried to black-mail her into giving me bigger roles, had become public and remained a hurtful memory. I'd heard she wasn't around much, so I wasn't likely to see her. I did fear that, if she did show up, she would not hesitate to rip into me. I decided to visit the studio anyway.

I went to the 10:30 advanced class, which was conveniently very crowded. I took a place at the back, so that, in the unlikely event Ms. Graham appeared, it would be difficult for her to spot me.

Well, halfway through class, Ms. Graham walked in. As she shuffled to the front, I could see her arthritis was worse than when I had last seen her. Her authority, though, had not diminished. Bodies became alert as she made her presence known to succeeding rows of dancers. The music stopped and we all acknowledged her with a small bow. She bowed back and class continued. Fight or flight. I had to choose.

I stayed put. I danced: plié sequence, brushes and leg fans. I could see that, as always, she was checking out each person in the room. Then she stood up from her sacred chair and began walking, making a beeline directly towards me. I expected disaster. In a minute, she was standing right in front of me. I could feel her dissecting my technical flaws, judging my character, thinking of the right words to finish me off.

"Kenny," she said," it's good to see you."

Then she turned emphatically and slowly made her way back to the front of the studio.

Two Best Friends

Hector

My life in New York would not of course have been complete without friends, and I had many in the Ailey Company. Hector Mercado and Mari Kajiwara became my closest. Hector and I had grown up in different worlds. His family lived in Spanish Harlem and had encouraged him to become a dancer, seeing it, unlike my own parents, as a profession that could lead to prosperity. They had already witnessed the success of Hector's uncle, Jaime Sanchez, who was a well-known actor and dancer and had been a Shark in both the Broadway and movie versions of *West Side Story*. Hector trained as a dancer from a relatively young age, as a student at the High School of Performing Arts. Soon after leaving school, he had performed in an Elvis Presley TV special, believing that commercial show-biz was his calling. It was actually Mari, a fellow Performing Arts student, who had talked him into going to the same Ailey audition I had attended.

He danced with bold strokes of joy and furrow-browed intensity. Always the babe magnet, his handsome face was featured on many magazine covers. It was often compared to those of the famous Rudolphs, Nureyev and Valentino (but not the reindeer).

We became roommates, starting in Russia, after my snoring companion had driven me from my original room assignment. Most of our big adventures were shared onstage, as Alvin often partnered us up in different pieces: we regularly danced "Sinner Man" together, and were both leads in the second casts of *Rainbow 'Round My Shoulder* and *Carmina Burana*.

At Helen and Hector's Wedding.
Amy Christopher, Sybil Burton,
Helen Greenford, the minister (name unknown),
Hector Mercado and myself (with eyes closed).
Author's personal collection

Hector also helped pull me out of my shell and into a bigger social life than I would normally have experienced. His partner was British-born ballet teacher Helen Greenford. I spent a lot of time with the two of them away from the company, usually sharing quiet visits in their apartment. Occasionally she joined us on tours. Her aunt was Sybil Burton, first wife of the great actor Richard Burton. Sybil had become the Disco Queen of New York after opening the elite discotheque, Arthur, on 54th Street, whose patrons included Andy Warhol, Princess Margaret and Rudolph Nureyev. She lived on Central Park West with her two daughters, Kate and Amy, and husband, Jordan Christopher, leader of the house band, The Wild Ones.[53] We often went to her apartment to drink beer and watch movies. This was in the days before videos and DVDs, so seeing a film in someone's home was a big event. When Helen and Hector married, Hector asked me to be his best man.

Hector left the company before I did. He had dreams of performing in Broadway musicals. And he was successful. His greatest achievement was performing the role of Bernardo in a Broadway revival of *West Side Story*. When I saw the production, I had visions of following in his footsteps, rumbling with him under the highway and dancing in the gym. It was a fun thought, but dancing with the Ailey Company was my dream come true and I hoped to stay where I was for a long time.

Mari

The artist I loved dancing with the most was Mari Kajiwara, my first New York friend. I met her when I was brand new at the Graham School and didn't yet know anyone. One morning before class, a beautiful young woman with sleek black hair, deep brown eyes and a warm smile, maybe seventeen, had walked over to the corner of the studio where I was hiding, reached out her hand and said, "Hi, I'm Mari. Who are you?"

She was still finishing her last year at The High School of Performing Arts. Too gifted to go unnoticed, she was scooped up shortly after graduation by the Ailey Company and danced as one of its soloists for fourteen years.

I partnered her in *Dance for Six, Myth, Hidden Rites* and, most memorably, in *Rainbow 'Round My Shoulder*. In *Rainbow,* I danced the role of a prisoner on a chain gang, who, in the section with Mari, acts out a dream of reunion with his lost lover. Choreographer Donald McKayle had created a passionate and driving duet for the characters. Because we were such close friends offstage, the duet always became personal and wild. Mari's intense eye-to-eye connection with me, as we stood on opposite sides of the stage before moving towards each other, always let me know that I would be in for the ride of my life. Her passion inspired in me a depth of emotion that, in turn, motivated me to give more than I ever dreamed I could. The *New York Times* described her as dancing with "technique that was both pure and powerful, enhanced by a luminous presence," and "with an emotional depth that seemed to grow out of the very depth of her consummate technique."[54]

Mari Kajiwara.
Photograph: Kenn Duncan/©The New York Public Library

My heart was always with Mari; she knocked me out. She was beautiful, generous and wise. We danced, walked, talked and played together. So at the time I often wondered, "Why aren't we getting together as a couple?" Alvin even thought we were an item. A few times on tour, I'd wake up in the morning and find a tray of breakfast goodies in front of the motel door. On it would be a note from Alvin: "Hope you two have a nice breakfast."

Partnering Mari in *Rainbow 'Round My Shoulder.*
Photograph: with permission from photographer Johan Elbers

I loved her. However, as with Georgia, it was emotionally easier for me to
continue on with my sporadic run of brief relationships than to embrace a dear
friend and hold her close.

In 1978, Mari married Israeli-born dancer Ohad Naharin in New York. When Ohad became artistic director of Israel's illustrious Batsheva Dance Company in 1990, she joined his group. She was still dancing beautifully when the company performed in Toronto at the Sony Centre in 1997.

In the spring of 2002, I joined a large group of former Ailey dancers and Ohad at a memorial service in New York for Mari. It was cancer that had taken her. She was fifty.

A company member performed *Journey*, a solo Mari was known for dancing, choreographed by Joyce Trisler. Many of us spoke. We watched Mari's exquisite dancing on film.

Images linger. Feelings too.

On the Road

Every year in the Ailey Company we packed our suitcases and headed out from New York for close to six months of touring, visiting our two-page list of cities and towns, many of which were unfamiliar. In the U.S. we would often dance in as many as five different places in a week, for up to three months. After a show, followed by a midnight dinner and a heavy sleep, we would get on the bus for a ride of up to five hours to the next stop. (If the trip was longer than five hours, the union said we had to fly.) Only in the larger cities, where we gave multiple performances, did we actually have time to unpack our bags. While the seemingly endless bus rides brought stiffness to our already sore bodies, we knew we were relatively pampered. We had a nice tour bus to travel in. Costumes and sets were sent in a truck. During the company's early years, the dancers had been packed into a station wagon and had shared their seating with all the sets and costumes, the legs of chairs sticking out of the car windows as they motored across America. Alvin told me that on a trip to Philadelphia, the company car had been stolen, sets and costumes included.

The motel rooms we frequented on the long U.S. tours—often reeking of mould and stale cigarettes, with house restaurants that served up wilted iceberg lettuce and pulpy tomato salads topped with Day-Glo French dressing that stuck to the roof of your mouth—inspired me to come up with inventive survival strategies. Because of the scarcity of vegetarian dishes on offer in restaurants, I began packing a hot plate and a couple of pots and pans so I could make meals of pasta and veggies in my hotel rooms. Some of my fellow dancers thought I was peculiar, but many came knocking on my door when the smells of soy sauce, garlic and ginger drifted down the hallways. After setting off fire alarms in my rooms a few times, I learned how to wrap wet washcloths around the smoke detectors before plugging in my hot plate, so that my cooking went undetected by staff. The few of us who cooked together and rarely ate out were able to save a lot of the money given to us as a "per-diem," a daily allowance to cover the costs of restaurant meals while touring.

During my time with the company, requests for overseas shows increased. We performed in Germany, Austria and Eastern Europe, including stops in Hungary, Romania and the former Yugoslavia. Summer festivals in Croatia included outdoor performances in Split on the Adriatic coast, in a theatre built into the ruins of Roman emperor Diocletian's summer palace. In the south of France, in Avignon's fourteenth-century Palais des Papes, the wind, the Mistral, was so strong one night we could barely walk. Performing the opening of *Carmina Burana,* our monks' cloaks billowed like sails, making us struggle to hold our balance even while taking the smallest steps. We visited the Sadler's Wells Theatre in London twice. There was, however, only one Canadian show ever scheduled—in Winnipeg. After receiving the two Gold Stars in Paris, the company was invited for an extended return visit. Also memorable were shows in Lebanon and Iran.

Out-of-country touring was easier than on-the-road touring in the U.S. in one respect: we almost always stayed in one place for a number of performances, and the hotels were usually central and often luxurious.

Two groups quickly emerged among us. The first included the majority of dancers, who stayed up late after shows to unwind and relax, and hid under the sheets until the last minute, staggering onto the bus in the morning, bleary-eyed, their lips attached to a cup of strong coffee. Those of us in the second group would wake up early once in a while and head out to explore the sights for a couple of hours. We always ended up feeling energized because of the excitement of discovering a beautiful garden, or a Renaissance statue, or from laying our hands on the coolness of a 500-year-old stone wall.

Days off were special. I remember an early morning walk with Mari through the Lavra, a monastery complex in Kiev. In Bucharest, Romania, a group including Hector and fellow dancer Peter Woodin went for a swim at a spa by a nearby lake. On the shoreline, we stepped into a roofless booth, with our heads protruding; an attendant pressed a button and suntan oil sprayed through a thousand tiny nozzles, coating our bodies. In Berlin, I went on a quick bus tour, visiting various palaces and the Berlin Wall; outside Vienna, I rented a car with Mari and our two gentle Japanese friends, dancers Mazasumi Chaya and Michihiko Oka, to drive along the Danube River.

While on tour, Alvin surprised me with a few new responsibilities. I was an inexperienced teacher, but he asked me to be one of the few company members to teach master classes in universities across the U.S. He also invited me to conduct the class portion of our many lecture-demonstrations. Finally, in spite of my fears of speaking in public, he asked me to talk at international press conferences overseas.

Postcards Home #2

Dear Mom, Dad and Wendi,

"Had a good day off yesterday. Went to the National Gallery. Then cooked dinner in the room. Watched Cat on a Hot Tin Roof with Paul Newman and L. Taylor. Okay, not really with them. Leaving now for Hampton, Virginia, then N. Carolina, Nebraska, Oklahoma and Texas." (Washington, D.C.)

"Drove 5 hours on the bus and have to rehearse now and perform tonight. Stiff and aching. Tomorrow to Charlotte, N. Carolina." (Winston-Salem, North Carolina)

"Day off. We're 20 minutes from the Mexican border, but they wouldn't let me in because of my hairdo." (McAllen, Texas)

"We finished our tour yesterday. Going to Judy Jamison's for my birthday dinner. Loving the company. Finally a place where I can be slightly mad, crazy and different." (Manhattan)

SOCIETY FOR
BATSHEVA DANCE COMPANY
9 SDEROT HAHASKALA. TEL-AVIV. TEL. 35587

האגודה למען
להקת מחול בת־שבע
שדרות ההשכלה, 9, תל־אביב, 11970

קרן בת־שבע
לאמנות והשכלה
BATSHEVA FOUNDATION
FOR ART AND LEARNING

23rd August, 1971

Mr. Kenneth Pearl
69 East 4th St.
NEW YORK, N.Y.

Dear Kenny,

    Following up our telephone conversation, Linda and I have talked again and she has reinforced my feeling that you would be good for us and we would be good for you.

    The four Graham pieces in the repertoire are:- "Diversion of Angels", "Cave of the Heart", "Embattled Garden", and "Errand into the Maze". With Efrati's retirement there are principal parts open in all those ballets. Also in "Mythical Hunters". Cranko is doing two pieces - one to Hebrew poetry ...... We tour France, Belgium and Holland starting November 5th in Brussels, with a week in the Paris Festival. After that there are performances all over Israel, a choreographic workshop, new productions and either a South American tour for six weeks, or Vienna and Paris for six weeks. November and December 1972 we will tour the U.S. with two weeks at City Centre.

    As I indicated to you, I am very ambitious for the company; it seems to have passed through a difficult, probably poisonous, period. Working conditions and atmosphere are fine now.

    Perhaps it would be a good idea for you to think of my offer for a limited time - i.e. a six months period. If Alvin will give you leave of absence for that length of time, you would be in a position to return to America if you were not happy here . If you think to join us in this way I can use you as soon as possible - the leading dancer position is open and I want to fill it as soon as possible. The man I mentioned to you on the phone is Michael Ries of Columbia Artists (Tel: CI 76900) who shares an enormous enthusiasm for this company - perhaps he can influence you as he also represents Alvin.

    Dear Kenny, I hope you have sleepless nights and decide in our favour.

Yours sincerely,

Brian Macdonald
D i r e c t o r

cc. Kennedy Centre

In 1971, Brian Macdonald, the Artistic Director of the Batsheva Dance Company in Israel, invited me to join his troupe. What a generous offer! Many sleepless nights followed, but I was happy dancing with the Ailey Company and decided to stay put. No regrets.

Adventures Overseas

Le Palais des Sports, Paris, 1972

Le Palais des Sports in Paris seats 4,200. Following the company's award-winning performances in Paris in November 1970, there had been enough of a buzz to encourage presenters to book us into a sports arena for a month, giving seven shows a week. The program, which was the same each night, began at 9:00 and finished at midnight. As requested by the producers, it consisted of four full-company works and two solos. *Streams* opened the program. Then Dudley Williams danced his eloquent Ailey solo, *Song for You*. The act closed with Donald McKayle's *Rainbow 'Round my Shoulder*. After intermission came three Ailey works, led off by *Blues Suite*. The solo *Cry* came in the middle of the act and, of course, we closed with *Revelations*. Most of the men danced in four half-hour pieces each night, making this run the most exhausting performance month ever.

Following our evening performances, we had to travel back to our hotel by Metro. We usually arrived around 2:00 a.m. for dinner and were in bed by 3:00 a.m.

It would have been nice to sleep in and have a relaxing half-day to see the city. But Alvin hadn't brought us to Paris to be tourists. He wanted us to be better, no matter how successful we were, no matter how hard we had already worked. So we did an hour-and-a-half ballet class every day and then, even though we were performing the same show each night, we rehearsed every afternoon except on Saturday, when we performed a matinee as well as an evening show. Sometimes rehearsals were needed so that injured dancers could be replaced. Sometimes we rehearsed pieces that were not a part of the show, but that we had to keep fresh as we would be performing them at our next stop. Usually we rehearsed to put our notes from the last performance into practice. Or just to get better. During the entire month, we had three days off.

Sitting on the Metro, our legs felt like rubber and we wondered how it would be possible to put enough sensation and steel back into them to meet the day's demands. But every night when the lights came up, making an illuminated diagonal pathway for the company's entrance in *Streams*, I felt the dancers' bodies around me straighten up, muscle up and energize. The hush, as the voices of 4,200 audience members quieted, created a space into which our energy would project. Fatigue and soreness vanished and, as the smoke from thousands of cigarettes drifted across the stage, we made our entrances.

"I've Been Buked" from *Revelations.*
The company, with James Truitte (centre) and myself (upstage corner).
Photograph: with permission from photographer Johan Elbers

Three Happenings at Le Palais des Sports

Fire

On our first night in Paris, I was too excited to sleep. After midnight, I went out alone wearing my tight cowboy boots, popular in those days, and roamed the streets. The air was misty and the boulevards wet and quiet. As I walked down the centre of one, a speeding car careened around a corner. Jumping out of its way, I tripped on the curb, slid on the slick sidewalk and went down on my lower back.

Later, in my room and feeling fine, I pushed down on the mattress, which felt like it was filled with straw. Usually, whenever I had to sleep on a soft mattress, I put it on the floor to protect my back. But it was now very late, and I needed to get to sleep.

I woke up, my body sagging into the bedding, and got dressed. The injury happened in an instant as I pulled on my tight right boot. I heard a high-pitched sound, and felt a painful ripple and fierce heat as my lower back tore. My roommate Mel Jones ran out to find the company manager.

Within an hour, I was being attended to at the physiotherapy clinic that treated the French Olympic Team athletes. I knew that I couldn't have been in better hands, so I was ready to accept the physiotherapist's diagnosis and recommendations, whatever they were. After he had made some painful manipulations, he told me I had a bulging disc. My sciatic nerve was screaming. Waves of pain were shooting down my butt and right leg into my foot. Any curving of my back, or bending of my body, which naturally occurs while sitting, for example, brought on the pain. I was almost pain free if I was standing upright or flat on my back. But I knew I wasn't going to perform four dances a night in either of those two positions.

The physio told me everything I had done the night before had exacerbated a pre-existing weakness in my back, which had been caused over the years by elements of my dance training and because of my body type. The previous night's plane ride, the walking for hours on cobbled streets in tight boots, the fall, the sleep on a sagging mattress and then, the fatal quick yank of the boot that morning—all had been the final blows. If I ever wanted to dance again, I had to rest, do a series of exercises that he would give me and return for regular treatments. Then the discs would slowly "roam" back to their proper place and I could be dancing again in two months. "But our opening is tomorrow. Please give me permission to dance," I begged.

The good therapist just shook his head and said, "No way."

I didn't make it to the theatre for the dress rehearsal that night. I lay on the floor on a few blankets, a towel rolled under my lower back and focused on the performance. I put out of my head the possibility of not being onstage the next night by imagining myself going through every beat of every dance, over and over again.

Later that night, Mel told me no one had covered my parts. Not knowing the extent of my injury because I hadn't told anyone, Alvin fully expected me to be ready for the first performance.

At noon the next day, I rode the Metro with my fellow dancers, standing, of course. At 2:00 p.m., we began our dance day with ballet class. Rehearsal and performance followed. I made myself do what I wanted and needed to do, counting on willpower, painkillers and a wave of adrenaline to get me through. Night after night. It took months for the pain to subside to a tolerable level, but I didn't miss a beat. I didn't understand why my spine didn't burst into flames.

Ice

At the beginning of our fourth week, the arena started getting cold. By Wednesday it was freezing. The producer told us that the *Ice Follies*, a show featuring figure skaters, had been scheduled next into the venue and that the temperature had to be lowered so the ice would freeze quickly right after we left. By the last weekend, we felt as if our blood was coagulating. Dressed sometimes only in a pair of thin tights, we were blowing ice rings.

Earthquake

On Saturday, after a matinee at the end of the third week, Alvin called a company meeting. He showed up tense, frowning his big frown. Alvin's hands, which were usually so soft, became claws, and he dug them into one of the best of us. He ranted on about how she was overweight and out of shape (she wasn't), wasn't dancing well (she was) and was letting everyone down. This exchange, had it been necessary, could have taken place in a private meeting, but Alvin chose to humiliate our gifted friend publicly. It was the first time I had witnessed one of Alvin's much publicized wicked mood swings. While holding back my anger, I saw a chair come flying out from our huddled group, aimed at our out-of-control boss. The chair missed its target, but Alvin was silenced. Then, John Parks, one of the company's stars, shouted, "I quit."

We all should have quit, but he was the brave one and, after the tour, he did leave.

Our wounded friend ran from the room in tears and someone followed to give support. Feeling shocked, unsteady and angry, we wondered how she, or in fact any of us, was going to get back on stage in a few hours and make the audience believe we were a family and in good spirits. We all did, because performing was the means by which we became whole and balanced.

That eventful night, our battered friend performed. As always, she was brilliant.

Pedestals

I had needed my mentors to be the alchemists who would take the raw material that was me and turn it into artistic gold. I had also needed them to be perpetually noble, wise and selfless. Placing my idols on pedestals, expecting them always to be on balance, had inevitably led to disappointment. As I saw, over and over again, everyone slips and falls. When I saw my mentors lose control, I felt deserted. How could I go on believing in the lessons their work communicated and in their perfectly stated philosophical aphorisms, if they were so capable of being the opposite of what they preached?

First of all, the hurtful behaviour was usually rare. Second, if I chose to accept the considerable gifts my leaders had to offer, then I had to learn to accept them as real people, with their own mix of strengths and weaknesses. The weaknesses were magnified because they were constantly in the spotlight and had responsibilities I could only begin to imagine.

I had once read the philosopher William James' line: "The art of being wise is the art of knowing what to overlook." I finally understood what he meant. But I had yet to figure out just how much I would overlook before I walked away.

Baalbek and Ulysses

Baalbek is a historical site, the ruins of a massive temple complex built in the hills, eighty-six kilometres northeast of Beirut. Even before the Romans built their soaring temple of Jupiter, Baalbek had already stood as the largest stone-block construction in the world, dating back almost 5,000 years. The cutting and placement of the largest stones are said to be beyond the engineering abilities of any recognized ancient or contemporary builders.

In modern times, a space for an international performance festival had been set into the ruins. Our shows there took place in 1974, a year before the start of Lebanon's bloody civil war, on a stage surrounded by ancient columns that rose into starry skies. Contrasting with this magical locale were the army tanks on the roads leading to the theatre and the soldiers in camouflage gear lined up on the ground below the stage. They were stationed there, we were told, to protect us. While we rehearsed and danced, the government's soldiers stood immobile, rifles pressed to their chests, fingers against triggers that, within the year, would be pulled back in a fight against the enemy.

Our moonlit performance opened with *Hidden Rites*, a new Ailey piece. It is a high energy and sensual work for nineteen dancers, evoking a series of imagined rituals of initiation, death and rebirth. Patrice Sciortino's percussion score of chimes, piano, drums and whistles establishes the atmosphere of a mythical world, which was fitting for the ancient stone upon which we were performing.

The event had great personal significance because Alvin had choreographed a seven-minute solo for me. It was an intricate mix of sharp hip and torso moves that exploded into what I thought of as a rampage of rhythmic traveling steps that connected me to every point of the stage, making sacred the ground the company was about to dance on. The movement signified the lighting of the fuse that would ignite the stage and set in motion the rites to follow.

As memorable as these performances was a quiet moment that took place off-stage in the heat of an early morning, before company class.

I had heard that there was a man who lived in Baalbek whose name was Moses. He was known for picking up and transforming small pieces of stone that had broken off from the buildings. With a penknife, he carved these discarded stones into little statues representing everything from figures in Greek mythology to nature symbols.

Walking with Alvin towards the stage one morning, we spotted Moses sitting on ancient steps with his penknife, working on a new creation. We walked over to watch. He was a tall gray man, dusty like the landscape, who because of his massive physique took on the permanence of the stones that surrounded him.

As soon as he caught sight of Alvin, as striking here, high up on a mountain in Lebanon, as he was on the streets of New York, Moses put down what he was doing. He picked up a stone about eight inches square, and began creating, alternately sawing at it and piercing it with the tip of the knife. We watched as a beautiful sun quickly emerged with wavy rays and a beautiful smiling face.

He handed it to Alvin, who said thank you with his own beautiful smile, and they embraced.

I desperately wanted him to sculpt a piece for me, too. I think he sensed my wish because I was making a fool of myself gushing non-stop about the sun. He gave me a mischievous smile and began carving again. He sculpted a smaller stone this time, about six inches by four. He worked swiftly, chips flying, and in ten minutes he handed it to me saying one word: "Ulysses."

Pistachio Nuts Lead to Indigestion

Selected once again by the State Department to represent the U.S. abroad, the Ailey Company visited Tehran, the capital of Iran. This was during the time when the Shah Mohammed Reza Pahlavi was still in power and the Ayatollah Khomeini was still dreaming and planning the Islamist revolution that would ban sinful American dance. Under the Ayatollah there would be no visits by companies with bare-chested men and bare-legged women dancing to the lyrics from *Blues Suite*: "My mother was a tailor. She sewed my new blue jeans. My father was a gamblin' man, down in New Orleans."

We were told that our week of performances in Tehran, in a vast, elegant theatre, would be attended mainly by U.S. officials and business types, and by the Iranian upper crust. I wondered if the Shah himself would attend. His photographed image appeared on half the postcards on display in our regal hotel lobby—clean-shaven, perched on a throne, jewel-bedecked. I knew the Shah was looked on favourably by the West, but his image, which projected wealth and secularism, starkly contrasted with the crowds of people I saw on the streets: men with beards, many women wearing veils, all looking poor. The high cost of the tickets would prevent these people from attending our performances, which disappointed us: We were a company "for the people."

Mari and I walked the chaotic streets lined with mosques and markets on the day we arrived, through crowds made up mainly of men; we felt as though we were swimming upstream against an unrelenting current, sweaty bodies pressing against us, hands reaching towards us for money, or touching our hair. We felt scared. Would we find our way back to the hotel? What if we got separated? We followed our map and found our way to some colourful market stalls. I bargained for a mirror with a silvery metal frame shaped into flowers and vines. We drank fresh-squeezed carrot juice from a street vendor, and gave coins to a dozen people of the many who were begging. Then we went back to our swank hotel to have a swim in our perfectly spotless pool. At night we visited a club to listen to music and to dance, a club that appeared as open and free as any back home, filled with attractive young people wearing skimpy outfits. There seemed to be two Tehrans.

I did not fully understand then that the Shah was a U.S. puppet, kept in place to help serve U.S. interests. From what I witnessed, I wasn't surprised that a campaign of civil resistance, partly secular, partly religious, would begin soon after we left.

Following the opening night performance, our well-healed audience clapped politely, conveying what was for us an unusually low decibel round of acceptance. The reception afterwards was grand. I wondered if the servers were looking at us thinking: "Your time is coming, Americans. We'll be taking over soon. Get lost!"

On our last day in Tehran, a day off before flying home, I decided to buy bags of local pistachio nuts as gifts for friends and family. Standing at the checkout counter of a little grocery store with my backpack at my side, the cashier smiled at me in a charming way. He seemed so friendly that I held out my hand to shake his. We shook. I paid. I packed my gifts and went back to the hotel.

Moments after arriving, as I was unpacking my goods, my heart leapt into my throat. My passport, which I knew for certain I had placed in my bag, was gone! It only took an instant for me to realize that the cashier had been smiling at me as he watched the man in the line behind me reach into my bag and remove that sacred, essential item that I would need to leave Iran and enter North America in two days. A Canadian passport was worth a fortune on the black market.

We were guests of the government, so I got deluxe service. I spent the next day with Iranian detectives, interpreters and government officials, but went back to the hotel late at night without a new passport. Early the following morning, my colleagues each hugged me, looks of concern in their eyes, and then filed onto the bus that would take them to the airport. I waited, nauseous, in the hotel lobby, Alvin sitting beside me with his arm around my shoulder. "Don't worry, we'll get you on that bus." But the bus left, with the two of us sitting there.

An hour before the flight, a police car screeched to a stop in front of the hotel. A man in a suit jumped out, waving his arms wildly. At the end of one, I saw a blue passport. He gave it to me, pushed Alvin and me into the car and, with the siren on full blast, got us to the airport moments before the gate closed.

A Bad Break

There were two casts for *Blues Suite*, which led off the program at London's Sadler's Wells Theatre during our second trip there. I was in both casts. The day of the opening performance, as always, we ran through the dances we would be performing. We did this, appropriately, with cast number one.

The front section of this London performing space had an unusual shape: at the front, it angled in sharply on each side. As a result, rehearsing the piece, we made a lot of adjustments regarding our spatial relationships. Opening night went well. A matinee had been scheduled for the next day. Because time was limited, we ran only a quick spacing rehearsal with the second cast. The company had performed all the dances so many times that quick rehearsals on a show day sometimes seemed like all the preparation that was necessary. So the dancers "marked" their movement, instead of dancing full out.

During the performance, five minutes into the opening section, the dancer in front of me backed up close to me because of the shortened stage, as he had in rehearsal. Only now, he was doing his movement with a big energy, not "marking" it. His movement included a violent swing back of his arms with his fists clenched. His left one whacked me on the left side of my nose. Towards the end of that first section, there came the moment when, along with fellow dancers, I draped my body over a stool as a soloist performed. Looking down, I noticed a pool of blood on the floor directly beneath my eyes. I wondered who had been injured. Then, watching red drops fall, I realized that the someone was me!

The section ended. I wiped the blood from the floor with my shirt sleeve, left the stage, and ran on a moment later to perform a quintet. My nose was still bleeding, so I did most of the dance with my head tilted slightly upwards.

After icing at intermission, I performed the two remaining pieces. It had never occurred to me to ask that I not perform them. I was still upright so I kept dancing. After the performance, I resisted going to the hospital as I was afraid the doctors would tell me not to dance. Alvin insisted I go. Ivy Clarke accompanied me. We went out to the street to hail a cab and, watching many taxis drive by, wondered why none would stop.

Then Ivy looked at me and started to laugh. "How you look is why no one is stopping. You're still in costume and you have all your makeup on, including your mascara, which is running down to your chin. You look mad." I disappeared behind a lamp post and in a few seconds she got a cab.

The doctor told me that I had a break and had to take a break. He said my nose would heal on its own without bandages, but that I should not think of performing for a week. Part of what he had said suited me fine: a bandage would have prevented me from going on stage. But I had every intention of performing, including that very night.

I got back to the theatre an hour before the show feeling lousy, but made light of the situation to everyone including Alvin. He tried to convince me not to perform and he could have simply said no. But I stated my case with such conviction that he finally gave in. For the week though, he did forbid me from doing any partnering in which I risked getting hit. With a swollen nose and black eye, I wasn't cute. But it was going to take more than a broken nose, and my everyday aching knees and back, to keep me from getting up on that stage.

Where is the Bermuda Triangle When You Really Need It?

During August 1973, the company was invited to perform in Bermuda for a week. We had been touring a lot, visiting small U.S. towns, staying in motels in strip malls. So a trip to an idyllic island was a treat we were all grateful for.

Even with five performances, our time on that lovely island was unusually relaxing. We rented mopeds and sped along the shady, winding roads that connected our hotel to the theatre—terrifying Alvin. We enjoyed fresh fruit, orange and lavender sunsets, the sight of pink and lime-green homes, and enthusiastic audiences. At the end of the week, arriving at the airport, we were relaxed, ready for an intense rehearsal period that would begin in a few days in the still steamy Manhattan.

Returning to the U.S. from international tours was always nerve-wracking for me. Even though I had a Social Security Number, I had not had a work visa since I had left the Graham Company. I was therefore an illegal alien once more, and every time I re-entered the U.S., I risked losing my job and being deported.

I developed a routine to keep myself safe: at the airport, before going through Customs, I collected all the New York receipts that were in my wallet and gave them, along with my U.S. address book, ID cards and dance clothes, to Hector to carry for me. I then filled my wallet with Canadian money and added a few old receipts from Canadian stores. Once the company landed in New York, I separated myself from my fellow dancers. I always had with me a one-way ticket from New York to Toronto, which I had carefully purchased before heading out from New York on tour, so I could show the Immigration Officer, as I had done on my first train trip from Toronto to New York, that my stop in New York was only for a short visit and that I would be heading back home in a few days.

Getting ready to return to New York, I did everything I had always done with the address book and the receipts. But this time, and for the first time, because the trip was so short, I had neglected to buy in advance a one-way plane ticket back to Toronto. Still, waiting in line for my U.S. Customs interview, I felt everything would be all right. Maybe that was because the Vietnam draft had recently ended. Or maybe because the sight of Bermuda's swaying palm trees had put me into such a relaxed state, I felt the whole world, including the U.S. Customs official, would also be relaxed. He would just nod a friendly hello and wave me through to the plane.

When the not-very-relaxed and exceptionally vigilant Customs official looked at my Canadian passport and asked me why I was going to New York and not to Toronto, I told him I would be going home after a brief New York visit. But I had no ticket to show him. He looked at me and simply said, "I don't believe you. You are sneaking into the States."

Was this guy good or what? Even as I began trembling, and fear started driving nails into my stomach, I felt admiration.

He picked up the phone and, a minute later, two uniformed men appeared. They led me through the crowd, every person staring at me, likely thinking I had just been caught doing something wrong, which I had.

The security guards led me into a room crowded with two more uniformed officers and a very large German shepherd, which growled quietly between them, madly wagging its tail, possibly sensing what easy prey I might be. My body was tingling. Adrenaline was kicking in, and I was praying I wouldn't do or say anything stupid.

First, they had me strip down and went ahead quite matter-of-factly with a full body search. No cavity was spared. The dog got up, wanting to sniff around, but thankfully one of the officers pulled it back. Then they let me dress and by that time my luggage had been delivered from cargo.

Two officers began a thorough investigation, questioning me about every vitamin pill and even about the white powder that was baby powder. They seemed fascinated by the fact that I used baby powder.

Then they began the search of my carry-on backpack. After they had gone through a couple of pockets, I suddenly remembered that my wallet was in the backpack and, in my wallet, I had left one bill, my phone bill from my Brooklyn address. If they found it (and they would) they would know that I had been living in the United States. I felt my skin grow prickly and hot.

What happened in the five minutes that followed, I could never have anticipated or planned. The adrenalin just took over and, without any thought at all, I went into action. Imagine that the theme music for *Mission Impossible* is playing. Pushing aside the officer's arm that was searching inside my backpack, I grabbed the wallet from my bag, ran for the door, threw it open (fortunately it was not locked) slammed it shut and began racing through the airport. I didn't know where I was going, but just ran to get as far away as possible from the dog and the men, shoving people aside who were again looking at me as if I were doing something wrong, which I was. The airport had two buildings, so I headed to the second one.

I rounded a corner and saw one of those large podium-style ashtrays filled with sand. Thank God, smoking in airports was still legal. Hearing the dog barking, I rescued some money from my wallet and then frantically dug into the sand, shoving my wallet into the bottom of the collapsing hole. After covering it, I looked up as nonchalantly as possible at the people who were stepping away as they glared at me. I smiled at them. "Bad egg salad sandwich. Had to get rid of it."

That made them step even farther away. Then, sweating, breathing heavily, I began walking back to the interrogation room as if nothing had happened. I didn't have to go far. Rin Tin Tin and *The Wild Bunch* were just around the corner. They grabbed me and led me back to their room.

"What's going on? Why did you run like that?" They were furious.

"I'm really sorry," I answered. "I felt sick to my stomach because of the body search (not untrue) and needed some fresh air."

Thankfully, the company had not yet boarded the plane. With the officers watching, I found Hector and explained to him what had happened. Then I told him where I had buried my wallet and asked him to please dig it up and courier it to me in Toronto. I told him if they asked why we were talking, to say that we were strangers; that he had seen me being led around by the officers and was wondering what was going on. I hoped they would leave him alone. They did.

The head officer walked me to an airline ticket agent. He watched as I exchanged my ticket for one to Toronto. Then he had two of his men follow me to make sure I got on the plane.

Desolate, I watched the company head out towards their plane. An hour later, I was on mine.

A Turning Point I Never Expected

Three days later, hoping to stay below the radar, I took a bus to Montreal, about five hours away, and flew back to New York from there.

Going through customs, I told the usual lie. I was relieved that I had survived and was still filled with wonder at the effects of my adrenaline rush. I was also a wreck. This event, and the pistachio-passport event in Iran, had me suspecting that the Dance Gods might be getting impatient with me. I had ignored them for ages; had taken them for granted. And gods of all stripes do not like being taken for granted. The years with the Ailey Company had gone smoothly, so I had been lulled into leaving my visa situation the way it was. But I realized I had to change my ways. It finally sank in that what I had been doing without a visa was selfish and irresponsible. Back in New York, only a few days after the Bermuda chase and heading out with the company to the familiar Kennedy Center in Washington, D.C., I realized that my capture in Bermuda could have hurt the company, possibly earning it bad publicity and unwanted scrutiny. Aside from that, I could have been deported and sent back to Canada with a criminal record.

These thoughts filled my head before the opening night performance in Washington, distracting me just moments before the curtain went up. I hoped the excitement of the performance would take over and help me forget my misgivings for a couple of hours.

Warming up on stage before the curtain opened, I called upon the Dance Gods and made one more request, hoping to appease them.

Me: "Please hang out with me a little longer. I'll get my visa problem solved. I'll go to a physiotherapist. I will, really. Just let me keep getting lost in the music and movement. I've gotten comfortable with all my problems. It's hard to change."

Dance Gods: "How much more time do you need?"

Me: "I don't know, a little. A day, a month, after the tour."

Dance Gods: "That's not good enough. We want specifics."

Me: "But Brother John's singing the overture. The audience is waiting. I have to focus. Need to stretch out this tight hamstring. Gotta go."

Admittedly, giving the Dance Gods such a quick brush-off, when until recently they had been generous, patient and helpful, was not a great idea.

The music began. Brother John Sellers, accompanied by a blues band, began to sing, "Good morning blues, blues how do you do?" Familiar words and melody took me to another place, to a bar in a hot southern town, a place to dance with muscle and sensuality, to partner women playfully. I was quickly immersed in the collective joy that always arose when the company danced. I felt at home.

The Dance Gods would have to wait.

Act Three

They didn't wait long.

Less than an hour later, during the second intermission, my knees were throbbing. I told our rehearsal director I couldn't dance *Revelations*. He urged me to perform, because readjusting at the last minute would have been troublesome, especially on opening night in a major theatre, when everyone's nerves were on edge. I felt he should have taken me seriously, as he knew I wasn't a quitter and never missed performing. I hadn't, in fact, missed a performance, not one of the more than five hundred, in almost five years. But there wasn't time to argue, so I got ready for Act Three, believing that my predictable adrenaline rush would dull the pain.

But sometimes an injury strikes that is different from all the others. During the last section of *Revelations*, during "Rocka My Soul," when my soul always did rock, my knees collapsed.

At the hospital after the performance, the diagnosis was damage to the knee ligaments, which connect bone to bone and stabilize joints. One doctor confidently recommended immediate surgery; another, equally confident, recommended only rest and physiotherapy. Both said I would have to stay away from dance for a long while and that I might consider the possibility of finding another career. The company headed northwest; I headed home on crutches.

The first communication I had with anyone, and it was to be one of our last, was with the unpredictable Dance Gods. As I lay in bed, they circled me, whispering their harsh judgment, their unforgiving verdict: "We helped you have a career, helped you move in no time at all from unconfident University of Toronto boy to hotshot Ailey dancer-man. Do you think that was easy? We were happy to do it because we believed you had something to offer, not just something to prove. We gave you plenty of time, but you took no steps to make your status legal. You also refused to be kinder to your body. You played the martyr, ignoring your pain and taking drugs, just to get on stage. Yes, you did it because you love dance, but you were also selfish and irresponsible. So now you're down for the count. Only a naïve fool would have held onto that '60s optimism for so long. 'Imagine there's no countries.' Ridiculous! And because you've been reckless, we're outa here. So what will you do now, broken ex-Ailey man, alone in your Brooklyn apartment?"

5

CONTRACTING AND EXPANDING

September 1975 – December 1980

Out of the Whirlwind

The day after my knees said "so long," I was confined to the stillness of my Brooklyn apartment. After living with the daily commotion, dazzle and pressures of the Ailey family, it was shocking to suddenly find myself alone.

My hoped-for magical healing did not happen. I stayed home, going out to shop when the fridge got empty, with my new companions, two oak crutches.

Many times during the day and in wide-eyed moments at night, I'd hear the shared negative words of those two very different doctors concerning my small possibilities of a recovery. It wasn't a matter of just working through pain—that I could have handled. But now it seemed as if all the connective tissue under my kneecaps had dissolved. There was nothing to hold me up.

The company was on tour for two months without me, and doing just fine. Missing shows, knowing that other dancers were filling in for me, was disheartening. I fully realized that no one is irreplaceable. I was determined to try to keep in touch with the ones closest to me.

Mari called from Detroit to report that a newspaper critic there had written in his review that he missed me. The information stroked my deflated ego, at least for a few minutes. A week later, she sent me a letter with a newspaper clipping in it, reporting that a high percentage of people in pain didn't seek emotional help, the result being that they grew tired, depressed and had a diminished quality of life. Subtle, no—but then, what are friends for?

Out of the whirlwind, I thought about my arrival in New York eight years earlier. I had been so pumped up with my passion for dance that everything had seemed possible; but my wildest dreams had not even come close to the high points I had experienced.

I had, of course, been knocked down frequently, making the worst choices regarding my injuries. However, I gave myself credit for something beyond my love for dance: an ongoing and unstoppable commitment to the work.

Like most young dancers, I had believed that I was indestructible. And the ability to persist through any challenge had seemed heroic to me. In dealing with pain, I had gone along with the dance world's conventional wisdom: suck it up. Or, as Peter O'Toole said while portraying the hero of the film *Lawrence of Arabia*, as he snuffed out a burning match between his fingertips: "The trick is not minding that it hurts."

To Dance or Not to Dance

For the first time in many years, I now had time to fill. For years I had been practising and reading about vegetarianism, the environment and animal rights, and had occasionally taken massage workshops. So I wondered if I could be happy being a practitioner in a natural healing discipline.

I began taking courses in nutrition and massage. But I soon lost my enthusiasm for spending evenings listening to lectures or sitting at a desk, hunched over a textbook. Thoughts about performing, being on the tightrope in the arena again, started bubbling up. I longed for the physical exertion, the opportunity for deep emotional expression and, especially, the collective joy. I missed the strokes of approval, too. I fell into sadness, living what I felt to be an emotionally bland, isolated life.

After a month, I exchanged my crutches for a cane. I started physiotherapy, then I began taking elementary dance classes and, around two months later, I went back to an Ailey rehearsal. My body still wasn't ready to dance, but I was going stir crazy and missed being with my friends. Yet again, my needs overwhelmed any common sense I might have had.

I still couldn't climb stairs without pain, but was determined to go directly into rehearsals for a new Ailey work, *Les Mooches*, which Alvin had just started to choreograph. I got by during the first couple of hours of rehearsal, but barely. Then I was asked to step up onto a chair, a prop Alvin was using in the dance. A simple enough move, but my knee wouldn't hold. I just couldn't step up onto that chair.

I spent the rest of the day watching a rehearsal of a large company dance in which, for the first time in five years, I would not be dancing. I had fought valiantly, but the panther in me had lost its prowess, and I couldn't honestly tell anyone that I would ever be able to dance the Ailey way again.

Later, after I had left the company, Alvin told me it had been difficult for him to watch me trying so hard to pretend I was healthy while I suffered through that rehearsal. I have to give him credit. He did wait a long time for me to get better, and I will always appreciate his patience.

The End of the '60s

Back in my apartment, I explored my shelves and cupboards, rarely sorted through during the busy Ailey years. Out of sight at the bottom of drawers and at the end of my closet rack, was clothing that looked familiar, but couldn't possibly have been anything I had ever actually worn. There were bright neon-coloured, tie-dyed T-shirts, wildly flared bellbottoms, a couple of Peter Max-style ties covered with rainbows, and a pile of multi-coloured beads and kerchiefs.

Just for laughs, I put on the loudest T-shirt, tied a bright orange kerchief around my forehead, decorated my wrists and neck with beads, and then took a look in the mirror. I could have been a cartoon character living on the Beatles' "Yellow Submarine." But it had only been a few years earlier that we had all been proud to be so flamboyantly adorned, the clothing identifying us with the free-spirited times that we were certain would go on forever.

Now, especially on my visits to Central Park, I could see that the spirit of the '60s, once a bright spark in a dark time, had largely disintegrated into merely a style, held onto by those possibly too stoned to realize that times had changed, or by younger participants who had been late getting to the party and still wanted to join in the fun.

I stuffed all my hippie clothes into a garbage bag, figuring they were just taking up space and would never be worn again. Then I changed my mind and saved the outfit I had put on.

Disco and the Blues

When I was dancing with the Ailey Company, I heard about "Funk Houses," located out in inner-city Brooklyn. These were big converted warehouse spaces where hundreds of African Americans would dance a style called Funk or Hustle. I had been advised not to visit these clubs, as the only white boy with his own version of the Afro might not be a big hit.

In 1977, however, the film *Saturday Night Fever* brought the Funk-House moves uptown. In the movie, John Travolta plays Tony Manero, a blue-collared disco dance champ in a white polyester suit. My friends and I all watched this picture many times to take in the sweet, crisp dance steps, steps that involved elaborate hand movements, and silky twists and turns. There was '50s Swing in these moves and bits of Salsa, too.

What *Saturday Night Fever* had helped give rise to was the short-lived, culturally transformative phenomenon called disco. And it was disco that helped me get through my post-Ailey blues.

To have fun, we went to disco clubs, including New York, New York with its grey-flannelled walls, and Infinity, where we were served complementary fresh pears. The women wore clothes designed by Halston and Gucci, halter jumpsuits fashioned from figure-moulding Lycra and Spandex. And the men? I can remember with embarrassing clarity dressing in tight stretchy shirts, unbuttoned half way down to show every available hair on my chest (think Tom Selleck). And on my feet? Forget Birkenstocks. I wore burgundy platform shoes.

At these clubs we dance lovers felt at home, because the energy was wild and the dancing furious. I especially needed to let go, to allow my body to find its own way back into movement. And on the dance floor, I had my chance. Listening to Donna Summer and Barbra Streisand emoting through "No More Tears," or Gloria Gaynor belting out "I Shall Survive," with a crowd of people around me jumping and twirling, never failed to fill me once again with joy. My knees limited my prowess, but I indulged as much as possible.

Searching

Getting Involved With Acting

During these disco-dancing times, as my spirits brightened, I decided to take acting classes. Having been told many times that I was a strong dramatic dancer, I thought that performing as an actor might fill more of my life's empty spaces and take me back into the world that I was missing.

I wasn't sure what it meant to study acting, so I read *Respect for Acting* by Uta Hagen and *On Method Acting* by Edward Easty. Method acting was used by many of the film heroes of my generation, actors such as James Dean and Marlon Brando. The technique, in part, entails exploring and using one's past emotional experiences, through structured classroom sensory exercises, to bring truth to a playwright's or screenwriter's words.

I enrolled in a method acting class, taking two four-hour classes a week and participating in many extra-curricular rehearsals. My teacher was the young, passionate, insightful and macho Mr. Terry Schreiber, who has since become the leader of a renowned New York school. When I studied under him, he was running a small studio, located in a basement in Greenwich Village, west of Washington Square Park.

These classes offered me a new way of learning and expressing my creativity; I was a beginner once more. Jeans and T-shirts replaced tights and leotards. The sounds of words spoken with a wide range of feelings replaced the emotional colours of the piano and drums. Yes, I was learning by participating, but I was no longer constantly physical. I was watching and listening more. In these classes, Terry could sense where each of us was holding back emotionally, and he gave us characters to explore that would help bring what we were hiding into view. Method acting, I realized, meant digging in and getting to know oneself.

During my second month at the studio, after having worked on some lighter fare, Terry asked me to perform a scene from a recent play, *Buried Child*, by American actor and playwright Sam Shepard. Engaging and visceral, it explores a fractured family's disillusionment with the American dream. I was to play the role of Bradley, one of two brothers, an aggressive man who has lost a leg in a chainsaw accident, and who feels emasculated.

I had experienced the loss of teeth, but never anything as life changing as the loss of a leg, so I didn't know how to prepare. Terry told me the loss didn't have to be of a body part. It could be anything that had been taken from me that had caused hurt. I immediately remembered my mom finding my saved stories when I was eight and throwing them out. With the help of a female student who sat in a chair opposite me, Terry helped me re-create in my mind my mother's presence: her lilac smell, her raspy voice, the bright colours of her clothing. He then led me down our narrow basement stairs to the storeroom where my stories were hidden.

Twenty-one years ago, when my mother told me she had tossed out my stories, I had barely reacted. Someone watching the two of us would have assumed those stories didn't matter to me at all. But in my acting class, a place where it was safe to explore, I tore up the stairs, found my mother in her kitchen mixing a batch of cinnamon-scented cookies and spoke what really had been on my mind. "Those are my stories. I wrote them," I shouted. "They are not yours. How could you do this?" I kept this feeling alive as Terry led me into the scene from *Buried Child*.

The anger that had tangled up my insides seemed wild in its delight at finally being allowed out into the open.

John Lennon Says It's Okay

Big, warm, nurturing hugs were truly what I had wanted and needed in class after Terry had gotten me to reveal private pieces of myself, hidden territory that was usually not on view. Instead of the hugs, though, facing the class after having been rocked by joy, laughter, anger, grief or tears, I, like everyone else, got a critique of my work!

I recognized that I was participating in an acting class, and I understood the reason for, and value of, being critiqued. It still felt truly bizarre to expose myself, vulnerable and raw as I was, to a room full of mostly strangers, and then listen to them offering their dispassionate evaluations.

In the dance companies I had worked with, I had been challenged to express a wide range of emotions, but now, in acting class, I was being led to reveal specific, highly personal experiences. A much fuller range of feelings poured out of me, making me realize that there was an unknown being deep inside. The experiences of feeling those unfamiliar emotions took me to a place where creating a believable character became less important than under-standing myself.

I was still confused as to why, even after all the confidence-building per-forming, wonderful friendships and several short-lived romantic relationships, I still felt so locked down.

Rehearsing a scene with a classmate at her apartment, I saw on a table a book called *The Primal Scream* by a Dr. Arthur Janov. All I knew about Primal Therapy was that it was one of the "in" therapies of the 1970s, part of the zeit-geist, brought to the public's attention by John Lennon. He had attributed the success of his *Imagine* album to his emotional recovery following only four months of Primal Therapy with Dr. Janov.

My scene partner, who was doing regular sessions with a therapist in Greenwich Village, told me they were helping her to resolve personal issues. I quickly read the book. I learned that the Primal therapist guides the patient to uncover buried childhood pain, the believed source of present personal conflict. The process involves regressing: discovering, exploring and re-experi-encing this pool of pain through sensory work, emotional confrontations and reasoned discussion. This layered journey ultimately leads to understanding and to the demise of the hurt, or at least to the dulling of its sharp edges.

I got the number to my scene partner's clinic and made an appoint-ment with Dr. Arnold Buccheimer, PhD in psychology and professor at Baruch College.

The Most Caring Man

My first impression of Dr. Buccheimer was one of roundness. Physically, everything about him was round. His face was round, his thick eye-glasses were round, and most round of all was his belly. His mind, however, appeared sharp, his perceptions, incisive and his intellect, fierce. The day we met I was nervous: Was this the person I was going to trust and with whom I would share my personal secrets? He told me he had seen me dance many times. Knowing he had knowledge of such a big part of my life helped me feel comfortable.

Dr. Buccheimer used Primal Therapy as one of his tools. During our first session, I noted that his treatment room was lined with mattresses. He encour-aged his patients to express their feelings physically, believing, as Martha

Graham did, that "movement never lies." If I felt like punching or rolling around, I would be free to do so safely.

Dr. Arnold Buccheimer.
Photograph: Kenny Pearl

For several years, every time I managed to put $50 together, I went for a private session. Some friends thought I was nuts, just wasting my money. They showed me magazine articles about the limitations of using techniques involving regression: getting angry just served to escalate, rather than diminish, anger.

Many of the methods Dr. Buccheimer used to encourage expression were similar to those used in my acting class. Their purpose, however, was different. One example: My acting teacher, Terry Schreiber, had helped me express my true childhood feelings toward my mother after she had thrown out my stories. Dr. Buccheimer, after helping me to re-experience the same moment, took me in a different direction.

Dr. B: "I'd like you to go back to your house and visit your eight-year-old self after your Mom has left. Can you see the hurt little you?"

Big Me: "Yes I can. He's expressionless. Just blank. I see him holding on to all the feeling I just let out."

Dr. B: "What do you want to do or say?"

Big Me: "I need to hug him." So I pick up a pillow and hug it. I really do feel in my arms the little me: a wiry, angular boy. He is numb. "You're right to feel so hurt. It's okay to express here what you feel and say what you need to say. Getting angry can be okay."

Little Me: "But my stories must be bad. Why else did she throw them out?"

Dr. B: "Just because she's your mom doesn't mean she's right about everything and you're wrong. What you wrote was beautiful. She didn't even read your stories."

Little Me: "But I want her to like what I do."

Dr. B: "Maybe one day she'll take the time to actually enjoy your creations. Maybe she never will. Don't let that stop you from doing what you love to do. Ask your mother why she did it."

Big Me and Little Me: "Okay, Mom, why did you do it? Those stories were not yours."

Me as Mom: "I grew up in a tiny house with seven siblings. There were piles of old clothes from my father's business everywhere. I saw a dusty binder filled with writing. I thought, 'who needs to keep all this stuff?' I hate clutter! So I threw everything out."

For three years, Dr. Buccheimer watched me act out what are generally considered to be negative emotions without making any judgments. He witnessed my jealousy, selfishness and impatience, accepting everything about me. Gradually, helped by his acceptance, my confidence began to overcome my feelings of doubt and harsh self-judgment. And I came to a few realizations.

My willingness to dance through every injury, even while experiencing horrific pain, was not only the result of my desire to give generously of myself for the good of the group. It also stemmed from my desire to not let my parents "win" the battle—to prevent them, at all cost, from having the chance to say, "We told you so. Dance is the wrong choice." Ironically, choosing to fight through pain, to show my parents that I was in control, had resulted in my losing control, succumbing to injuries that finally did bring my career to my much-feared screeching halt.

As well, I slowly began to come to terms with my parents' rejection of my work. I had always thought that it was *they* who would have to change, that *they* would have to finally realize the error of their non-supportive ways and come to support my decisions. I realized, however, that it was *I*, and not they, who had a better chance of changing and making matters better between us.

How did I come to this realization? I began to see the world through my parents' eyes and accept the reasons why they felt and behaved the way they did. I thought, for example, about the poverty they had endured as children, and their fears that I, too, could suffer from its deprivations. I also recognized that they couldn't easily accept any choices made by me or my sisters that they couldn't understand or control. The unknown made them feel vulnerable. And finally, I saw that they likely would not take up any activities that might lead them to self-discovery and change, such as an expressive art form or therapy.

I hoped that these lessons would help prevent me from carrying out self-destructive behaviour patterns in later life.

Working with Dr. Buccheimer, I also began to understand why I continued to run for cover whenever any of the wonderful women whom I had been crazy about (like Georgia, like Mari), expressed loving feelings for me. A part of the reason was my deeply embedded anxiety that those who loved me would be unkind: that they would negate my accomplishments in the way that my parents had harshly responded to my creativity. I hoped this spark of fresh awareness would lead me towards stability.

For the most part, I booked private sessions with him, but not long after beginning them, I began to take part in more affordable weekly group therapy meetings as well. In these sessions, I became aware that thoughts and feelings that I was uncomfortable with, which I had even felt shame about and which I felt were unique to me, were shared by others. I wasn't the only person, for example, who had difficulty accepting loving feelings or who didn't always feel deserving of his creative accomplishments. I began to feel less isolated.

Initially, I had given myself a year to be miraculously "healed": to feel more deserving of success as a performer, to feel comfortable in a long-term romantic relationship and to resolve peacefully all the issues I had with my parents. (Only that!) I came, however, to understand how difficult change really was and how subtle shifts, not the rare big breakthroughs, were the norm in therapy.

I saw, too, that I slowly grew, not only because of the kind of therapeutic practice I was engaged in, but also because of the healing nature of my therapist. No matter what kind of therapy Dr. Buccheimer had used, his knowledge and caring attitude would have made our sessions effective. Knowing that someone kind and bright was guiding me, who had no personal agenda in relation to me, encouraged trust. This trust, in turn, allowed for risk-taking and for opening up, which led to growth.

Garbage Points the Way

The praise that I had received in my first acting classes made me think I was heading for stardom. I hit the audition trail and quickly came down to earth. Most of the auditions I attended, particularly the non-union ones, were "cattle calls," in which hundreds of hopefuls were rarely given more than a minute to perform a monologue. Often we were just glanced over and instantly dismissed, without the opportunity to speak a single word.

Despite the fierce competition, I did get roles in three well-directed and well-received Off-Off Broadway plays, all performed in small theatres around town. In one of them, I played alongside Jerry Zaks, a future Tony Award-winning director.

One morning, in front of my apartment door, I noticed, along with all the other garbage, a photo of a handsome smiling face looking up out of a box. Taking a closer look, I saw that the box was filled with a foot-high stack of actors' headshots and résumés. A hundred actors were looking up at me through discarded McDonald's wrappers, banana peels and greasy napkins, waiting for the garbage truck. Disposable talent. About to get the toss.

Then, not long after, I went to an audition after seeing a notice that called for men between 5' 10" and 6', with brown hair. When I arrived an hour early, I was given number 387. There were already almost 400 men sitting in the theatre, many of whom, if I squinted tightly enough, could have passed for me.

The experience of seeing so many Kenny look-alikes, as well as the thought of my headshot ending up in a cardboard box awaiting garbage pickup, made me skeptical about cattle calls and got me wondering about other ways to approach my too slowly developing acting career.

Halston and Pearl

Wandering the streets, feeling drained as always after a session of therapy, I suddenly had this peculiar thought: "Why don't you create a cabaret comedy act?"

Though cabaret was wildly popular at the time in New York clubs, my idea surprised me for several reasons: I had never been to a cabaret performance. Also, I was shy in group settings and imagined myself the least funny person in the room. Furthermore, I had always danced the choreography of others and never had thoughts about creating my own work.

I figured my inability to initiate, something I had easily done as a little kid in all my creative activities, might have been rooted in my fear of having that creative activity put down. Lots of artists I knew shared this fear, but could initiate in spite of it, sometimes even because of it. My fear, however, had, up until this point, dominated me and had left me always having to follow the impulses of others.

But the laughs and good feedback I had received doing comedic scene work in acting class had given me some confidence. And, during improvisation sessions, when I was "on the spot," I was able to create humour. As well, I had gained a lot of self-acceptance through Dr. Buccheimer's sessions. So I decided to act on my fantasy.

Blonde, slim and quirky Julie Halston, a fresh grad of the theatre program at Long Island's Hofstra University (and newly married), had recently arrived in acting class. She had the rare ability to move convincingly from dramatic to comedic roles. We all watched, fascinated by how she created a fresh physicality for every character she portrayed, how the quality of her voice changed and how vulnerable she allowed herself to be. After sitting down for a meal with her, hearing her hilarious stories about events that would have been mundane without her keen observations, wit and spontaneity, I became convinced that she was the one to help create what we would soon call "The Act."

We rehearsed at my place, three or four days a week for several months, whenever our free times overlapped. We improvised, choosing different settings, situations and characters as starting points. Our skits were mainly character driven, not wild and wacky. They featured the dilemmas people find themselves in when they pretend to be something they're not. In one skit, two "tough" New Jersey teens flirt on a subway:

Vince: "Joanne, I can tell you really like me."

Joanne: "Oh yeah, how do you know that?"

Vince: "I happen to be very septic."

We came up with a dozen skits and eventually auditioned for a well-known club called Tramps, and were accepted for a single show. That night, the room was packed with our laughing, cheering friends and, unbeknown to us, a cabaret producer scouting for fresh talent. He offered to help, and soon had us performing in two other downtown venues. During one show, we shared the bill with future Broadway sensation Nathan Lane, and his partner, Patrick Stack. Then, through our acting teacher, Terry, we auditioned for an award-winning comedy writer, who volunteered to do some directing. Soon after, we produced our own show, *Halston and Pearl* in *An Evening of Dilemmas,* at a small theatre in Greenwich Village. Our act was featured favourably in one of those clever *Village Voice* cartoons, and we received a great review.

Over a six-month period of performing, the full houses, big laughs and generous applause encouraged us. We began to talk about shaping a play out of some of the characters that we had grown to love. [55]

PHOTO BY AMANDA KREGLOW

WEST BANK

HALSTON & PEARL

IN

AN EVENING OF DILEMMAS

COMEDY ENTERTAINMENT

FEATURING:
SUBWAY LOVE
MOTHER KNOWS BEST
FIRST KISS, 50'S STYLE

THURS. AT 11:00
AUG. 9, 16, 23, 30
$4 COVER $4 MIN.

RESERVATIONS SUGGESTED

CAFE
On Theatre Row
407 West 42nd Street
New York, New York
695 6909

Photograph: Amanda Kreglow

The Secret of a Recipe or a Dance Studio

Therapy, physiotherapy, acting classes and "The Act" were all happening at once. Life was expensive but I didn't want to cut out anything. So, although it seemed like I was returning to my Under the Table Agency housecleaning activities, I took a job as a waiter at The Cauldron, a kosher macrobiotic restaurant, the first of its kind in North America, perhaps the world. It was run by a Hassidic Jewish couple, Gloria and Marty. Located on East 6th Street, it was the East Village successor to the Paradox. However, in 1976, with the hippie era over, there were no communal tables. During the week, not-so-stoned artists and students filled the neat booths; but on Sundays, the place was packed with Hassidic Jews. I was intrigued by the families in their black suits and dresses, whom I always associated with chicken soup and bagels, figuring out chopstick co-ordination to chow down on plates of kosher tempura.

After having danced around the world with the Ailey Company, spending days and nights walking on hard floors, with bad knees, and waxing eloquent about the virtues of seaweed and kidney beans, I felt a little disheartened, but did what I had to do to pay the bills. Of course, I also ate very well.

After a month, the owners asked me to train as a chef. I accepted. The food was delicious, and I longed to know the secret of their pink but tomatoless salad dressing (they used beets). With the bigger salary, I would be able to cover all my expenses. As an aspiring cabaret performer and a soon-to-be New York chef, I would once more be living the romantic and dramatic New York life.

So it was interesting timing when, two days later, I suddenly got a call from the Ailey organization telling me that Alvin wanted me to teach at his new school, the American Dance Center, which he was co-directing with Pearl Lang. It felt great to know that he was still thinking about me.

I was interested but skeptical. I couldn't be both chef and teacher as the schedules conflicted. Also, the full-time chef salary would give me more income than the few dance classes could provide; and my knees were still shaky. My response to the caller was, "Sorry, I can't do it."

However, a week after being invited, I was back on East 59th Street, teaching my first class at the American Dance Center.

Starting Out as a New York City Teacher

A Rare Audition

Alvin had asked me to teach the Graham technique three times a week. Walking into the studio for the first class, I was elated, and soon it was clear that I could do extra classes, as long as I made adjustments to accommodate my knees. If I took on more, I would be able to stop being a waiter at The Cauldron. But the school, then just the seed of what it is today, could not offer me more teaching hours. I had to supplement my income by teaching somewhere else.

I took a stroll exactly four blocks north to the temple of the pelvis, the Graham School, to apply for a teaching position. This was a few years after my studio reunion with Ms. Graham. Teachers there at the time were all former or present company members, so I felt my request was reasonable. But Ron Protas, Ms. Graham's assistant, gave me a flat "No."

I heard soon through the grapevine that he hadn't wanted me to teach because he felt I would denigrate the purity of the technique with a lot of Ailey moves. He was partially right. I knew I would of course teach Ms. Graham's floorwork as faithfully as I could. The floorwork, which constituted the first third of class, contained the building blocks of her technique. But guided by the classes of my former mentor Donald McKayle, I did plan on breaking away from traditional Graham movement patterns once the dancers were moving across the floor. The movement would be based upon Graham principles, but would also be influenced by all the choreographers and dancers who had positively affected me.

During the next year, I taught for Alvin and picked up some classes at the High School of Performing Arts (now LaGuardia High). This was the school that would soon inspire both the film and the TV series *Fame* and that my friends Mari and Hector had attended. Around that time, a former teacher, Kazuko Hirabayashi, took over as the Graham School's director. She knew my dancing, and was the person who pushed for me to teach there.

But even after her recommendation, Mr. Protas, who made the final decisions, was still reluctant. Finally, somehow, he gave an inch. For the first time in the history of the school, a prospective teacher was going to have to do a teaching audition, with Martha Graham as a jury of one!

A few days later, surprisingly calm, I stood beside Ms. Graham, about to begin teaching an elementary class of twenty dancers. She sat on her director's chair, kimono clad, black hair pulled back tightly, cheekbones still flaring, looking as formidable as when I had taken my first class with her nine years earlier.

As class proceeded, I fully expected Ms. Graham to interrupt to impart words of wisdom, or to shock a student with an utterance of how he or she did not have the passion to be a dancer. That was her style, Clytemnestra on her throne. But she remained quiet. In all my years at the school and in the company, I had never experienced her being silent for such a long time.

So I taught, not getting too complicated, as these were beginners. Ms. Graham's presence did not make me shy. I taught the way I felt was right for the moment, demonstrating the movement I had planned, speaking about the technique and giving corrections. Because she remained so quiet, I kept glancing over to see if she had fallen asleep. But she sat upright and alert, taking in every student, and every word I was saying.

At home a few nights later, the phone rang. It was a member of the Graham School's Board of Directors. Sweaty palms time. "We had a meeting last night," she began. "Ms. Graham told us you taught with a great sense of truth and reality and she wants you to teach as many classes as possible."

How bizarre and wonderful! The last time Ms. Graham had talked to her board about me, she had told them I had tried to blackmail her into giving me big roles.

In many classes since, when I have felt my words not connecting and my movement phrases a shambles, the memory of that one sentence from one of my heroes has given me courage.

A Reference Letter I Couldn't Write

A few days later, I began teaching twelve classes a week, and it was truly awesome to stand at the front of the studio, in the same place as the great teachers who had taught me, and look out at twenty hopeful dancers.

My new schedule was challenging for several reasons. First, it was physically demanding for a modern teacher who doesn't just indicate movement, but demonstrates full out throughout most of each and every class. As well, it was creatively demanding. Before my New York teaching began, I had mainly experienced being a guest teacher for Ailey while on tour. And teaching a single class as a guest teacher is a "honeymoon" experience: you're fresh and mysterious to your students. You can enjoy the buzz of teaching one exciting class, without having to worry about developing in a group of students the technique and aesthetic qualities that require nurturing over a sustained period of time. Now, I felt the pressures of my new responsibility, and worked hard to prepare classes that I hoped would excite, challenge and instruct the dancers over many months.

Meanwhile, my knees got stronger. I was able, along with ice, physiotherapy, a knee support and Pilates, to manage the short bursts of activity that were required to demonstrate movement.

I loved every group of dancers I taught. In spite of the odd dark cloud, there was always an abundance of potential, energy, spirit and beauty in every class. These were young adults setting out on a journey. I felt privileged to have been chosen as one of their guides.

At the beginning of my teaching career, I felt some fear. My students were counting on me to help lead them towards their artistic goals and, in dance, there is so little time to attain them. So, I thought about dancers I had admired: Mari, Linda, Powell, Bertram, Cohan and so many more. And I tried to understand the qualities that made them special. How did they sustain or attack movement? How did they direct their energy? How were they able to communicate their power beyond the stage's footlights? How did they manage to stay alive in their stillness? To use a little to say a lot? These were some of the questions I considered. The slowly emerging answers became the core of my teaching.

Despite my initial fears, I felt from the start that I was teaching well. I tried to be extra supportive: I had not wanted to damage the confidence of my students the way my parents had done through their lack of recognition. But before class one night, a young woman asked if I could write her a reference letter for an audition she was planning to attend. I said "sure," but the blank look on my face must have broadcast something peculiar. I really had no impressions whatsoever of how she danced.

I asked her how often she had been taking my class. She surprised me by saying, "Three times a week for the past two months."

Despite the many hours spent together, I knew I was totally incapable of writing her the letter she wanted.

I looked at the twenty other dancers who were preparing to take class. I had strong impressions of most. But there were several whose dancing I could only vaguely visualize. And I realized, as class began, that my eyes kept wandering, seemingly out of control, to a half-dozen students, both men and women, whom I felt were the most talented and the most beautiful. I realized they were the ones whom I had encouraged nearly all the time.

The mystery was solved. I hadn't noticed the dancer who wanted a reference because she did not stand out to me. Even though she worked hard, showed up regularly and paid the same for class as all those I had unconsciously favoured with my attention, I had ignored her.

In that moment, I knew that I may have been capable of teaching an exciting class, but I had not been a fair teacher; I had not treated each hardworking student equally.

That was the day my teaching began to change.

Obviously, my first challenge was to pull my attention away from the most talented students and spread it around the room. After a while, I started noticing how those I had once ignored began growing in confidence, and how that confidence began affecting favourably the quality of their work, helping them to open up and give more.

I realized that no one is "a lost cause." I knew dancers who had been told they weren't going to dance and then went on to have big careers. I remembered how I had felt when I was looked over in many of my Toronto ballet classes as the awkward latecomer, all attention going to the favoured nine-year-olds.

Even if a student chooses not to dance, skills learned in class are highly transferable: how to work with great effort for a designated time, complete tasks, take direction well. Who is to say that time spent with the unlikely one isn't as important as the time spent with the "obvious" talent?

In the course of my teaching, I saw that, in fact, most aspiring young dancers did not fulfill their dreams of dancing professionally. The reasons were many: there were relatively few paying positions available; they never met a choreographer they were suited to; they got injured; they lost patience, interest, hope; or they wanted stability. On their behalf I also began to think about life beyond the walls of the studios and stages.

Teaching thus became the act of doing my best to empower young people to take charge of their lives, to feel good about themselves, to experience confidence, so that no matter what they chose to do in life, the dance class would have served them well. It would not be a place where they "failed" because they did not become one of the few who found a place in the profession.

It was largely through dance that I still projected myself into the world, so, in the beginning of my teaching career, I still felt the need to be the "star." It didn't take me long to realize that real teaching involves a collaboration between student and teacher, and is based on mutual trust and respect. I also came to recognize that one teacher cannot teach everything, and I had to leave it to different teachers, gifted in other areas, to do what I couldn't.

The Life and Death of a Loft

Roger

After and Before
During these teaching years, I got lucky.

On a dance studio bulletin board, a place from which good things often happen, I read a notice about a loft for rent. The rent was a miracle, even in 1975. The ad read: "West 26th St. loft with 2,500 sq. feet of renovated space, including a dance studio. $300/month, including heat. Call Roger (architect)."

At $300 a month, I figured it couldn't have been in very good shape, but I decided to take a look anyway.

The next afternoon, with our appointment set up for 2:00, I waited for Roger outside the building on 26th Street. This address was just south of Madison Square Garden and west of New York City's Flower District.

At 2:30, still waiting, I reached into my pocket to find some change. I wanted to be ready to help the dishevelled street guy, matted curls hanging over his forehead, shopping bags slung over his wrists, who was careening on the edge of the curb, almost falling in my direction. It was a warm spring day, but he was wearing layers of decomposing clothing, probably everything he owned. He was his own suitcase. When he stuck his arm out, I handed him the money.

"How the hell are you?" he shouted. The syrupy smell of alcohol wafting towards me with his exaggerated "h" sounds had me backing up a step. But he shot out his arm at me once more.

"I'm sorry," I said. "I don't have any more to spare. Really. I'm just waiting for someone."

"I know. I'm Roger," he stammered. "How are you?"

He pulled me into the building and inside an old industrial elevator. He grimaced, studying the buttons, and jabbed number 6. The heavy door shuddered to a close and with a jolt, the elevator lumbered upwards.

Arriving, I pushed open another challenging door. I couldn't believe what I saw. Stretched out in front of us was a beautiful dance studio with a golden oak floor reflecting the afternoon light.

Roger announced, "My former beautiful wife was one hell of a good dance teacher. Taught here for seven years."

The studio was roughly sixty feet long and twenty feet wide, with four tall windows set in the long wall to my left, and a row of mirrors positioned along the wall to my right. Walking onto the floor, I could feel right away that the oak floorboards had been laid on widely spaced beams, so there was lots of air-space beneath them. This is the hallmark of a "sprung" floor, the kind of floor that makes for softer landings when a dancer jumps on it. Even walking on a sprung floor reduces strain on a dancer's joints.

We walked across the studio and continued for a few feet down a narrow passageway under a very low ceiling. Navigating around a ladder, I stepped into a room at least fifteen feet high and twenty feet square.

In the middle of Manhattan, Roger had created a country kitchen. Wide planks of grainy wood lined the floor. Wooden shelves, which ran along two of the walls, were three inches thick, some almost twenty feet long. They were suspended from the ceiling with thick rope, creating a feeling of both solidity and lightness. The kitchen's crowning touch was a cast iron, antique, wood-burning stove. Across from it was a ladder, leading up to a sleeping loft.

As he stacked the fridge with bottles of beer from his shopping bags, Roger grinned, revealing two unruly rows of yellow teeth. "Hell, I could use a couple of these. I'm thinking too clearly." He then chugged back a Schlitz of Milwaukee.

"Just look at the rest of the loft so we can go, okay? I don't live here anymore. Can't stand the place."

I walked up three steps that led to a small, enclosed dining nook. In it was a wooden table, with a bench on either side. Beside the table was a window that opened onto a little screened-in platform, a sun deck for a cat or small dog.

"That's it. Les go," Roger slurred, as he finished off another beer.

I held onto him as we headed back across the dance floor and into the elevator. Just as I was about to press the button, he interrupted, "Wait, I forgot to show you the rest of the loft." He pointed to the right. "I'm 'stayin' here," he mumbled, his body folding in on itself.

I was surprised to see that, after leaving the elevator and turning right, there was another large room with four tall windows. Eight stairs led up to a second loft bed. Under it were bookshelves and a long desk upon which three photographs lay scattered. The one face-up was a picture of a Siamese cat lying on the little deck outside the kitchen window.

Then there was a thud.

I grabbed the pictures and ran to the elevator. Roger was lying in a heap. As I helped him up and into the elevator, he saw the pictures in my hand and grabbed them. His body unfolded. Surprisingly erect, his mouth hanging open, he just stared at one for a few seconds. "You keep 'em," he said abruptly, shoving them back into my hand.

On the street, I waved down a cab and gave him $10. "This is to take you home. Get some sleep."

I examined the photographs. Under the cat picture was one of the building that I was standing beside. The third was the one that must have hypnotized him. In it, a beautiful man and woman, maybe twenty-five years old, stood in front of one of those giant west coast trees, arms tightly wrapped around each other. With their long blonde hair decorated with love beads and their smiling tanned faces, they looked like poster people for flower power. They were perfect.

Key Money

Renting a renovated loft in New York was tricky. The $300 a month rent was a bargain for the beautiful space that Roger had created. Many had been interested. So why had I been the one lucky enough to get it?

The simple answer is: I came up with $10,000. Yup, $10,000 up front, which was meant to cover the cost of the conversion of the formerly bare warehouse into a beautiful living and working space. The upfront money was called "key money," the cost of getting the key. When I left the space, the next renter was supposed to pay at least $10,000 to me, so I would have my costs cancelled. Roger was conscious enough the day after we had met to strike a deal, giving me ten days to come up with the total amount.

People think I'm crazy when I tell them I got the loft because of my vegetarian diet. But it's true. The $3,000 savings I had in the bank were there largely because, for years, I had saved money cooking in my room during Ailey tours. The bank wouldn't give me a loan to cover the rest, so I appealed to friends who had some extra bucks, hoping I could reach the total in bits and pieces. I figured that, if I could rent the studio to various dance companies and teachers, offering them an appealing, lowest-in-the-city rent of $3 an hour, I could make back the missing $7,000 in five years (the length of the lease), and pay everyone back with a little interest.

Only hours before Roger's deadline, after ten days of phoning and running around the city, I handed him the cheque. Then I immediately got the word out, tacking rental notices up on the bulletin boards of all the city's dance studios, places from which good things often happened, and waited.

Loft Fulfilment

Getting It Right

Offering the space for $3 an hour, I didn't wait long for friends and strangers to begin calling. Soon, the loft was filled with sound and movement, day and night.

The space became known as, simply, "The 26th Street Studio." Its warm and bright open space was inviting. One dance company, Bowyer and Bruggeman, named after its founders, Bob and Joanne, rented it for most of its available hours. Bob, the choreographer, was from Hollywood, California, and was as subtle as a shoulder-length pair of rhinestone earrings purchased on Rodeo Drive. His wild and wonderful dances were satirical, wickedly funny take-offs on dance styles and choreographers. The space also accommodated modern and folk dance classes, rehearsals by other choreographers, as well as juggling and massage workshops. I had been afraid that the constant traffic, with music and voices booming at all hours, would drive me nuts. But I liked all the people involved and felt good having so many creative spirits around. Julie and I also rehearsed our act there. As well, I used the space to work out and to prepare movement for my classes.

And we had some amazing parties. Every Christmas, I set up a tall tree and hosted celebrations for all the out-of-town people I knew, who, like myself, didn't go home for the holidays. More than a hundred dancers and actors regularly showed up to dance to the rock music played by a friend's band. Dozens of candles brought out the warmth of the oak floors, and long picnic tables barely supported the weight of the exotic platters of food that beautiful people from a dozen countries prepared. After seeing everyone mainly in classes, it was wonderful to have the chance to see all of them dressed up and relaxed.

One of the most appealing features of the loft was the garden that I created on its roof. I had picked up my love for flowers as a kid playing in my mom's garden at our Toronto home, and I had wanted for years to have a garden in New York. With the roof only a short flight of stairs away, I finally had my chance. So, for years, I regularly explored the Flower District, just a few blocks away and collected dozens of garbage-bound pots, which were filled with hundreds of pounds of soil, and discarded three foot square loading platforms, the latter of which I used to create the floor and pathways. A lush oasis of peace gradually emerged, about 800 square feet in size.

My garden was not subtle. There were five rose bushes coloured pink, orange and red, lots of purple and pink petunias, yellow and orange zinnias, sunflowers and marigolds, blue morning glories and lobelia, lilac and blueberry bushes, and a very pampered rhododendron.

Besides Central Park, this roof garden was an outdoor place of escape for Julie and me, as well as for Bob and Joanne and their company. Lounging on deck chairs after rehearsals, we were always calmed by the expansive views of West Side Manhattan. The calm, however, always led to hysterical laughter:

Bob and Julie were the two funniest people I had ever met, and no politician, entertainer, choreographer or teacher was spared their penetrating wit.

Up on the Roof

Bob Bowyer (top)
Marianne Claire, Scott Bryant, Joanne Bruggeman

Wendi and Paul Bonder, my sister and brother-in-law.
Photographs: Kenny Pearl

While I was enjoying some of my best Manhattan times, the rental fees that I was earning were slowly adding up. In 1979, less than four years after I had paid Roger the "key money," and more than a year ahead of schedule, I had made back more than the $10,000, enough to pay back all my friends with interest.

Fighting to Keep Our Home

My situation would have been perfect; in 1978, however, the building was sold. Our new landlord, Michael Sandler (we called him Sandler), wanted the whole place for himself. He immediately evicted the three tenants who had used their lofts only for work: a moving company, a furrier and a clothing manufacturer. As businesses without long-term leases, they had no legal claim to stay in the building. The two other renters and I received only eviction notices, as we each had five-year leases and lived in the building.

Judy, the artist on the third floor, had a boyfriend who was a lawyer. He told us that the residential loft situation in our part of the city was a recent phenomenon. But certain precedents had been set in earlier eviction cases. If we went to court and proved that half the floors in a warehouse building, one traditionally reserved for businesses, were permanently occupied by tenants who had signed contracts to live there, we could stay. We all had leases that ended in 1980. So Judy, Katherine (the potter on the fourth floor) and I got together and decided that we would fight.

We contacted a young hotshot tenant lawyer, Peter Goldstein, whom I had read about in *The Village Voice* newspaper. He had earned a reputation defending desperate cases.

Before taking up arms, however, I accepted an invitation from Sandler to meet with him in his Park Avenue apartment. He greeted me with a smile, wearing an immaculately tailored suit. If money were power, he was letting me know that he had it and that I, in my standard not-recently-washed jeans and T-shirt, didn't.

He led me into a room with a gloomy "manly" decor. Dark walnut panelling rose halfway up the wall to meet green paisley wallpaper upon which hung amber-toned paintings of racehorses, and heavily framed photos of Sandler and his buddies, paunchy guys with fat faces holding up big fish beside a monstrous yacht. Standing in front of me, Sandler pulled a cigar out of a case: "You want one? They're Cuban."

I declined.

He then sat back in his black leather armchair and stared down at me. Sitting on a low bench, I felt like a toad on a toadstool. I felt knots tightening in my stomach; I began to sweat.

He paused before striking, enjoying my obvious discomfort. "I love the smell of these beauties. How about you?" he asked, carefully puffing smoke into my face.

"Yeah they're great," I answered, fighting back a cough.

"Listen, Kenny," he began, biting hard on his slowly diminishing prop. "I like you a lot, more than those bitches that are trespassing in my building."

"You mean Judy and Katherine, right?" I asked, emphasizing their names. "I don't believe we're trespassing. That's why we want to go to court."

"To court?" he laughed. "We're not going to court and I'll tell you why."

I felt the spring snap on the trap he had been setting.

"We're not going because I'm about to offer you money, a lot of money, to pack your bags and get out of there."

"How much are you offering here?" I asked.

"I'm going to give you $15,000. Cash. You'll have it tomorrow. Get out by the weekend and I'll take care of the girls."

It was a lot of money, especially since I had already made back my key money. "What happens if I don't take the money?"

"Then you're screwed."

"If you offer Judy, Katherine and myself $10,000 each, then I think we'll all agree to leave our places."

"*Your* places? What do you mean *your* places?"

"They're ours as far as I understand, until a judge tells us we have to leave."

"Well, I'm the judge here and I just told you when to leave." He was shouting now, punctuating his words with jabs of his cigar aimed at my heart.

"You little prick, I'm offering you good money. Take it before I make your life hell."

My anger took over my fear: "Mr. Sandler, I will not desert my friends. I'm tired of rich guys like you with their big dollars pushing artists out of their homes all over this city. It stops here. We will fight you in court until we win, because you are wrong and we are right."

He looked stunned. Before he could recover and perhaps do something to make my life hell, I walked quickly from the room, down the hallway and out the door.

Moments with Ms. Graham

More Inspiration

While precariously living in and overseeing the 26th Street Studio, I was also keeping up my teaching. And during this time an interesting pattern developed: Ms. Graham began telephoning me at home to ask when I was teaching, and she would show up at my classes regularly, often remaining for the entire hour and a half. We got along well.

Her presence was a gift to all of us because she would often break in and speak about dance and theatre, illuminating her remarks with images from the Bible, the Greek epics and other works of literature. She liked quoting T.S. Eliot, speaking about the "simplicity costing not less than everything," when describing the intense work it took to choreograph a good piece, or to dance well. One day, while speaking about the evolution of her technique, she leaned towards me and whispered confidentially, "Kenny, I only steal from the best."

Her own sayings, especially the short aphoristic ones, most of which I had heard her express numerous times, and many of which are well known today, flashed like lightning to cut through any confusion: "The only sin is mediocrity;" "The body is a sacred garment;" "First we have to believe and then we believe;" "The body never lies;" "Misery is a communicable disease;" "You are unique, and if that is not fulfilled, then something has been lost;" "Great dancers are not great because of their technique, they are great because of their passion."

Being Clytemnestra One Last Time

One night, when I was teaching a beginners' class, Ms. Graham appeared along with an attractive young woman. I was surprised to see her, as she usually didn't show up at beginners' classes. "Kenny," she proclaimed in her most bombastic, theatrical voice, "I'd like you to meet Cecilia Peck, the daughter of Gregory

Peck, the famous actor, whom I once taught, you know, at the Neighborhood Playhouse, along with Bette Davis."

Yes, we all knew he was a famous actor; and yes, we knew she had once taught him along with actor Bette Davis. It was clear that she was trying to impress everyone by dropping names and that made me nervous about what might be coming next.

Apparently, Mr. Peck had told his daughter about a sequence of movements that had impressed him, which were sometimes done in more advanced classes. The sequence involved a number of falls, during which the dancer began standing upright, and then enacted a variety of moves, descending to the floor and, finally, rising to finish. The falls were done at different speeds, with the first one being quite leisurely, and the final one, almost impossibly quick, challenging the dancer to move down and up through eight different shapes on two slow counts.

Even though the dancers in my class were at least two years of steady work away from being able to accomplish that sequence, Ms. Graham was determined to have them show Ms. Peck what her father had talked about. I explained quietly to Ms. Graham that these beginning dancers had no idea how to do the fall, but she insisted. I said I would do them myself, but no, the class had to perform.

So I demonstrated the quick fall reasonably well for the dancers. Then Ms. Graham ordered the twenty beginners in class to repeat exactly what I'd done. Of course everyone was too intimidated not to try, and so, with looks of terror on every face, including mine, they got ready as Ms. Graham gave the pianist his cue.

Imagine the moment when fishermen bring up their nets filled with live fish and dump them on the deck of their boat. The fish, for the first time ever out of the water, bounce off the deck, flailing, bumping into each other, and finally just lie there helplessly, twitching uncontrollably. That was what we watched as twenty beginners tried desperately to do the fall on two counts.

After a pause, during which no one breathed, our audience of two turned to me looking horrified. After all, I was the teacher and how could I possibly have taught these students so badly? To save face, Ms. Graham left the young dancers with parting words of "encouragement" that went something like:

"You're all either stupid or you belong in an insane asylum." Then she and Ms. Peck made their exit.

I tried to explain to the dancers, who were still lying in a heap on the floor, too devastated to get up, what had happened. To their credit, they all came back to class the next night.

The patient Ms. Graham, the one who usually showed up, was sitting beside me again soon, and never asked beginners again for "The Fall."

Rising From the Ashes

Ms. Graham's temper was legendary. She often said, "I was a heller!" I believed she needed to hurl down bolts of lightning every now and then at those who displeased her to remind herself that she was still powerful. Maybe the occasional outburst helped dull the pain of her arthritis as well. I think Ms. Graham felt that her searing criticism was good for dancers, inspiring them to do their best. She believed in the survival of the fittest; no runts in her camp. Her victims did not protest. Everyone wanted to remain in her orbit and would fight through tears to keep open the possibility of being chosen to perform in her work.

However, since her near-death experience, she had become not only kinder and gentler, but also creaky and fragile: she struggled getting up from her chair and shook while bringing a cup of tea to her lips. She must have had help at home, because she continued to show up dressed neatly, hair always set in place with theatrical hair clips, makeup still dramatic enough to remind everyone that she had once embodied Jocasta, Medea and Joan of Arc.

After classes, she always retired to the company teachers' lounge, where she could relax before going back into the studio for a company rehearsal. I often went back with her to make her ritual cup of tea.

During this period of shuffling and quivering, when her creative prowess was nowhere near as formidable as it had been twenty-five years earlier, her fame grew. More than her great body of work, more than the fact that she had broken barriers by giving women in dance a humane, passionate voice, it was perhaps her defiance, her ability to survive against all the odds, that captured peoples' imagination. Her near-death experience, after drinking herself into a coma following her final performance in 1970 and, then, her miraculous recovery and return to her simple chair at the front of her studio were the events that, more than anything, elevated her standing to that of celebrity.

The rich and famous came calling: fashion designer Halston and dance star Mikhail Baryshnikov. The singer and actor Liza Minnelli rehearsed her stage act in one of Ms. Graham's studios and was featured as the narrator in a new work, *The Owl and the Pussycat*. Film stars Woody Allen and Diane Keaton dropped by; a closing scene from *Annie Hall* was shot in Studio One. Around this time, Ms. Graham also created a new work, *Lucifer*, for ballet stars Rudolf Nureyev and Margot Fonteyn. I watched her coaching an eager and adoring Nureyev one afternoon. He brought out the nervous, star-struck teenager in her, which was lovely to see.

And, just in case anyone in the dance world hadn't yet noticed the now risen-from-the-ashes Martha Graham, in 1976, a glamorous and memorable Blackglama photo ad appeared in *Vogue* magazine. Ms. Graham appeared on one side of the ad with Mr. Nureyev and Ms. Fonteyn on the other, all dressed in black mink. Ms. Graham's hair shines, jet black. Her shoulders are dropped, revealing an elegant neck, and her cheekbones jutted more emphatically than ever. Makeup, lighting and airbrushing took care of the wrinkles. She was eighty-two but looked fifty-two. Dance's Joan Crawford. Tagging the photo was the ad's famous line: "What becomes a legend most?"

Ms. Graham certainly tackled some fierce personal demons to reconcile herself to the fact that she would never dance again, so that she could resume being Martha Graham, diva, and more than ever, a cultural icon. Although none of her later dances revealed her to be at her creative peak, many of them, such as *Acts of Light* and *Maple Leaf Rag*, still remain in the company repertoire.

She said many times, "The centre of the stage is where I am." With a literally death-defying willpower and determination, she made it clear that it was going to take a lot more than illness, pain, age and a coma to keep her away from her studio.

During her early years of presenting her work, some audience members had booed her, thrown rotten fruit at the stage, called her work ugly and hateful and criticized every ground-breaking idea she had courageously realized. An artist who rarely compromised, she broke with traditions, survived the critics who mocked her and lived thirty years longer than people thought she would, choreographing for seventy years.

In the late '70s, fifty years of devotion later, she was having the last laugh. After each of her company's performances, when the dancers had finished their bows, she emerged from the wings and shuffled back to the place she missed, centre stage, and took a slow bow before wildly cheering audiences. Once considered a pariah, she was hailed as a legend.

My own most moving memory of Martha Graham is this: I have finished teaching class, one she has attended. The dancers have all gone. I am kneeling down in front of her to help her change from her studio slippers to her street shoes. With her tiny arthritically contracted hand resting on my shoulder, she is repeating, over and over again, "Thank you, thank you," her deep resonant voice reduced to a whisper.

April

And She Was Cute

April was a student at Merce Cunningham's school who worked as a server at a vegetarian restaurant that I visited frequently. A theatre graduate, she had recently fallen in love with dance. She was talented, funny and cute. Her eyes were an unexpected pale blue; shoulder-length red hair and pale Irish skin made me think that when summer came, there would be freckles. We began talking and joking around as she carried trays of steaming stir-fries to my table. I told her I lived in a loft with a dance studio that I rented out cheaply.

After booking it a few times to work on her choreography, she approached me one day, accompanied by her boyfriend, who looked like George Harrison. She explained, "Aaron's an actor and he's going on tour for ten weeks. We can't afford to keep paying big rent, so how'd you feel if I slept in that space over the kitchen while he's away? When he gets back we'll find a new place. I can afford $100 a month."

April was smart, seemed responsible and made me laugh. She would be good company. Also, on a dance teacher's salary, putting as much money as

I could into acting classes and therapy, it would be great to have help with the rent.

And she was cute.

Another Innocent Coming Together Bites the Dust

April moved in and slept in the loft space above the country kitchen. We became great friends quickly, talking about dance, laughing a lot, making meals together and going out once in a while for dinners, performances and movies. A month into her ten-week stay, I was already feeling sad that she would be leaving soon. My heart began beating a little faster whenever she appeared, and I found myself wishing she didn't have a soon-to-be returning boyfriend. But I kept my feelings for her to myself, determined to do nothing to jeopardize her relationship with Aaron.

She worked late at the restaurant and was always sleeping just above me as I quietly ate breakfast before heading out to teach morning class.

One morning, however, I was sitting in the kitchen nook finishing my oatmeal. My cat Coconut was, just as always, sitting in the square of morning light on the bench across the table from me. Looking up, a distance of about twelve feet from where I sat, I suddenly saw April climbing down the ladder. She liked climbing down, not in the usual way, facing toward the ladder, but with her back to it, gripping it behind her. She said she felt more secure seeing where she was going. I'd seen her climbing down many times. However this time, north of her pyjama pants, she wore nothing and, like a figurine carved into the prow of an ancient ship, her stunning naked torso reached out towards me and shouted good-morning.

I lost the grip on my spoon, which bounced off the edge of my bowl and rattled to the floor. Coconut jumped down to investigate and I followed.

"Hi," she yawned as she headed for the bathroom on automatic pilot.

I looked up from under the table to make my attempt at a casual "Good morning," but forgetting the location of my head, whacked it on the bottom of the table and, tipping it slightly, sent the oatmeal bowl clattering onto the floor.

By the time Coconut and I were back on our benches, April was already up on the top rung of the ladder. "Are you always this noisy in the morning?" she asked with a chuckle as she disappeared over the top.

The Honourable Thing to Do

Two months went by and boyfriend Aaron's return was two weeks away. Each morning, a topless April descended the ladder as I ate my oatmeal. I could have changed places with Coconut so that I wouldn't see her, but I wasn't that monk-like. I thought of little else but April all day. Eyes open or closed, I saw her beauty floating in front of me. I lay hopelessly awake every night and became so tired that, one day, I fell asleep on the subway, missed my stop and was late for class.

I couldn't decide whether April was trying to send a signal to me, or was just relaxed about nudity. I debated making a move: I liked boyfriend Aaron, and the thought of hurting him made me wonder what kind of person I really was. I decided not to think about that. Then the thought that April might respond in the affirmative made me question what kind of person she really was. I decided not to think about that, too.

Finally, honour broke away from its short leash; one morning as she climbed back up the ladder, I asked, "April, can I come up?"

Fun in the Sun

She broke up with Aaron. On summer weekends we headed off on the train to play in the waves at Jones Beach on Long Island, not far from Manhattan. Because the days at the beach were so much fun, we decided to save our money and, when winter came, head south for a beach holiday. A friend of mine recommended going to Key West, the end of a chain of little islands off the southern tip of Florida. He even recommended a guest house, run by a fun guy named Brent.

In Key West

Winter came and we took off according to plan. We arrived on a late flight, so by the time we got our car and found the highway, it was dark. I'd been looking forward to driving to Key West in daylight because I'd heard that the route, leading across narrow bridges that connected the Key Islands, was spectacular. I had imagined it from above, a silver ribbon pulled tightly across a gift of sparkling navy and turquoise waters.

At 11:00 p.m., we pulled up in front of our neat, pink guesthouse on Duval Street. Brent, the proprietor, decked out in bright pink shorts and a leopard spotted shirt, was all smiles. A golden halo of curls gave his chubby face an angelic look. "Darlings," he exclaimed, greeting us in a way that would have been appropriate for members of the royal family, "I'm so pleased you're here all safe and sound."

He led us up one flight of stairs to our room. It wasn't difficult to tell who had been the decorator. "I just love the leopard motif," he said. "Gives me energy. But of course, no real leopards involved. Everything's made from rayon." The curtains and the bedspread were the same material as his shirt. The walls and bureau were pink.

April chatted with Brent as I walked over to the window, which faced a small garden. It was lit with spotlights using enough energy to light up a small town. There were dense borders of tall hibiscus and bougainvillea trees that reached up to our window. The flowers on every tree were, not surprisingly, neon pink. On a small stone patio stood three pink plastic flamingos and two lounges upholstered in leopard spots.

It was close to midnight by the time we got our bags unpacked, with Brent supervising.

"C'mon kids, let's get outa here. I wanna take you to a cute little club." April was ready to go, but I'd been doing all the driving while she had slept, and I was exhausted. The two of them headed out, and I collapsed.

I woke up at 4:00 a.m. and felt April sleeping soundly beside me. I went out to the garden. With the lights off, colours were soft. I lay down on a leopard spotted lounge, a pink flamingo at my side, closed my eyes and took in the spicy aroma of tropical flowers. I had been living for ten years in a city where street lights erased the night sky. Here, when I looked up, the pulsing star-filled sky startled me and took my breath away.

Wildlife

I was up for breakfast while April slept. Brent was all smiles, wearing a French parlour-maid apron and flipping pancakes with the skill of a circus performer. He gave me a map and I set out to do a little exploring. Duval Street was Key West's main street. It had a small town atmosphere, filled with lots of restaurants, and shops selling seashells and beaded jewellery. After reaching the pier, which faced west, and noting the times of some snorkelling outings, I walked through a residential area. The houses were painted in pastel shades of blue, pink and yellow. Most had white gingerbread trim with flower-covered vines growing up their walls.

I got back to the guest house just before noon. April was up, dressed in tight leather pants and a T-shirt. "Hi. How'd you sleep?" I asked.

"Great," she answered. She was looking into a mirror putting on makeup, a surprising amount for a tropical day. She then put on a black leather jacket. "Um, I'm no fashion expert," I said, "but we *are* in the tropics and it's actually around eighty-five degrees out there."

"Who cares about the heat?" she responded, beads of sweat already finding their way through the makeup coating her forehead. "We're in Key West. I want to dress up."

She did look adorable.

As we walked down the road, even though I was sensibly dressed for the heat and sun in sandals, shorts and a wide-brimmed hat, I couldn't help feeling self-conscious. I looked like the gofer, the one who knocks on the movie stars' trailer doors and takes them to the set.

After lunch, the movie star and her chauffeur visited the Botanical Gardens, and took in the sight of orchids growing out of mossy tree trunks, and blue and purple butterflies darting in and out of flowering shrubs. We were the only visitors.

We sat down on a bench under a palm tree.

So what do lovers do when sitting alone on vacation under a palm tree? We grabbed each other and began a passionate kiss. April's lips felt oily from her lipstick and her cheek had a powdery sweetness, both unfamiliar sensations. My hand struggled towards her breasts, reaching upward between sweaty, sticky skin and a very tight T-shirt. We rolled off the bench onto the ground.

We heard a cough. But it sounded far away, so we paid no attention to it. We then heard a louder cough. Looking up, we saw an elderly couple wearing bright Hawaiian flower-covered shirts, glaring disdainfully down at the two of us. He held a guidebook; she carried binoculars. I had a feeling April and I weren't the wildlife they had come to the gardens expecting to see.

I tried to remove my hand from underneath April's T-shirt, but it wouldn't slide out neatly.

Both of us smiled like clowns and kept saying, "Sorry, excuse us." The woman actually picked up her binoculars and stared into them to get a closer look. The man, recovering slightly, said he was going to report us.

With me looking like Tom Sawyer and April like punk-rocker Deborah Harry, we must have seemed like the most unlikely couple, especially magnified twenty times. But to give some legitimacy to our moment, my quick-witted friend confidently replied, "Kenny just proposed to me. We're getting married. Aren't you happy for us?"

The woman put down her binoculars and through an uncertain smile said, "Well, isn't that nice." Looking at her husband, who was just about comatose, she added with more certainty, "Well isn't that lovely, dear?"

As they walked away, we saw the woman give her husband's bum a quick squeeze. We smiled at each other, figuring that she'd be leading him to the first available bench for a wildlife session of their own.

Out of the Blue

Three years after leaving Ailey, in 1978, I felt certain that my future role in dance would be exclusively as a teacher of group classes. Then, just when I thought I was too busy to do anything else, within a period of one month, I got four other dance opportunities.

One: Martha Graham recommended I teach private classes to one of the world's wealthiest women.

Two: Ms. Graham asked me to become one of her company's rehearsal directors.

Three: Pearl Lang almost ordered me to drop everything else I was doing and replace the great Bertram Ross in a revival of a much acclaimed full-evening dance work she had recently created, called *The Possessed.*

Four: Alvin Ailey invited me to appear as a guest artist in the company's big twentieth anniversary celebration.

Private Lessons to the Rich and Famous

An elegantly dressed doorman, wearing a peaked cap and white gloves, led me upwards on a sparkling elevator to a penthouse apartment high above Park Avenue. A more modestly dressed butler directed me to a washroom to change and, moments later, I stood in a vast living room, ready to teach my first private dance class to a woman named Doris Duke. Ron Protas, Ms. Graham's assistant, had set it up, telling me Ms. Graham had recommended me. Not knowing a thing about high society, I had no idea who Doris Duke was. Ron only told me that her Manhattan home was one of five of her residences, which included a 2,700-acre estate in New Jersey, a hillside mansion in Beverly Hills and a "palace" in Hawaii named Shangri-La. Her staff for these homes numbered over 200.

While I was checking out a shelf displaying gemstones, I suddenly felt a pair of eyes on me and turned to see a strawberry-blonde, slender Doris Duke (she liked to be called Doris) dressed in a plain black leotard and faded pink tights. She seemed suspicious of me.

I pulled aside a tiger-skin rug to clear some space to begin teaching her some Graham floorwork. She sat down gracefully beside a grand piano upon which rested a vase of saucer-sized, multi-coloured dahlias. After I remarked how beautiful they were, which pleased her, she informed me that they came from one of her gardens in New Jersey.

She then told me that Peggy Lyman, a Graham soloist, long and lean like Doris, was the artist whom she wanted to emulate. Not an easy task, as Peggy was a star performer in her mid-twenties and Doris was a beginner in her mid-sixties. Still, she was paying me $50 an hour, a great fee for a modern dance teacher in the '70s (even now); I wasn't about to discourage her.

Before beginning, she told me that she studied belly dancing and performed with a Middle Eastern dance company. She was also taking voice classes and sang with a Black gospel choir. I cynically pondered in silence all the opportunities money could buy. I also figured that Ms. Graham must have been courting her as a patron, or that she already was one.

But during our first hour together, I started to admire Doris. She may have bought her way into being a performing artist, but she was, in our relationship, humble, gentle and courageous. And she had talent. She picked up quickly and worked hard. Later on in our class, as she practised a movement combination down a hallway lined with Japanese screens and the most stunning Buddha statues I had ever seen outside the Metropolitan Museum of Art, I marvelled at her lithe grace.

I learned what I could about her: that she was a tobacco heiress who had inherited close to a hundred million dollars from her father, who had died when she was twelve. She was an astute businessperson, and had increased her fortune to over a billion. A foreign correspondent during the Second World War, she had written for *Harper's Bazaar* in Paris.

Her two marriages, the second to a notorious Dominican playboy, had been brief. She had experienced the ups and downs of many affairs. A reluctant celebrity, she became a great philanthropist, environmental conservationist (notwithstanding the tiger-skin rug) and apparently the first woman to compete in surfing (not the web) competitions. I also came across a horrifying story about how she had accidentally run over and killed her interior designer. The event had been ruled an accident.

Doris and I shared simple, easy-going times together and chats on the telephone (she always initiated the calls), and after a little while, she began referring to me as her "pal." At Christmas for a couple of years, when she was in Hawaii, she would send me a gift, special delivery: always a gourmet box of macadamia nuts. And after Romanian gymnast Nadia Comaneci had wowed the world by winning three gold medals at the 1976 Summer Olympics, Doris invited me to a special performance the great gymnast was giving on her 1978 world tour at Madison Square Garden.

We rode together in her chauffeur-driven Mercedes, along with another guest, apparently an oil tycoon. On the way downtown, they spoke of their friend, Greek shipping zillionaire Aristotle Onassis, of oil deals and million-dollar transactions. Naturally, right in my zone, I contributed significantly to the conversation.

During one of our private classes, Doris permitted a woman who said she was a psychic to watch. She claimed to see energy fields around people and wanted to see if what I was doing was giving energy to Doris or draining it from her. I got the thumbs up. Later, Doris told me the woman had also requested money to sponsor her work. I realized how vulnerable a wealthy, good-hearted person could be.

After I had taught her for almost a year, I sensed she wanted to be sure I was doing right by her. Or maybe Ms. Graham wanted to be sure. One day, the legend showed up to watch. So there I was, teaching class to one of the world's richest women, hands shaping her back, head and legs, with one of the world's most renowned dance artists looking on!

My time with Doris ended abruptly. After less than two years of classes, she announced that she wanted to go to the Graham School and take the advanced class. Doris had done surprisingly well. She could have gone into an elementary class, the level above beginners, and not been out of place. Someone had let her sing in a Gospel choir after a year of studying voice, but there was no risk of her getting injured standing in one place and singing. However, she wasn't nearly ready to be in a class with professional dancers. She could easily hurt herself.

After explaining myself to her, she became impatient: "What am I hiring you for if I can't be in the advanced class?" She remained convinced that after her sporadic classes, she should be at that level.

So she fired me. She never showed up at the Graham School. Maybe what I had said eventually made sense to her. But as the messenger, I took the hit.

Rehearsal Directing

Joseph Wiseman's Emotion

As a Graham Company rehearsal director—along with leading studio rehearsals—it was my responsibility to watch the male dancers during performances and give them detailed notes the next day, to make sure that their dancing reflected, to the best of my knowledge, the choreographer's wishes, technically and dramatically. As much as you rehearse and perform, there's always more to do.

My most memorable moment as rehearsal director took place, not in the studio, but in the theatre, after a performance. One night during a Broadway season, Pearl Lang was appearing as a guest artist, dancing the lead role of the Bride in the 1937 Graham work *Appalachian Spring*.

Pearl's husband, Joseph Wiseman (he liked to be called Joe), was standing at the back of the orchestra section next to me, watching the performance. He was a great actor, credited with an almost endless list of movie and Broadway roles. In spite of the fact that he had built his reputation performing parts in works by Shakespeare and Chekhov, he was perhaps best known for playing the evil Dr. No in the first James Bond movie.

At the end of *Appalachian Spring*, the Bride, having danced through many conflicting and anxious scenes, sat in front of her new husband, staring off into the future, ready, as protagonists are in many Graham pieces, to accept her fate after lessons learned.

The lights softened. Blackout. Joe ran to the wall behind us, threw himself against it, and began to sob, deeply and unrelentingly, caught up in what his wife had just revealed about herself as a young and innocent bride.

Possessed: Dancing in the Footsteps of a Hero

Soon, thanks to Pearl Lang, I would be playing the role of an exorcist. In 1977, she had choreographed an adaptation of the 1914 play, *The Dybbuk*, which she called *The Possessed*. Written by Belarus writer S. Ansky, the original was a seminal play of the European Jewish theatre, chronicling the life of a community of Hassidic Jews living in an Eastern European village in the late nineteenth century. The main throughline concerns the possession of a young bride by a malicious spirit, the dybbuk of the play's title. The story ends with an exorcism by a powerful rabbi. Ms. Lang's dance was a full-evening piece, performed in three acts. I had seen it after it had been brought back by popular demand. The theatre had been packed, the reviews ecstatic. With Ms. Lang performing the role of another bride, it was her biggest triumph.

When I originally saw *The Possessed*, the great Bertram Ross was performing the roles of both the Messenger and the Rabbi. The Messenger appears in Act One, a visiting peacekeeper who tries to guide the community towards justice. The Rabbi makes his entrance in Act Three. Like the Messenger, he is a trusted leader and guide. When performing the exorcism, he becomes possessed by God's will, channelling the compassion and power of the Almighty to overwhelm the dark forces that have taken root in the bride.

Pearl asked me to take on these two roles for a revival of the dance at Joseph Papp's famous Public Theater, and then to tour the U.S. afterwards. I was thrilled. I had loved the piece and would be challenged to follow in the mighty footsteps of one of the greatest dancer-actors in the modern dance world, the man who had inspired me as St. Michael in Rochester almost fifteen years earlier.

I couldn't dance the way I used to, but felt that if I worked on the roles both as a dancer and as an actor, I could bring a sense of personal reality to the work. I had not, however, forgotten the way Ms. Lang sometimes bullied the dancers with whom she worked. After five years of experience with the Ailey Company and years in therapy, I was able to confidently look her in the eye and say, "Yes, I'd love to perform with you again, but you have to be nice."

Becoming Who I Was Not

I knew from my recent training as an actor that, in order to embody both the Messenger and the Rabbi, I had to first do some research—to gather sensory information that would connect me to the characters I was to play and the settings on stage I was to inhabit. So I took the subway to the depths of Brooklyn, to the heart of New York's ultra-Orthodox Hassidic Jewish community, to attend an intense Saturday morning Sabbath service at its main synagogue in Crown Heights.

Arriving, I found my way to a seat in the men's section in the back row (men and women sit separately in Orthodox synagogues) and waited for the head rabbi to appear. All the people around me, men, women and children, were dressed in black. The men wore fedoras. They had gangly traditional sideburns, called peyos, and bushy beards; the women wore wigs or head coverings. I was dressed in a beige corduroy suit and a red tie, decorated with shooting stars. My outfit made me feel like the only lit Christmas tree ever to appear in Crown Heights. People were curious; I felt ridiculous.

Suddenly, a hand landed on my shoulder. Certain that I was about to get kicked out for ignoring the dress code, I had my apology ready as I turned around. Behind me stood a tall, handsome, burly man, with a big smile finding its way through the bushiest beard.

Him: "Hi Kenny, it's Barry."

Me (to myself): "Hi Kenny, it's Barry??? Who are you? How do you know my name? What's going on?"

Me (to him): "Excuse me. Do we know each other?"

Him: "Kenny, it's Barry Gold from Forest Hill Collegiate."

Me (to myself): "Barry Gold from Forest Hill??? What the . . .! You mean Barry Gold, the high school celebrity a year ahead of me, captain of the football team? That Barry Gold? Are you kidding me?"

Me (to Barry): "Oh, hi. Nice surprise to see you."

Barry: "Come to my home for lunch after services and we'll talk."

Soon, the white-bearded rabbi, leader of the congregation, entered and made his way through the reverential crowd to an elevated platform, the "bimah."

The service began. While praying, the congregation alternately sat and stood. Over their black coats, the men wore voluminous fringed white prayer shawls with blue trim. They rocked back and forth, sometimes doing a quick knee bend followed by a big bow forward. Their movements stirred up the dusty air, sending out a musty scent that reached me way back in the last row. Mid-service, the Torah, the holy scrolls, was lifted out of the ark. The scrolls were draped in a blue velvet fabric embroidered with shimmering gold threads, and carried around the sanctuary by a man. There was joyful singing and clapping. Each of us kissed our prayer book and then touched the scrolls as they were carried by. The scene was lively and theatrical. There was plenty of sensory detail here that I knew I could use to deepen my characters in *The Possessed*. I really felt as though I had been cast back to a little Jewish village in nineteenth-century Poland, one that could have been the birthplace of my father.

On the walk to Barry's home, all he could tell me about his joining this Hassidic sect was that he'd "seen the light; discovered my truth," and that he hoped I would too!! After arriving at his home, a dozen family members and friends gathered around his long dining-room table. Lunch was *Fiddler on the Roof* without the great score. Songs began, hands beat against the table. The men celebrated, the women served (they did sit down with us once the food was out, at the same table, unlike in the synagogue where they had to sit off to the side). At lunch, chicken ruled: there was matzo-ball soup with a chicken broth, sliced cold chicken, chicken fricassee, challah (egg bread) and steamed cabbage. My plate of bread and cabbage caused concern. Feeling that this was not the right time or place to explain my vegetarian diet, I just said I was allergic to chicken.

Having survived my initial shock, I discarded (for a few moments anyway) any tendency to judge. Hey, Barry was doing what felt appropriate to him. He had reconnected with his religion, which was more than I could say about myself, a person who ignored his. Okay, the outfit was extreme and the apparent sexism abhorrent, but Barry appeared engaged and full of life.

The Messenger
Author's personal
collection

It was just as the desserts of sponge, coffee and poppy-seed cake were being set on the table that Barry rose, stood behind me and put a giant hand on my shoulder. "Kenny, welcome to our community. We know you'll return often and pray with us."

I smiled politely, thanked everyone, then raced to the subway that took me uptown to the land of theatres and dance studios.

Soon I would be gluing on a beard and sideburns, and living on stage in a world that resembled the one I had just escaped.

The performances of *The Possessed* were a success. Ms. Graham even came to one of the shows and, visiting backstage afterwards, told me, "you were very dramatic," which I assumed was a good thing. But it was Joseph Wiseman, who had acted the part of the Messenger when the play had been presented on Broadway, who encouraged me most, praising my acting of the roles. His words made me think that, even though I had run from former football star Barry Gold's attempts to indoctrinate me, I could convincingly carry his world inside me and project something of that world on stage for the many performances to come.

The Possessed, in rehearsal.
Pearl Lang and I are in front.
Photograph: Martha Swope/©The New York Public Library
With Permission from B'nai Brith International

Sandler Declares War

My tasks as a teacher, rehearsal director and performer in *The Possessed* filled my professional life. Offstage, my relationship with April was growing. There was, however, a pervasive sense of gloom that dimmed even my brightest days. The cause was the ongoing and seemingly never-ending court battle against my loft's landlord, Michael Sandler. I learned from our lawyer that Sandler, a former lawyer himself, had only recently been released from prison. He had served a year's sentence for defrauding the U.S. government. Sandler not only fought me and my fellow loft inhabitants intensively in court; he did everything that his surprisingly inventive imagination could conceive of to make our lives difficult on our home turf.

He began by shutting off the heat in December; we walked around in winter coats, blowing ice-rings. Next, he turned off the loft's water supply so we couldn't use our sinks, showers or toilets; I ate off paper plates, peed into bottles, emptying them at night into street sewers, and showered at dance studios, filling a water bottle so I could brush my teeth at home. He smashed our mail boxes and stole the mail. He repeatedly put crazy glue into the locks. The locksmith told me the money he was making putting in new locks for me was financing his new truck. Sandler also took the doorknobs off the front doors at night and piled garbage in front of them so we couldn't get in. When I confronted him about his actions, he threatened to kill me. In order to run up our legal bills, he postponed court sessions with false reports of ill health and fires in his office. And these were just some of his dirty tactics. We couldn't leave our lofts and stay elsewhere because we had to show the court we were permanent tenants.

I also believed that it had been Sandler who had stolen my dance momentos. I had once again filled a box with my dance photos, reviews and programs. Returning to the loft one night I saw that it was gone. The only other person besides April who had a key to the loft was Sandler. I did manage eventually to recover a few of the photos from the Alvin Ailey archives, from photographer Johan Elbers and from the New York Performing Arts Library.

Paradise Lost

The worst, however, was yet to come. One stressful evening, after returning from a meeting with my lawyer, April and I decided to head up to the rooftop garden to breathe in its colours. It was late September, and the garden was at its peak, with its roses and zinnias in full bloom.

At the top of the loft's stairs, I opened the door. There were no colours; there was nothing.

The garden was gone. Every plant and piece of decking had disappeared.

Later, a neighbour told us that Sandler had ordered a dump truck to park in front of the building and had led a couple of guys onto the roof. They had then tossed everything into the waiting trash bin. I thought of my flowers falling swiftly downwards, experiencing an acceleration that was the opposite of what they had known in their summer of slow growth upwards.

Letting Go

One day in court, after a year and a half of legal argument, a mere seventy-six weeks longer than our lawyer had estimated, the judge blew up: "Would all of you just settle this? I don't want to see you again!"

It was the painter, Judy, who made me let go. She was on medication to deal with the stress of the battle and couldn't handle it anymore. She wanted to take a settlement in exchange for our lofts. I didn't argue. I had tried to be the strong guy, the one that Sandler couldn't bully, but I had been waking up with those stomach cramps for the first time in almost ten years, and my friends were all commenting on my weight loss and on the worry lines taking shape on my forehead.

I should have been excited about the settlement: we each received a whopping $36,000. But it was our lawyer who was the real winner, earning enough to score a Mercedes. After legal costs, I ended up with $10,000, much less than I would have likely received for selling the key to the loft to a new tenant. Still, my bank account was the fattest it had ever been. Time to relax and enjoy life. But fatigue overwhelmed me and I stayed close to home, wanting to savour my remaining time in that beautiful space.

Alvin Ailey's Twentieth Anniversary Party

During my final days in the loft, the thoughts of one more recent dance experience brought a smile to my face: my return to the Ailey Company as a guest artist for its twentieth anniversary celebration. The gala, which was held at City Center, had been set to feature highlights from many of the company's most popular pieces, followed by *Revelations*. The present company members and guests from the past twenty years had been engaged to participate. Alvin asked me to perform in the male quintet from *Blues Suite*, and gave his blessing by asking me to dance in "Sinner Man."

Based on the condition of my knees, I didn't think I'd be able to dance the pieces well. That, however, did not stop me from enthusiastically saying yes. To have the chance to leap and dive through these dances once more was thrilling; a minute after agreeing, however, I began wondering if I was going to make a total fool of myself in front of a couple of thousand people.

I had two months to prepare. I developed a training routine: I took ballet and modern classes, and I joined a gym and started to work out with weights. I had the studio space in the loft in which to rehearse. Even though I had performed "Sinner Man" a hundred times, I broke it down again into its basic phrases, worked on the movement in slow motion, and focused on how I related to all parts of the performing space and on how the lines of energy in the movement phrases were directed.

In addition, I used techniques from my acting classes to create a life for my character. I built a past for him. I imagined fresh images, based on the lyrics of the song, to fill the stage. By creating a fuller world, rich in sensory detail, my hope was to discover and convey an emotional life that might compensate for the lessened physical depth of my dancing.

During the performance, at the end of the second intermission and before *Revelations*, dancers who had performed with the Ailey Company over the course of twenty years came to the stage for a group hug. My arms wrapped around old friends I hadn't seen much for three years: Mari, Hector, Linda, Sylvia, John, Dudley, Judith, Sylvia, Chaya, Oka, and so many more. All dedicated, tough, gifted people with whom I had been blessed to share five of the best years imaginable: years of exhausting and joyful bus tours, ginger-soy meals shared in hotel rooms, trips to faraway lands. We were all crying, makeup running. Once you have danced with Ailey, you are considered family and will always be family.

The stage manager called, "Places, please, for *Revelations*." It was time to focus. In twenty minutes, I would be out there dancing alongside two of the company's former all-stars, Miguel Godreau and George Faison, remarkable dancers who would possess the movement and thrill the audience. All of a sudden, panic set in. They were in dance-shape and I felt I was not. I stood in the wings praying for everything to go well, for the Dance Gods, whom I had not called upon for ages, to swoop down once more and carry me along.

The time came for our entrances. The energy was fierce. Afterwards, all I could remember was that energy. I had no idea how well or poorly I had per-formed. I only knew I had gotten through it and felt fantastic.

After the finale, a smiling Alvin appeared, gave me a hug and said, "Great first variation." Pearl Lang was there, too, and was over the top with her praise. I remember her saying, "You danced like a demon."

My favourite comment came indirectly from someone I didn't know. My friend Mark Hammond was in the audience. He told me that after "Sinner Man," an African-American man sitting beside him had turned to his partner and said, "Wow, that white boy sure can dance!" Black or white, I knew it shouldn't matter. But I loved the personal review anyway.

In *The New York Times* Arts Section the next day, dance critic Anna Kisselgoff wrote:

"What Alvin Ailey has just celebrated is twenty years of humanity. Other companies have stood for other things. But no other companies or their publics could have radiated the warmth on both sides of the footlights as the Ailey Anniversary performance did on opening night."[56]

"Rocka My Soul" from *Revelations*.
Twentieth Anniversary Gala Performance, December 17, 1978.
Top row - Lucinda Ransom, Ella Thompson Moore, Loretta Abbott, Linda
Kent, Hope Clark, Dorene Richardson, Sylvia Waters, unknown dancer,
Alma Robinson.
Bottom Row - Miguel Godreau, Charles Moore, myself, Kelvin Rotardier,
James Truitte, George Faison, John Parks, unknown dancer.
Photograph: with permission from photographer Johan Elbers

6

RELEASING

October – December 1980

Pushes and Pulls

October 15. The phone rings. It's Julie, my talented friend, co-creator of "The Act."

"Hi Kenny. I have to talk to you." She is in full Brooklyn accent mode, which usually signifies a heightened state of emotion. "Are you sitting down?"

"I am now. How are you doing?"

"I have to say this quickly so it will be easier."

My pulse starts racing. Julie's sick. She has to have surgery. Some rare blood disease.

"Kenny . . . I have to quit working with you."

I wait for her to speak. My chest is tight.

"I know from my therapy sessions that I have to leave my husband. I need a break from all the men who are controlling me. I need to manage my own life."

Julie often plays the funny girl, but she is thoughtful and deeply intelligent, so I know she is not messing around. I also know that, more often than not, I have pressured her to work. The irony of the situation does not escape me: I am the one who had suggested a year ago that she do some therapy to help deal with her marital woes. I had recommended her to one of Dr. Buccheimer's associates.

An hour of conversation later, my last words before I say goodbye are, "Okay, I understand." I hope I sound supportive and am not projecting the despair I feel.

I walk up to my sad, gardenless roof and sit on the top step of the fire escape. Staring out at the grey, treeless cityscape, I hope for the mid-October coolness to clear my head. But I can't shake off my anxiety. Julie's decision to leave "The Act" is a real kick in the gut. With the court case over, I have been feeling upbeat about the show's growing popularity and have also been looking forward to our writing a play together. I am so fond of Julie and in awe of her talent, so used to her rhythms and good nature that I can't see starting all over again with someone else.

Then I have an unexpected thought: "Why don't I make a fresh start by moving back to Toronto?" I have a good laugh, because I love New York and need New York and know that whatever happens for me, it will happen right here. But as I sit, that surprising thought sets my imagination in motion, and I begin to think about why a move to Toronto might just be a good plan. There are pushes and pulls.

The first push is the realization that if I stay in New York, I will have to find a new place to live by the end of November, a month from now. I have been having nightmares of thieves and nasty landlords finding me wherever I go.

As well, only weeks before Julie's phone call, I had received two pieces of unexpected information—unsettling for different reasons. The first—shocking news about Robert Powell, the dancer who had inspired me like no other, the one who was remarkable even in stillness, who had encouraged me to audition for Alvin Ailey. For years, I had been watching him disappear in stages, drowning himself in alcohol. Unlike many alcoholics who get pale and emaciated, he became, first, red faced, then, paunchy. Physically, he became his opposite. A few days earlier, I had been sitting in a restaurant when a dance friend had approached me. The story he told was brief: a week earlier, Powell had invited his mother to visit him. While visiting her in her hotel room, he threw himself out the sixth floor window.

The next day, overwhelmed, I had received the second piece of information. It was actually good news, although not for me. April had recently auditioned for a California dance company based in San Francisco and learned that she got the job. She was ecstatic. I was happy for her, but desolate. I nevertheless encouraged her, because I knew how hard it was to get work and that she would be unlikely to find a comparable job in New York. I thought of following her, but after investigating the few teaching opportunities there, realized there was not much work available for me.

Sitting on my roof, I think: "With April in San Francisco, I have one less reason to stay here."

And then I realize I am not only being pushed away from New York, but pulled toward Toronto, by my need to connect with my family. My kid sister, Wendi, who had been only eleven when I left home, is now twenty-four. When I close my eyes, I see her as a child, not as a grown woman who has recently married Paul, whom I hardly know. I want to get to know both of them before they take off somewhere and become unreachable.

Because of my work with Dr. Buccheimer, and because my Dad is about to turn seventy, with Mom not far behind, I also feel it is time to make peace with my parents. I believe I now have the ability to communicate calmly and knowledgeably, and to keep the conflicts of the past from completely colouring my interactions with them. I realize I can't do something as intimate as rebuilding my relationships through long-distance phone calls and brief visits.

During the next month, I explored the situation. I spoke with April. We were optimistic. Toronto was not much further by air from San Francisco than New York. No matter what, we would make the situation work. I telephoned the directors of the Toronto Dance Theatre to make sure that if I did decide to move, I would have a place to work. They invited me to teach at their school.

I began to see my possible move as a way to make a difference: to contribute to the growth of a vital and quickly growing dance scene. I felt like I would be an explorer again, and began to feel excitement for this new adventure. So much had fallen into place so quickly, I felt as though my long-absent Dance Gods may have been behind it all.

My last weeks in New York, during an icy December, were mainly low key. I had a loft sale and then gave a party so I could say goodbye to my friends. Dancers from the Ailey Company, teachers and dancers from the Graham Company, and fellow acting students all showed up. My heart just about burst as we danced, laughed, remembered, hugged and said our goodbyes.

The night before my departure, bags packed, I wondered what single dramatic event might happen and convince me not to leave. Sitting in my neighbourhood bar, drinking my last New York beer, I gave the possibility of staying one more improbable chance. I closed my eyes and waited for a sign. If I opened them and April was there, telling me she had been unhappy with her life in California and had returned home, I would stay. But when I opened them, standing beside me was a burly guy with a snake tattoo spiralling down his arm. It was time to go.

The next night, on New Year's Eve, 1980, I was on a plane heading to Toronto. I stared out the window, catching a last look at Manhattan as it disappeared under clouds and had a final moment of panic, wondering what I was doing.

But as I settled back in my seat, I closed my eyes and imagined myself living in one of Toronto's maple-tree-lined, Victorian red-brick neighbourhoods. I saw an empty backyard and there I was walking into it, ready to dig a garden into new ground.

Dedication

Dedicated in memoriam to those in New York
who taught and inspired me,
and who were my friends.

Alvin Ailey   Mary Anthony   Amy Antonelli   Consuelo Atlas
Talley Beatty   Bob Bowyer   Enid Britten   Dr. Arnold Buccheimer
Sybil Burton   Ivy Clarke   Ulysses Dove   Doris Duke
Noelyn George   Miguel Godreau   Martha Graham   Mary Hinkson
Mari Kajiwara   Pearl Lang   Bernard Lias   William Louther
Edward Love   Michihiko Oka   Ernest Pagnano   Robert Powell
Lar Roberson   Bertram Ross   Phillip Salvatori   Ramon Segarra
Brother John Sellers   Warren Spears   Joyce Trisler
Matt Turney   David Hatch Walker   Dudley Williams
Morton Winston   Joseph Wiseman.

Acknowledgements

Dance artists Terrill Maguire and Jen Cole and many curious students all encouraged me to write *The Dance Gods*. I offer big thanks to my first editor, Susan Turner, for her astute guidance and belief in me; to Wendi and Paul Bonder for their non-stop support; to readers of early drafts, Grace Miyagawa, Jonathan Bonder, Toba Pearl, Ellie Kester, Marilyn Biderman, and Dorothy and Jeff Simon; to Miranda Forbes, for her design work; to Eddie Kastrau, for technical help; to Dana Mills, Code Workun and Meaghan McAneeley, for their patience and assistance; to everyone at FriesenPress. I have not been able to locate Vladimir Bliokh, a photographer I met in Moscow, and I want to thank him here. Susan Sperling asked me some important questions and then sent me, after my editor became unavailable, to a new editor, Karen Shenfeld. I extend to Karen deep bows of gratitude. She was more than an editor; she was a mentor whose knowledge and rigorous work ethic guided the book to its finish. Carol Anderson and Susan Berger gave me many helpful suggestions. Thanks to Alvin Ailey archivist Dominique Singer, photographer Johan Elbers and Tom Lisanti of the New York Public Library. Max Wyman, Paula Citron, Deborah Jowitt, Peggy Baker, Molly Johnson and *The Dance Current Magazine* all showed me their generosity. Much love, always, to Sylvia Waters and Linda Kent. I am in debt to my lifelong friend Barbara Laskin for her detailed work as copy editor. Thanks to April for her support and to Julie Halston, who remains a pal and still makes me howl with laughter.

Endnotes

1. This chapter subheading is from the song "With a Little Help From My Friends," written by John Lennon and Paul McCartney and released on the Beatles album Sgt. Pepper's Lonely Hearts Club Band in 1967." on page" on page 261

2. The dancer I still remember from that ballet class was the great Lawrence Adams.

3. Dancers in the Graham class included Lilian Jarvis, a soloist with the National Ballet of Canada, and future company members of Toronto Dance Theatre Barry Smith, Amelia Itcush and Donald Himes.

4. During my time in New York, the area around St. Mark's Place was referred to as both the Lower East Side and the East Village. Now it is usually referred to as the East Village. The area called the Lower East Side is further south and east.

5. John Lennon and Paul McCartney, "Strawberry Fields Forever," *Sgt. Pepper's Lonely Hearts Club Band*, 1967.

6. Joseph H. Mazo, *Prime Movers: the Makers of Modern Dance in America* (London: A & C Black Ltd, 1977), p. 157.

7. Merle Armitage, *Martha Graham: Early Years* (New York: DaCapo, 1937), p. 9.

8. Stephen Stills, "Love the One You're With," *Stephen Stills* (Atlantic, 1970).

9. Ballet terminology derives from the court of Louis XIV, the 17th-century French monarch who was a leader in the development of the art form. In 1661 he formed l'Académie Royale de Danse, followed in 1669 by l'Académie Royale de Musique, which later

gave rise to the first professional dance company in Europe. Much of the terminology is used in other forms of dance, including modern dance.

10. Joseph Campbell and Bill Moyers, *Follow Your Bliss: Conversations with Bill Moyers* (Vanderbilt University, Dec.1989).

11. From Lennon and McCartney's 1967 hit, "With a Little Help From My Friends."

12. A slogan that became common during the '60s in the U.S., attributed to youth protesting the Vietnam War, young people rebelling against the Establishment, and Black Panthers protesting domination by the ruling classes.

13. From "Woodstock," the 1969 song by Joni Mitchell that was featured on her third album, *Ladies of the Canyon* (Los Angeles: A&M Studios, 1970).

14. From "Won't Get Fooled Again," written by Pete Townshend of the band The Who in 1971 and included on the band's album, *Who's Next* (Track, Decca, 1971).

15. From Bob Dylan's 1962 classic, "Blowin' in the Wind," included in his album *The Freewheelin' Bob Dylan* (Columbia, 1963).

16. From John Lennon's revered song, "Imagine," written in 1971 and included in his second studio album of the same name (Apple, 1971).

17. ibid.

18. From "Age of Aquarius," a medley of two songs written for the 1967 musical *Hair* by James Rado & Gerome Ragni (lyrics), and Galt MacDermot (music), released as a single by The 5th Dimension.

19. See 13

20. A hippie expression attributed to Henry David Thoreau, poet, naturalist, abolitionist, 1819–1862.

21. Jennifer Dunning, "William Louther, Virtuoso Modern Dancer, Dies at 56," *New York Times*, May 17, 1998.

I only saw Bill a couple of times after he moved to London. When we met, he was frail and shaky; arthritis was slowing him down. He became friends with a journalist, Sharon Atkin, when she interviewed him for the Caribbean Times. They married in 1996. Two years later, at age 56, he died; the cause was oesophageal cancer.

22. George Harrison's song, "Piggies" from the *White Album*, (EMI & Trident, 1968), was written as a social commentary on class and corporate greed.

23. Clive Barnes, "Graham, Great and Not So Great," *New York Times*, April 20, 1969. Arts section.

24. Anna Kisselgoff, "Ailey: Dancing the Dream," *New York Times*, December 4, 1988.

25. Alvin Ailey, quoted in *Black Visions '89, Movement of Ten Dance Masters*, Tweed Gallery Exhibition Catalogue, 1989, p. 9.

26. Joseph H. Mazo, "Ailey and Company," *Horizon*, July/August, 1984.

27. Thomas De Frantz, *Dancing Revelations* (Oxford University Press, 2004), p. 87.

28. Clive Barnes, "As Long as They Have Talent," *New York Times*, April 14, 1968, p. 23(D).

29. "Brown V. Board: Timeline of School Integration in the U.S." *Teaching Tolerance*, Number 25, Spring 2004. http://www.tolerance.org/magazine/number-25-spring-2004/feature/brown-v-board-timeline-school-integration-us

30. Debora Obalil, *Dancin' to Freedom: A Historical Analysis of the Rise of the Alvin Ailey American Dance Theater*. Hope Project: Paper 26, Illinois Wesleyan University, 1995.

31. Clive Barnes, "A Great Lesson in Race Relations," *New York Times*, April 26, 1970.

32. Robert Tracey, *Ailey Spirit*, (New York: Stewart, Tabori and Chang, 2004), p. 26.

33. Alvin Ailey with Peter Bailey, *Revelations* (New York: Carol Publishing Group, 1995), p. 106.

34. ibid

35. Robert Fleming, *Alvin Ailey*, (Los Angeles: Melrose Square Pub./ Holloway House Publishing, 1998), p. 126.

36. Deborah Jowitt, "Does it all add up (or should it)?", *The Village Voice*, December 16, 1971.

37. Martha Graham, *Blood Memory*, (Doubleday, August 1, 1991), p. 238.

38. Judith Jamison, *Dancing Spirit*, (Doubleday, 1993), p. 125.

39. A matryoshka doll, also known as a Russian nesting doll, refers to a set of wooden dolls of decreasing size placed one inside the other.

40. Anna Kisselgoff, "Dance: No One's Sitting on His Hands," *New York Times*, April 27, 1971.

41. Don McDonagh, "Dancers Crackling Again," *New York Times*, April 28, 1971.

42. George Hall, "Bernstein's Mass," *The Guardian*, July 12, 2010.

43. Peter G. Davis, "The Religious Composer," *High Fidelity Magazine*, February, 1972.

44. "Rio festival Views Ailey Dancers," *New York Times*, September 6, 1963, p. 35.

45. Anna Kisselgoff, "Dance: Ailey Returns," *New York Times*, April 19,1972, p. 37.

46. The Alvin Ailey American Dance Theater building, the Joan Weill Center, opened in March 2005. It is an eight-storey, 77,000 sq. ft. building, with 12 studios and a 255 seat theatre. <http://www.alvinailey.org/about/visit-us/joan-weill-center>

47. Program note for *Cry*.

48. For instance, *The River* for American Ballet Theater and *Carmen* for the Metropolitan Opera Company.

49. From the foreword to the Robert Tracey book, *Ailey Spirit*, p. 10.

50. Tracey, p. 78.

51. Fleming, p.126.

52. Clive Barnes, "A Great Lesson in Race Relations," *New York Times*, April 26, 1970 30(D).

53. Kate Burton is an acclaimed Tony nominated actor. She is perhaps best known for her ABC TV portrayals of the mother of Dr. Meredith Grey on *Grey's Anatomy*, and Vice-President Sally Langston on *Scandal*.

54. Anna Kisselgoff, "Mari Kajiwara, 50, Dancer Known for Pure Modern Style," *New York Times*, January 12, 2002.

55. Julie Halston is still a great friend. She is one of the busiest actor-comedians working in New York today, appearing on Broadway, Off-Broadway, in films, on TV and in comedy clubs. *The New Yorker* magazine called her "a force of nature."

56. Anna Kisselgoff, "Has Ailey Really Gone Commercial?" *New York Times*, Dec. 17, 1978.

About the Author

Photograph: Courtney Vokey.

Kenny Pearl began formal training in dance at the age of eighteen in Toronto at the National Ballet School of Canada and with the co-founders of Toronto Dance Theatre. He moved to New York City to train and, subsequently, danced around the world with the companies of Alvin Ailey and Martha Graham. He has taught regularly at schools across North America, including at the Juilliard School of Music, the Martha Graham School and the School of Toronto Dance Theatre. He was Artistic Director of Toronto Dance Theatre from 1983-87 and, since 2002, has held a faculty position at Ryerson University. He wrote *Dance/Life*, a handbook for emerging artists, in 1990. Kenny lives next to the Scarborough Bluffs in Toronto, where he enjoys gardening, photography and taking long walks.

About the Book

When Kenny Pearl arrived in New York City, determined to succeed as a dancer, he was penniless, friendless and jobless. His memories shine against the backdrop of the turbulent '60s and '70s, including Vietnam War protests, the military draft and the rampant crime that once plagued the city. From humble beginnings in the hippie-populated Lower East Side, to performing with the greats of the New York modern dance scene—he danced with the companies of both Martha Graham and Alvin Ailey—Pearl's life is one of tenacity, hard work and passion. This is the engaging story of the hurdles he faced on his unique journey and the remarkable people he met along the way.

CPSIA information can be obtained
at www.ICGtesting.com
Printed in the USA
LVOW12s0142221217
560472LV00001B/197/P

9 781460 262702